THE MIDNIGHT
ECONOMIST

THE MIDNIGHT ECONOMIST

Little Essays on Big Truths

THIRD EDITION

William R. Allen
University of California, Los Angeles

Introduction by Milton Friedman

THOMAS HORTON AND DAUGHTERS
26662 S. New Town Drive
Sun Lakes, Arizona 85248
(602) 895-0480

Library of Congress Catalog Number 96-79710

ISBN 0-913878-57-X

Contents

Mainly Microeconomics:
Analysis of Relative Prices and Resource Allocation

Contents

Mainly Macroeconomics: Income and Monetary Analysis

MONEY, INFLATION, AND MONETARY POLICY

GLOBAL THINKING:
TRADE, FINANCE, DEVELOPMENT

Introduction

I have always been fascinated by what seems a puzzle about economics. On the one side, the fundamental principles of economics are elementary—simple common sense, seemingly accessible to every intelligent person. On the other side, many very intelligent persons fail to understand them and err egregiously in applying them to specific problems.

Surely, it is the simplest common sense that a low price for any product will encourage buyers and discourage sellers; that a high price will discourage buyers and encourage sellers. Whence then the indignation, the uproar, the charges of fraud and villainy when the legal fixing of a *maximum* price for rental quarters—that is, an artificially low price—produces more prospective buyers of rental space than prospective sellers? Or when the legal fixing of a *minimum* price for an hour of unskilled labor—that is, an artificially high price—produces fewer prospective buyers of more labor than prospective sellers?

Economics, it seems, is more than obvious common sense. It is also a way of reasoning, of thinking about problems. Many are the occasions in which I have participated in discussions about policies involving economic issues in which those participating have included economists of all shades of political opinion together with noneconomists of all shades of political opinion. Almost whatever the subject of discussion, the outcome after a brief interval is predictable. The economists will be found aligned on one side of the subject— the free enterprisers along with the central planners, the Republicans along with the Democrats, libertarians, and generally even the socialists—along with a few allies; the bulk of the group—academics, businessmen, lawyers, you name it—generally on the other. I have been amused to observe the same phenomenon, if in somewhat muted form, emerge even when the subject of discussion has been rather far removed from economics—foreign policy, or academic policy, for example.

Some people have a natural instinct for economics and the economic way of reasoning, and some people are completely lacking in such an instinct— just as some people have an aptitude for mathematics or an ear for music and other people do not. And just as a great man may lack an ear for music, so also he may lack a feeling for economics. My favorite example—for economics, not music—is Winston Churchill, surely one of the greatest men of our time or any time. Yet when it came to economics, he came a cropper every time he had occasion to get involved, whether before World War I when he played a leading role in the early development of the welfare state, between the wars when as

Chancellor of the Exchequer he decided to return the British currency to gold at the prewar parity, or after World War II when as prime minister he decided to retain a fixed exchange rate for the pound instead of permitting it to float.

A striking example on the opposite side—a noneconomist who had a real feel for economics—was Leo Szilard, a famous natural scientist who played a key role in persuading President Franklin Roosevelt to initiate the Manhattan Project to develop the atomic bomb. Leo, a colleague of mine at the University of Chicago, was always coming around, tapping me on the shoulder, and saying "You know, I've been thinking about . . ." and out would come a sophisticated economic proposition, original with him though generally well known to professional economists. More surprising, it was usually correct—he was almost the only physical scientist, I may say, with whom I have had that experience.

While some people may be tone-deaf to economics and other people born economists, for most people economic reasoning is an acquired skill—and taste. That, at least, is the only way I have been able to justify spending the best years of my life trying to teach elementary common sense—often dressed up, it is true, in fancy mathematical clothes—to successive generations of students.

William Allen is a professional economist with a natural ear for economics. He reasons like an economist, eats, sleeps, and breathes economics, as a good economist should. But he has something else, a quality that is far rarer—the ability to explain his economic reasoning to others, in language they can understand, and in language that will intrigue and interest them. He has demonstrated his skill over the years in the classroom. He demonstrates it even more dramatically in the gems of radio and television commentaries reprinted in this book.

Bill's commentaries are not sugarcoated pills to be swallowed by the listener with no questions asked. They seldom tell the listener the answer. That is not Bill's aim. His genius is in bringing into the open the elementary principles involved in an issue so that his listener or reader will be induced to think about the problem on his own and to think about the economic principles in a different way. As the poet has it, "He that complies against his will is of his own opinion still." No one else can persuade us. We must persuade ourselves. But someone else can help us find the right way to think about a problem, to break it down, recognize the familiar ideas in an unfamiliar guise, enable us to make up our own minds.

That is what Bill Allen does over and over again in these commentaries. I marvel at his versatility, the wide range of problems and issues he covers, and even more at his skill at finding a fresh and arresting way to present each item. He is equally skillful at finding arresting turns of phrases precisely applicable to the particular issue he is addressing.

Few people will be able to read—or read widely in—this book without being both educated and entertained, without finding themselves questioning beliefs they have long taken for granted, and forming new beliefs. Best of all, some will even end up reasoning like economists.

MILTON FRIEDMAN

Foreword

The Midnight Economist has long provided—on radio and television and in newspapers and magazines—purported pithy pearls on various aspects of Truth to a mainly lay audience. He has thereby followed a long and splendid tradition of political economists exploring and explaining the nature and workings of the social world.

Some—including giants of the economics fraternity—have been concerned, not only with explication of real phenomena through scholarly lectures, journals, and monographs, but also through reaching wide audiences of nonspecialists.

In a world of scarcity, economics is important, and good economic guidance can lighten the costs and burdens of living together civilly and sensibly. The world has suffered more tyranny and poverty than need have been because it has clutched, or had thrust upon it, lousy economics. It behooves competent economists to bestir themselves, to share what they may have learned about what works best, to instill some feel for (and tolerance of) "the economic way of thinking." What economists have learned may be deemed not much, but even a small candle can at least help to make the darkness visible. A wider appreciation of the analytic approach of economics may contribute to that greater acquiescence in sense and rejection of foolishness which will enable this nation's grand but vulnerable experiment in freedom and productivity to continue.

The Midnight Economist syndicated radio series began in January 1979 and continued for nearly fourteen years, through November 1992. Most of the brief essays were published as monthly flyers and twice-yearly pamphlets, first by the International Institute for Economic Research (Los Angeles), then by the Institute for Contemporary Studies (San Francisco), and finally by the Reason Foundation (Los Angeles). A book compilation of broadcast scripts into early 1981 was published by Playboy Press (1981). A second book, presented by ICS Press (1989), drew on scripts prepared from 1981 through 1988. This volume, offered by Thomas Horton and Daughters, contains pieces broadcast from 1989 to 1992, along with a few later magazine and newspaper discussions in *California Political Review, The Freeman,* the Greensburg (Pennsylvania) *Tribune-Review,* and the *Washington Times.* Smaller collections have been distributed by the Private Enterprise Partnership, an economics education institute of Pittsburgh, and by the Dryden Press to accompany its textbook by James D. Gwartney and Richard L. Stroup.

Reaching wide audiences requires assistance. It is hardly feasible to mention all who have helped with words and acts over the years, and there are delicate difficulties entailed in mentioning only a sample. But propriety and appreciation require noting a splendid long-time friend and associate, William Dickneider. Bill is a first-rate economist, insightful in applying elemental analytics to real questions, imaginative in pursuing information, and effective in exposition. The Midnight Economist program would not have continued so long and so well without his loyal, substantial help. (The several diagrams and charts in this book—as well as some of the substantive content and drafting of a good many of the essays—are his contribution.)

The Scaife foundations have generously subsidized from the outset my educational efforts to save Western Civilization, with Richard M. Larry being my patient, sympathetic, and sophisticated contact. A grant by the Carthage Foundation, one of the Scaife institutes, to the Pacific Academy, directed by J. Clayburn La Force, was instrumental in production of this book.

But it is hard to be a hero to everyone.

A major television station was invited to add Midnight Economist pearls to its news programming. After all, the station presents three hours of news each evening, and matters of economics inevitably bulk large in what is reported. But the station replied that it was "not interested in doing economic commentary ...." Perhaps it was felt that meditations of a professor of economics would not meld well with the happy talk of anchor types, weather clowns, and sports sorts.

And there was the conspicuous policy-studies institute. It was invited to sponsor these broadcasts. But the institute held that it was "wedded to the print medium," for while broadcasting has "certain impact as an *entertainment* medium," it has very doubtful "impact and effectiveness . . . as an *educational* tool ...." So reaching the general community with thoroughly reputable but readily manageable economics smacks too much of education for the television station and too much of entertainment for the institute.

Few radio and television program directors—or newspaper op-ed editors—have a coherent notion of what economics is about or what economists do or how and why they do it. But they are sure that economics is difficult, dull—and (gasp) controversial. Striking boldness and high cultivation do not universally characterize the broadcast industry. Few who manage policy institutes are persuaded that the perspective, the priorities, and the predilections of society generally are sufficiently important to cultivate. They approach—through only the printed page—just the in-group, the power brokers in government and journalism and the academy. And people in philanthropy, in both private foundations and corporations, if they can be attracted at all to wide dissemination of economic education, commonly (blessed are the exceptions!)

have limited staying power: They quickly become bored or grow faint, and then cavalierly abandon their troops in the trenches.

Still, some of us missionaries persevere. The intent of the Midnight Economist is to provide laymen capsules of reputable economics, useful applications of well-established, elemental analytics. The analysis itself, the substantive content, is to be dispassionate utilization of those fundamental concepts and techniques which economists have laboriously developed and quite generally adopted. The exposition, however, may at places be rather more vigorous and colloquial than usually provided by an academic. While the words of the Midnight Economist are mine (with the aid of William Dickneider), the essentials of content come entirely from the common heritage of economics scholars.

General Meditations

৶৶৶৶৶৶

Introduction

According to a famous definition: "Economics is the science which studies human behavior as a relationship between ends and scarce means which have alternative uses."

Some may gag a bit over reference to economics as a science. And some may sense from the definition a lack of sex appeal, with economics appearing as a deadly dull, dry, and dreary field of arcane doodling and diddling—sort of like accounting. In actuality, there is, in good economics, much of feel and flair, of instinct and intuition: Economic analysis is not a purely mechanical exercise of grandly grinding out uninteresting answers to artificial problems. And much the same can be said of chemistry and physics. In any discipline of analytic application to important matters, elegant tools and rigorous techniques of thought must be supplemented with accumulated learning and developed wisdom in order to distinguish the profound from the superficial, the appropriate from the inapt and inept, and the feasible from what cannot work well.

The foregoing definition of economics, even if deemed a bit pretentious or portentous, does suggest the core of the broad, versatile field of study and use. It all starts with scarcity: In this world of limitations, we cannot produce all we want. The fact of scarcity has implications of the most fundamental seriousness. Scarcity implies the necessity to pick and choose, for we will never fully satisfy all desires; choice-making implies cost-bearing, for cost is what we must give up or trade-off in order to obtain the thing preferred. A world of scarcity and choices and costs is a world not only of dealing with stingy nature but of dealing with people; in dealing with other grubby people, we sometimes coordinate our efforts to mutual advantage, and we persistently compete in many ways as each tries to get a bigger slice of the finite social pie.

A world of scarcity is inherently a hard world. But with some civility and sense, we can make our lives easier than they otherwise would be. How are we to organize ourselves as a community, what ground rules and institutions can we evolve and adopt, which will enable people, with all their grasping grubbiness, to live together peacefully and productively?

By and large, people and their governmental leaders and masters have not answered that central question well. History is not an impressive story of progressive sophistication in formulating rules and procedures which enable the great bulk of the world's people to live without fear of oppression and want and with reasonable hope of personal fulfillment. But the human spirit is remarkable: People have been denied many options, their initiative has been severely curtailed, they have been abused and oppressed—and yet they have not only stubbornly survived, but commonly have shown much sense in adjusting and making do within the limited alternatives available to them.

People usually have done as well in their personal affairs as they have been permitted to do. How can they be permitted to do better? Much of what we do is "economic" in nature—what we do and how we do it, that is, in allocating "scarce means which have alternative uses." Many sorts of influences impinge upon the human condition, and many sorts of analysts—from the anthropologist to the zoologist—contribute to understanding human potentialities and prospects. But much of our misery has stemmed from dumb economics—inefficient institutions, inappropriate property rights, wasteful processes, debilitating policies.

Dumb economics has included, also, lousy instruction. While people commonly are shrewd in handling their private business, they are not accomplished economists in the broader context, where their expertise and experience are necessarily limited. And they have been taught—by politicians, journalists, academic poets, and even some purported economists—much mythology, including:

- we could have enough of everything if we were fully to exploit our fantastic productive power;
- economic efficiency is a matter only of technology and engineering;
- agricultural and other surpluses stem from productivity outrunning demand;
- capitalism requires a social "harmony of interests"; but also capitalism is the source of competitiveness and conflict;
- property rights commonly conflict with human rights;
- business people are self-centered and rapacious, while government people are self-sacrificing and altruistic;
- labor unions protect the natural brotherhood and collective wellbeing of workers against their natural enemies, employers;
- charging a higher price always increases the seller's profits;
- the American economy is increasingly dominated by monopolists who arbitrarily set prices as high and wages as low as they please;
- minimum-wage laws raise the income of the poor;
- rent control improves and expands housing;
- there is unemployment because workers outnumber jobs;
- government "jobs" programs increase employment;
- a government budget deficit reflects failure to tax enough to finance needed government services, and increasing tax collections will surely reduce a deficit;
- inflation is caused by greedy domestic monopolists, irrational consumers, and disruptive international cartels;
- inflation is required for full employment, and full employment must lead to inflation;
- fluctuating prices create wasteful uncertainty and rising prices constitute inflation, so government should make it illegal to change prices;

- the optimal size of various key measures is invariably *zero,* e.g., zero budget deficit, zero foreign trade balance, zero unemployment;
- tariffs increase domestic employment and wages;
- we cannot compete in a world in which most foreign wages are lower than wages paid domestic workers;
- international trade cannot flourish in a setting of market uncertainty, and fixed exchange rates reduce uncertainty, so exchange rates should be pegged by government;
- economic sanctions against our enemies are highly effective, and economic aid is necessary and sufficient for our friends to grow.

Mythology is a legitimate part of romantic and arational life, but it leads us astray—making us poorer and weaker and more quarrelsome in a stingy world—when it is made part of economic analysis and policy.

Good economics of description, diagnosis, and prescription will not solve all our problems. The best of achievable worlds will still be a world of scarcity—and thus a world of choices, costs, and competition. But good economics will help us to do best, even if not well, in a hard world.

There are important things economists can explain in part. Most commonly these are things to be explained at quite a formal level—things dealing with production relationships, uniformities of human behavior, the structure and operation of market institutions, the repercussions (not all of which were intended) of government policies. Such conventional investigation and deduction is reflected mainly in the essays of Parts II and III.

Ultimate decisions in our messy world of hopes and fears are not generally made elegantly at a formal level. To be sure, technical analysis can help to set the stage and provide some framework and focus for final choices: Theory and its applications help to define options and identify returns and costs. But then, in determining just what to do and how to do it, we lean heavily on habit and predilection, trial and error, mores and preconceptions, the instinct of the race.

Theory is an exercise in logic. But logic without application remains only an intellectual game. A given theorist at a given time can legitimately confine himself to pure abstraction: It is important to get the logic straight. But sooner or later, directly or indirectly, there is to be some tangible payoff to the community if the community is reasonably to continue to subsidize the navel contemplators.

All of the essays presented here are oriented toward interpretation of real-world phenomena. But those of Part I go beyond the traditional domain of economics, confined basically to marketplace institutions and activities. As these "general meditations" of Part I illustrate, the modern economist is hardly confined to sharply delineated boundaries. He has found it useful to follow "the economic way of thinking" into any area of activity which entails the use of means which are scarce and versatile.

The Quality of People

Bunnie Rabbit, Winnie, and the Grand Plan

With their uncertainties and fears and aspirations, people do much fretting and flailing. It is a hard world, to be sure. The best things in life may be free, but the multitude of second-best things are costly. So we work and save and plan—and we compete, struggling with one another as well as with stingy nature. And in our scheming and striving and struggling, the veneer of civilization is worn very thin. The veneer is worn completely through at times and in places, exposing our greed and gaucherie and petty preoccupations.

A vastly more attractive and assuring aspect of being is provided by furry friends. I have been blessed with companionship of my rabbit, Bunnie, and my dog, Winnie. Bunnie had to leave me some while ago; and now Winnie, too, has gone.

Both little Bunnie—she of the dainty face and long ears and button tail and velvet coat—and dear Winnie—pretty and cute and sweet and nice—like the lilies of the field, neither spun nor sowed. They directly contributed nothing to gross domestic product. They were consumers, not producers, absorbing a bit of the world's scarce resources and returning nothing—nothing but an example of poise and patience and grace and affection.

The poet assures us that they also serve who only stand and wait. Presumably, we shall never fully comprehend the Grand Plan of the Universe. But much of what we suspect and infer is to be gained—if we are willing to learn—from the humble likes of Bunnie and Winnie. While people meanly scheme and worriedly strive and struggle, the Bunnies and Winnies seem instinctively to have found their role and purpose. And they play their part with an innate dignity and beauty of nature which should humble us.

There are many ways in which we can do ourselves in, individually and collectively, and the human race has worked assiduously to discover and utilize them all. Occasionally, a Shakespeare, a Rembrandt, or a Beethoven reminds us of our angelic heritage. We have laboriously accumulated some successes of medicine and mechanics. And a few of the world's peoples have grudgingly permitted some experimentation in social arrangements of freedom and individualism which can ease the pains and constrictions of our plight of scarcity. But it is not surprising that progress in reclaiming our heritage is, at best, slow and unsure, for it is perversely protested and opposed by most. Unlike the Bunnies and Winnies—the supposed lesser of God's creatures—people persist in rejecting their role and subverting their purpose.

Certainly, it is a world of scarcity. But the scarcity is not confined to iron ore and arable land. The most constricting scarcities are those of character and personality. All our cleverness and wit, all our tools and technology, will leave us poor, indeed, a disgrace in the eyes of the Deity, as long as we lack the goodness and grace and gentility of Bunnie Rabbit and Winnie.

"The Quality of People"

ᴈᴈᴈᴈ

Surely, among the determinants of economic growth is "the *quality* of people." But personal quality is a sensitive subject, and some object to treading such terrain.

Some seem to suppose that economic progress relies not at all on a variegated human factor: supposedly, production and its allocation and use are determined simply by oil and iron deposits, harbors, arable land, and climate. But, around the world, there is only a loose correlation between standards of economic living and endowments of nature. It can be argued persuasively that the *major* determinant of the quality of life is not geography, but the quality of people.

To emphasize "the quality of people" is *not* to repair to notions of a "master race." The reference here is *not* to innate genes and hormones which destine some ethnic groups to be brighter and more imaginative and harder-working than other groups. Whether or not nations and races can be distinguished on such grounds, people assuredly do differ in their histories, habits, and institutions. And so they differ also in their perceptions, their anticipations, their ambitions, their attitudes, and their mores; and they confront different ground rules, they perceive different options, and they respond to different incentives.

So what is the nature of the ties which can bind self-interested individuals into a coherent community characterized by high productivity and sensitivity to civilizing proprieties? The police power of the state to maintain aspects of order and the authority of courts to adjudicate disputes are necessary ingredients of social cohesion—but such power and authority are far from sufficient.

Among the required complementary ingredients of order and efficiency are *discipline* and *confidence*.

Discipline pertains largely to acceptance of and commitment to civil, coordinated behavior, which helps to generate predictable, reliable activities and responses. But, for many, discipline is highly specific, for only a severely delimited context, not an orientation and guidance of general applicability. Marines, football players, and scholars supposedly are distinguished by uncommon discipline. But often discipline evaporates when the people step an inch outside their circumscribed, well-defined professional activity. Their specialized discipline has little relevance for their general behavior.

And confidence stems in part from community discipline. An economy will exhibit much inefficiency when individuals find other people to be unreliable, erratic, cavalier in fulfilling responsibilities. And confidence—the basis of making plans and choosing strategies—is further diluted by uncertainties of the future purchasing power of money and of the clarity and stability of property rights.

We in this country were born relatively free and prosperous. Whether we progress, stagnate, or retrogress will be determined mainly by the quality of our people.

The New York Times, English Majors, and Reality

◌◌◌◌

In important respects, *The New York Times* is a fine and useful paper. But it has peculiar attraction for a certain kind of confused clientele, and persists in publishing little philosophic and psychologic essays by intense, articulate types—commonly women who majored in English in college—who purportedly long for a better world while nobly reveling in their sorrow over what they perceive as the actual world.

If they stumble across a clue of how the real world works, they camouflage it or put it out of mind. For to deal with the actual, working world is to analyze it in terms of scarcity and uncertainty, alternatives and tradeoffs, incentives and payoffs, frustration and unfairness. Analyzing the world requires a sober mind; and it leads to sober assessments, conclusions, and prescriptions. But solid sobriety in dealing with the world is not the way or the ideal of former English majors too anxious to do good.

One of these sensitive souls has ruminated in *The Times* about the 1960s, which she acknowledges were sometimes silly. And she is sadly bemused by kids of today who long for a 1960s which they never knew—and which never existed. Mistaken nostalgia conjures visions of "mellow celebrants at Woodstock," of "everyone ... totally cool and lazy and self-indulgent," or retching but fetching wretches "brain-damaged beyond hope of repair by years of peace marches, LSD and other forms of navel-gazing ...."

What is incorrect about this picture of the past? There *was* the orgy of Woodstock, even if more coarse than cool; and there *was* self-indulgence in LSD. One inaccuracy of the picture. of course, is that not everyone—not even everyone under age thirty—was a practicing slob in the 1960s.

But "mostly," the English major tells us, "we can forgive the excesses of our youth—except ... our youthful, excessive faith in the future." So *that* was the problem: the young and young-in-heart of a quarter century ago were simply too good, too pure, too idealistic and trusting for a degenerate world. "... we wanted ... all the right things," we are told—"enough to eat for everyone and equal treatment for all," good schools, cheap rent, and full employment. But the flower children, who put a premium on "compassion," have been surprised and stymied "by the ascendancy of greed ...."

Not a word is offered as to where the outpouring of goodies was to come from and how it was to be distributed. It is asserted simply that "all of us would be free to make up our lives as we went along," and "work would resemble play."

The author is a bit embarrassed about the innocence of her generation. But the failing—and continuing failing—is hardly "naiveté": it is massive ignorance and stupid, stubborn refusal to learn what the world really is and how it really works. And we are not helped in our coping with reality by insipid silliness of former English majors in *The New York Times.*

The Free Society, The Open Economy

Tomorrow and Tomorrow and Tomorrow ....

øøøø

The pattern and process of historical happenings is rarely a simple *chain*, no stronger than its weakest link; rather, it is an elaborate *web* of innumerable strands, no one of which is of critical significance.

All is temporary and transitory. History is largely a humbling story of minor contributions and marginal changes. Life is a play with incessant turnover of characters and seemingly quite random shifting of scenes. Even at the moment of activity, what one does and how well one does it has little discernible impact on the wider world beyond one's personal view and experience. Little of what we do is well noted or long remembered. Few are heroes, and those who are stars today are forgotten tomorrow.

If all the toil, trouble, and trauma of our short survival in this veil of tears signifies so little, if hardly anyone is conspicuous in the Grand Scheme of Things, why bother? Neither the Deity nor the Government — if we are permitted to distinguish the two — has appointed me to decree what you should deem important. You are free to be disturbed by your lack of fame or distressed by mortality of your body and reputation. But permit a small word of comfort.

Fame comes from power, and fame is power. Power sometimes is used for good, making the community healthier, wealthier, or wiser. Most of us do not begrudge a generous allotment of fame to those who are most useful to us. But power, like nitroglycerin, is a tricky substance, capable of harming as well as helping, even when innocently used in trying to help. Indeed, power corrupts, and initially pure intentions can readily degenerate into obtrusive and oppressive tyranny.

But incoherent anarchy is not the only alternative to imposed totalitarianism. We best be wary of power, which enables some to suppress and exploit others. But society requires order and coordination. How can we conduct our personal and social affairs efficiently in seeking purposeful ends while retaining a dominant individualism? There are societies and societies. What are the conditions and characteristics of a *free* society?

The answer surely has many aspects and ingredients. But, in a world of scarcity, life inevitably is largely economic. And the economic aspects of freedom necessarily are bound up with the open market, with private decisionmaking in the use of privately owned resources. A flourishing market embodies much power, to be sure, but in an open market the power is very widely diffused.

A free society, based on an open market, may have few heroes, and fame is fleeting. Some may be frustrated by failing to attain tyrannical power; but all can rejoice that no one else can tyrannize. And most of us are quite content to participate, even though modestly, in the continuity of the community, as did our forebears and as will our progeny.

Economic Order: Big Brother Versus Mutual Bribery

ॐॐॐॐ

We dream of a world in which no one has to work, where nature lavishes on us all the goods we could desire. But this is not the kind of world in which we actually live. The means to satisfy wants are *scarce:* we want more than we can have.

Scarcity gives rise to *competition* and *conflict*. And yet in a viable society we must live together with coordinated activity. How can there be peaceful and efficient co-existence of acquisitive and uncooperative people in a stingy world?

The *motives* of people are essentially the same every place—to increase material welfare and to express personality. But *social arrangements,* including *economic systems,* differ greatly in the ways specific goals may be pursued. *Scarcity* exists in all societies; how *adaptation* to scarcity is made varies from community to community.

Use of *violence* is one way of resolving conflicts. Thomas Hobbes, the English 17th century political theorist, explained the problem of order when people seek to satisfy diverse desires with scarce resources. "... if any two men desire the same thing, which nevertheless they cannot both enjoy," he says, "they become enemies." And in the anarchical state of nature, "the life of man [is] solitary, poore, nasty, brutish, and short."

Hobbes resolves the problem of order by introducing a ruler to whom each man shall "give up [his] Right of Governing [him]self." People are to enter into a social contract with an absolute sovereign, Hobbes tells us, "to keep them in awe, and to direct their actions to the Common Benefit."

One may reject violence as a mode of interpersonal relations and still be dissatisfied with the Hobbesian Big Brother resolution of the problem. Instead of state-imposed order, how about *mutual bribery?* We tend to class as immoral all bribery. But is it immoral to *induce* people to do what you wish by making them better off?

Let Adam Smith, the Scottish thinker of the 18th century, explain:

> Man has almost constant occasion for the help of his brethren, and it is in vain for him to expect it from their benevolence only. He will be more likely to prevail if he can interest their self-love in his favor, and show them that it is for their own advantage to do for him what he requires .... Give me that which I want, and you shall have this which you want .... It is not from the benevolence of the butcher, the brewer, or the baker, that we expect our dinner, but from their regard to their own interest. We address ourselves not to their humanity but to their self-love.

Is this a grubby view of the world and how to adapt to scarcity? Well, the world *is* grubby. We *are* confronted by scarcity. And so conflict *does* exist. Are we to adapt through giving up our individual freedom and responsibility to Hobbesian central control—or adapt through mutually beneficial coordination of self-interested actions in a free market?

The Decline of American Civility

ℒℒℒℒ

Have we become more nasty and brutish, or have the media just developed a keener eye for beastly behavior?

Steven Knack, doctoral candidate in economics at the University of Maryland, cites evidence that civility has declined. "... think of voting as just one particular type of socially cooperative behavior," he suggests. But the proportion of eligible voters actually going to the polls has fallen dramatically in recent decades.

There are other signs. Crime rates are much higher now than thirty years ago. A smaller fraction of adults read newspapers or watch television news, which may mean that today's citizens are less well informed. The proportion of college students who cheat on exams reportedly has nearly doubled since the 1960s. Charitable contributions, adjusted for income and other factors, have been declining since 1948. Income tax compliance also has fallen. All this, along with casual impressions of rudeness of the highway and crudeness in public expression, suggest a dismaying decline in civility.

Why? Mr. Knack suggests a weakening of traditional sanctions on abusive, self-indulgent behavior. Families, neighbors, and community institutions like churches have less influence today. And greater urbanization and mobility make it easier for individuals to escape accountability for the costs they inflict on others.

Still, Mr. Knack overlooks another likely, and perhaps more important, cause: a marked increase in political competition.

Competition occurs in all societies, for people want more than available resources can supply. The pie is smaller than combined appetites, so people compete for slices. But while competition is a fact of life, the *method* of competition varies widely.

In *market* competition, people compete for a slice of the social output pie by offering something in exchange. But an individual will have more to offer in exchange—and thus be able to acquire more—by first *producing* more of what the community values. So market competition encourages people to *produce* and thereby contribute to others. By competing for some of the pie, people end up baking a bigger one for the community.

How different is political competition! Here, rivals try to persuade government to *give* them slices of the pie produced by *others*.

This method of competition brings forth belligerent conflict, for it directs efforts from *producing* the pie to demanding its political *redistribution.*

Insidiously, it subverts appreciation and respect for other people and their property rights. Victims, too, are manners and morals, which share with formal property rights the task of controlling and coordinating individuals' behavior for the community's benefit.

Political competition has been edging out market competition for much of this century. Perhaps we should pay attention to this lamentable fact when trying to explain the decline of American civility.

Self-Esteem and Self-Hypnosis

◿◿◿◿

The young scholar approached with exam paper in hand and fire in the eye. Flashing her grade of D, she informed me, with feeling: "I am a graduate of Beverly Hills High, and never before have I received a grade of less than B+."

I doubt that her bad grade wounded her self-esteem. After all, at fault was surely the teacher, not the student. But many—politicians and psychologists, in particular—worry much about self-esteem and how to protect and nurture it. A large California Task Force to Promote Self-Esteem has finished three years and spent over $700,000 of state money in preparing a 140-page report on how to feel good about oneself and be nice to others. Most of the counties in California and many other states have joined, or may be joining, the bandwagon of satisfied navel-contemplation.

The essence of the human situation is scarcity; thus, the essence of our being is competition; and the essence of our salvation is coordination. If we are to survive well, we must evolve and adapt procedures and attitudes of resolving conflicts and combining productive efforts.

To prosper, we must pursue desires to do well, and enable people to perceive and exploit options and to anticipate reward from productivity. We have to produce what we consume. We produce by sweat of the brow and by planning and sacrificing and organizing. Production is not generated by convincing ourselves that we "deserve" much because we all are perfectly splendid fellows and that we surely will receive all we deserve. Both incentive and guidance in productive activity are to be found in a society and its economy which rewards most those who are most useful to the community.

Scarcity does, indeed, give rise to competition in any social order. But an open-market arrangement, based on private rights to use of property, gives rise also to efficient coordination. When people perform well in such price-directed activity, when they provide valuable things to others, doubtless the resulting rewards of wealth and applause will be accompanied by sense of self-esteem. But the esteem is a by-product of valuable performance. With lousy performance, there is no warranted esteem.

The sweet smell of success and the fear of failure are powerful fuel for the engine of endeavor. But self-esteem by simple-minded self-seduction conduces contentment, not commitment. There must be sufficient confidence to try, of course, but self-sustaining, growing confidence had better reflect experience—experience of effective effort resulting in acknowledged accomplishment.

Do not bother to tell the community of the esteem you deserve or the pride you feel or how singularly precious you are. And do not tell me you deserve an A in my course because you went to Beverly Hills High. We are looking at your performance and achievement. And then *we* will tell *you* your appropriate reward and the esteem you warrant in our eyes.

Midnight Knockings on the Door

ȘȘȘȘ

It is hardly to be expected that respectable economists—those brooders over scarcity—would have many friends. But I have a few. Several have immigrated from behind the Iron Curtain.

These friends from lands of tyranny have added to my understanding of government condoned and conducted brutality—of political thugs permitted in the streets and police raids on homes in the night. But even when the mind is instructed by trusted associates, full emotional comprehension is not attained when personal experience is lacking.

In a small way, I recently had a taste of the midnight pounding on the door by armed men. The door in question was that of my hotel room. Not only was there beating on the door, the door was actually opened as far as the chain would allow. A voice from the corridor claimed to be from "hotel security."

I reclosed the door and called the front desk. Yes, they were aware that "security" was operating on my floor. I informed the desk that "security" would be called off at that moment or I would utilize legal mechanisms to put the hotel into a state of great financial regret.

It all turned out to be only a breakdown in hotel staff communications. There were no truly bad guys in this episode—just some who were confused. But in many instances in many places around the world, there have been thoroughly bad guys—ruffians of government who could not be deterred by appeals to constitutional protection and by threats of legal reprisal.

How big a step is there between physical coercion and economic domination?

A non-profit institute once received a message from an agency of the government of California. The letter said, insinuatingly, that an informer had reported that the institute had failed to take out a required personnel insurance policy. The president of the institute was ordered to appear "precisely at 9:50 AM" at a specified address to account for his transgressions against society. In the government's version of magnanimity, the bureaucrats would permit any relevant papers, lawyers, and accountants to be brought along. (No mention was made of clergy to administer last rites.) As if in trivial afterthought, the possibility was acknowledged that the informer had been incorrect, in which case a copy of the insurance policy could be (and was) forwarded in lieu of a personal appearance.

Even by uncivilized standards of government, it was a coarse performance. The belligerent message implied that the recipient was presumed guilty, and seemingly rejoiced that a culprit had been discovered in his dastardliness. Little Brother—state and local government—can be as intrusive and officious as the Big Brother feds. At any level, government is government, and it persists in commonly playing the role of enemy.

Reasonable thought suggests and experience illustrates that a community cannot be politically free and economically slave, or politically slave and economically free. If political authority can coerce and dominate in the one dimension of activity, it will do so in the other.

Patriotism: Sacrifice and Hope

Valley Forge ... But <u>We</u> Were <u>Born</u> Free

There is more to life than economics. To be sure, man does not live without bread. And the way he organizes activities of production and exchange has critical political and social, as well as economic, significance. But man is not sustained by bread alone—or even by bread and circuses together. Indeed, what most ultimately distinguishes one person or one people from another has less to do with material wealth and power than with qualities and characteristics of the mind, the heart, and the soul.

Our current public heroes are disproportionately represented by pampered clowns and gladiators. But the world's most vital work is done by those of courage and integrity and judgment and dedication and perseverance, most of whom are largely unsung and unfavored with extraordinary reward.

Perhaps the community's conception of the heroic is modified as the condition of the community develops. Perhaps what is deemed exemplary and worthy of emulation when a nation is young and lean, with future promise dominating present attainment, and yearning for independence, is heavily diluted and substantially replaced when the nation seemingly runs short of frontiers to explore. Some have been obliged to *earn* their freedom, with both sweat and blood. But most of us were *born* free. Perhaps inheritances are not as well comprehended and prized as what we ourselves have won and produced.

It would be naive to suppose that all the American colonists were revolutionary heroes—or that the revolutionists were regarded as heroes by all the colonists. Indeed, the revolutionists were a minority of the community—and not all of the revolutionary zeal reflected political idealism and philosophic purity. The revolution was conducted by people, not deities, so there is to be found in the history of the grand adventure more than 200 years ago a sufficiency of coarseness, ineptitude, and fear.

But the inherent frailties of people and the confusions and uncertainties which divided the young community serve to make more visible the strength and the sense of those who bore monumental burdens to make us a nation. Certainly, the burdens of those men and boys at Valley Forge in the terrible winter of 1777-78 were monumental—quite beyond full comprehension as one now serenely surveys the lovely landscape in a warm summer day.

No shots were fired at Valley Forge. But while the enemy forces comfortably occupied nearby Philadelphia, more than 3,000 of the 11,000 troops under General George Washington perished from cold, disease, and starvation.

They died for us. Truly, I have trod hallowed ground. We shall deserve damnation if—through failure of *our* courage and integrity and judgment and dedication and perseverance — we meanly lose our noble inheritance.

Military Power: Global Obligations and Fairness

ØØØØ

I can be bewildered and bemused both by the callow younger generation and by the confused of my own ancient cohorts.

Consider military service. A good many years ago, the military draft was dropped in favor of the voluntary military. To many, this seemed a sensible shift in procedure.

In its nature, the draft is ham-handed. People are shanghaied by lottery. This enables the government to pay wages far below market rates; the government budget is helped, but at the financial expense of those who also provide their bodies. In contrast, under the voluntary arrangement, people are induced, not coerced, into signing up, and the whole community foots the bill.

The voluntary arrangement of the market seemed to work well — at least until the prospect of extensive shooting. Evidently, the great bulk of those who had willingly enlisted have had little emotional or intellectual difficulty in facing up to their contracted obligations. But a few (and their parents) have publicly cried of dirty pool.

They candidly say that they enlisted for employment and educational benefits, but they had not counted on the military being called upon to fight! Indeed, some have belatedly come to the realization that they conscientiously object to fighting. Given the often demonstrated unfriendly nature of the world, one is hard-pressed to provide a coherent and flattering explanation of a supposition that national defense forces will never be called upon to defend the nation.

It is no easier to applaud those senior statesmen who fear the purported unfairness of voluntarism. Voluntary enlistment, they say, is more attractive to the poor and to those of relatively limited career options. If this is permitted, we end with a military of mercenaries who are disproportionately black and brown.

Even in periods of peace, we are informed, a democratic nation should be protected by a military reflecting the ethnic and economic configuration of the entire community. So we should willy-nilly draft people — whites as well as colored, wealthy as well as poor — pulling many out of more productive activities and paying them little. We will thereby supposedly help the downtrodden by reducing and making less attractive their employment options!

Even if substituting market demand for governmental decree in filling military personnel requirements is acknowledged as normally sensible, it still is held that a draft is democratically in order in times of trouble. Faced with impending war, we are to pause — and have the rest of the world wait for us — to reinstitute the draft and train a civilian army and navy. It is difficult to take such silliness seriously.

It makes sense to raise military manpower through the market, with individuals choosing that occupation as the best of their perceived options. Drafting manpower means wasting manpower. But the military is not to be simply a social welfare program for times of peace. Those who choose the military must realize that their duty may be hard.

The Bastille and Thermopylae

◇◇◇◇

To live is to fight many foes, to battle at varied barricades for prizes and causes of numerous sorts. We often fail to win, suffering either loss or stalemate. Even when we deem ourselves victors, we must commonly conclude in candor that the fight was an incidental skirmish rather than a decisive struggle or that the gains are smothered by the costs or even that we chose to contest a bad issue at a bad time on a bad field.

It is exhilarating to pump up the troops, to radiate seeming confidence even while comprehending the desperation of our actual situation, assuring comrades that, come the revolution, all will be well. Theologians, Marxists, politicians, and others have found it convenient to hold out hope of great things to come, even though they are vague on when those great things will come, how they will get here, and what they will consist of.

The young are particularly susceptible to hope; the old, having long been frustrated and frequently disappointed, tend to be cynical and gun-shy. The young fantasize about glorious and successful storming of the Bastille; the old realize that often we are doomed to fight and fall at Thermopylae and Corregidor.

Not all this — neither euphoric champing at the bit nor subdued dedication to duty — is all bad. Without some happy anticipation, there will be little effort and investment. And there is basis for hope that we can do better than we have done; we can discern some places where we have gone wrong, and we have deduced procedures which, if effectively implemented, could improve our performance.

And yet, the analyst looks with dispassion and calculates with a sharp pencil. He will note how very hard it has been, over six thousand years of poverty and tyranny, to improve our lot, and he is mightily impressed with the variety and magnitude of our difficulties and handicaps, including weaknesses of community character and deficiencies of societal sophistication.

For all our shrewdness in our limited personal affairs, we can be seduced and corrupted on grand issues of the free society and its efficient economy — an arrangement of freedom and efficiency which may, therefore, be only an enormously attractive but transitory aberration of history we have not had the sense and strength to nurture adequately.

While there must be some hope to make constructive action fully rational, we best beware excessive self-delusion, lest the subsequent frustrations and disappointments destroy the basis of continuing effort. We walk a fine line between hope and despair. Are we engaged in real attack of advance or only in delaying rearguard action? Still, we are obliged to battle, to respond to our own versions of the rallying cry of Shakespeare's King Henry V:

"Once more unto the breach, dear friends, once more;
Or close the wall up with our English dead!"

Communism and its Collapse

Pernicious Potentialities of Contriving Cloud-Places

∅∅∅∅

A century ago, the American author, Edward Bellamy, published his utopian novel, *Looking Backward.* The popular book pictured a collectivist paradise in the year 2000 which resembles a smoothly managed prison — or zoo — populated with docile inmates.

There was little room for individualism in this ideal world, for there was little room for registering personal preferences, for private rights to use of property, or for productivity to be reflected in rewards. With brotherly cooperation replacing beastly competition, the objective of imposed organization and the criterion of decreed rules were solely "the welfare of society."

Bellamy's simplistic vision is of simple but sensitive people of limited ambition and little self-interest enjoying a pleasantly zombie-like existence in a simple world. He rebels against and rejects the realities of risk, uncertainty, change, cost, ambition, greed, conflict. For him, an efficient social system requires personal purity — and individual acquiescence to centralized direction in a military-type of egalitarian organization. And, despite all evidence, he was confident that people *are* innately pure, but are corrupted by bad institutions — and that purity would be restored with correction of the institutions. Individual subservience to integrated social structure and consolidated control would be the triumph of common sense.

The author provides glowing general assessments of *conditions* and *results*, but little of how the arrangement is to be *established* and how it then is to *operate*. Success requires human characteristics which in actuality are not characteristic of humans. Ignored is the admonition of David Hume that the proper starting point of social analysis is to take men as they are; and rejected is the vision of Adam Smith that appropriate ground rules and procedures of society can meld and channel activities of combative competitors to the benefit of all.

The gentle Bellamy acknowledges that he had had "no thought of contriving a house where practical men might live in, but merely of hanging in mid-air, far out of the reach of the sordid and material world of the present, a cloud-place for an ideal humanity." "Ah," a poet instructs us, "but a man's reach should exceed his grasp, or what's a heaven for?"

It need not be wholly in vain to seek the impossible — if what we seek would prove desirable if attainable. It is useful as inspiration and guide to strive for more than we can achieve — if the manner of striving itself does not preclude attaining as much as is possible. It is proper and appropriate to strain to reach beyond our grasp — if, in fact, we reach toward heaven. But if the reach is grossly misconceived and fundamentally misdirected, then what is grasped will be quite the opposite of heaven.

The Socialistic Mind

ᴥᴥᴥᴥ

The market provides production and consumption options, incentives and guidance in making efficient choices, and devices and procedures through which preferences are registered, costs calculated, and communication facilitated.

These functions — functions of surveying alternatives, making choices, and carrying out transactions — *must* be performed somehow. In a world of scarcity, we best strive to produce much of what we desire most. In a world of want, inefficiency is a sin. How to enhance productivity and avoid waste?

The socialistic mind replies in terms of decrees from a Big Brother elite. Why? Why must some czar and his bureaucracy be in charge, directing and subsidizing here, prohibiting and penalizing there, regulating, taxing, and mandating everywhere?

Is it because government is staffed and advised by creatures who are brighter, wiser, more knowledgeable and insightful, more sensitive and genteel than real people?

Is it because the socialistic mind truly cannot grasp the effective and attractive consequences of market arrangements which engage individual aspirations in coordinated activity for community accomplishment?

Or is it because the socialistic mind does not embrace criteria of individual freedom and responsibility and objectives of personal and community well-being, but, instead, hungers for authority to whip us all into the party line and rule our lives?

To suggest that government types are morally and intellectually superior to the rest of the community is surely to jest. In their brain-damaged condition, would-be masters of mankind may, indeed, fail to grasp the sophisticated essence of the price-directed open market. But along with lack of analytic subtlety, there is a domineering aspect: socialists like to subvert, and dictators like to dictate.

Karl Marx, the father figure of so-called scientific socialism, actually said little about *socialism*. His message to the masses pertained to the degenerative weakness and exploitative machinations of *capitalism*. Although capitalism had been enormously productive, acknowledged Marx, its day was done: It had become nothing better than a lurching, self-destructing engine of repression.

Marx, the theorist, gave little hint of what was to replace capitalism. It was left to Lenin, the revolutionary, to improvise a government and an economy. He botched the job. His successors barely tried. Stalin and the rest of the boys to come never were fundamentally concerned with economic efficiency. Instead, observed the late Warren Nutter, an insightful analyst, "they ... sought ... to fashion an economic system that would promote their political goals without threatening the authoritarian nature of the state."

Beware the road to socialism, which shapes the economy "to serve political ends, not the other way around."

Silly Slogans: Abilities, Needs, and Work

✍✍✍✍

Few of us rigorously analyze much, and none of us analyzes constantly. We have neither time nor temperament to be solely pure logic machines. Commonly, we think in slogans, and act in habit. Such short-cuts can usefully simplify life and save effort. They can also mislead. There is often much silliness in slogans.

Political slogans are bad enough. Slogans of political economy can be worse. Among the analytically most curious slogans of pop political economy is the radical absurdity: "From each according to his ability, to each according to his needs."

What a macho motto that is! Come the revolution, we all will pitch in, working assiduously and effectively, and sharing appropriately. But neither Karl Marx nor his socialist predecessors or his communist followers have explained in principle or demonstrated in practice just how the centralized state is to achieve both efficiency and equity. We must take their vague assurance on nebulous faith.

A mere rallying cry in terms of abilities and needs provides neither organizing principle nor operational procedure for a complex economy. It tells us nothing of required institutions and the incentives and guidance they must provide to use the resources of the community well in satisfying as best we can the preferences of the community.

To speak in terms of giving by ability and getting by need not only fails to instruct us in what we must do, it basically obscures what we must do. Production and distribution are not separate acts or separate functions of the economy. What we produce with our limited resources, how we organize our intertwined productive efforts, and how we share the social product are all interwoven aspects of one huge economic operation. We cannot resolve any of these questions in isolation from the others.

The massive melding of myriad activities can be coordinated only through market calculations with market values. Prices reflect both costs and demands. Without open markets and the market-clearing prices they generate, costs are ignored and governmentally decreed "needs" replace individual initiative and personal preference. And tyranny replaces liberty.

Although no lover of liberty, Marx recognized the ridiculousness of distribution now on the basis of "needs." For him, that supposed ideal must wait indefinitely for the full-blown paradise of Communism. Meanwhile, until we somehow some time evolve into that perfect state, the hard-nosed slogan must be, he tells us: "To each according to his *work*."

"Faith," we are instructed by high authority, "is the assurance of things hoped for, the conviction of things not seen." Faith of some sophistication can be a source of strength. But faith reflecting simply silly slogans is a poor excuse for analysis.

Emigrants and Visitors to Communistic Utopia

ØØØØ

"... what fools these mortals be!"

Few have been so foolish as the several thousand Americans who left their country in the early 1930s to resettle in the Soviet Union, the workers' paradise, the utopian land of Lenin. A feature story in the *Los Angeles Times* recounts the pathetic story.

The Great Depression was, to be sure, a time of terrible troubles in western democracies. Faraway, mysterious Russia seductively promised employment and security to foreigners who were presently suffering and fearful of the future; it promised cooperation and coordination instead of competition and conflict; it promised, indeed, not only a new earth but ultimately new heavens.

But seduction it was. The idealistic, hopeful immigrants from the west were initially welcome: their coming was a propaganda coup for the Soviets. But, we are told, "by the late 1930s, those Westerners remaining had become a people displaced, often shunned by Soviet neighbors and co-workers, feared as subversives, in some cases jailed or even executed." Authorities made it difficult to leave, and the expatriates were marooned in a crude, harsh land.

There was another type of migration to Russia in the 1930s — indeed, from the 1920s to our own day. These were self-styled intellectuals — novelists, playwrights, entertainers, journalists, clergymen, even some scholars — who visited the Soviet Union.

"Political pilgrims," they are called by sociologist Paul Hollander, confused crusaders on a Messianic quest.

Appalled and alienated by lack of appreciation of them by lesser folk at home, these precious people ignored realities and adopted ideologies of innocence and naiveté, with poetic perceptions of possibilities of personal and social perfectibility. Not every intellectual is a consistent and dispassionate logic machine. And precepts of morality and standards of analysis can become flexible and selective, with hard-bitten assessment and cold criticism reserved for their own rejected societies while denying or forgiving the cruelties and disasters of glorified communism.

The pilgrims were deliberately deluded by their hosts, but they wanted to be deceived. A German ex-communist remarks sadly and in awe on "the lengths to which a man can go, who, though neither stupid nor vicious, deliberately ceases to see, to listen, to think critically ... so as not to doubt the cause he serves ...."

The suckered common people were no sillier than the intellectualoids. The two groups — the largely forgotten and stranded emigrants and the visiting Beautiful People — did differ in two regards. First, the visible visitors had public forums and thus were in a position to spread poison. Second, they enjoyed staged excursions and then returned to comfortable homes, while the ordinary people were tragically stuck in hell.

Capitalism and Its Concerns

Capitalism and Comedians

❧❧❧❧

Bill Cosby is a very able man in his trade. He is one of the finest of TV comedians and an effective pitch man in commercials. He also has a Ph.D. in education. But evidently his study was not in *economics* education. And, like many other conspicuous show biz sorts, he expansively and aggressively uses his public forum to pontificate on matters about which he knows little.

Mr. Cosby once was interviewed at length in a major newspaper. Much of his commentary pertained to the condition of black Americans. He is distressed by basic aspects of that condition. To the mortification of many of us, much of his distress is warranted. But, even if predictably and understandably, his concern and chagrin lead him to vacillate between racial pride and persecution complex, between justified indignation over discrimination and unjustified denigration of institutions which represent our best hope of improvement.

Commendably, Mr. Cosby castigates the person — including the black teen-ager — who "finds it easy to blame other people, or the government, for having no faith in yourself...." But in the next paragraph we are told: "This country governmentally thinks we still need slaves. In terms of capitalism itself," he goes on, "if you have poor people, that's how you make money. You have a group of people you want to keep working for less; the way to achieve that is not to educate them."

If the intent is really to equate, or closely relate, the economics of slavery to the economics of capitalism, the comedian is inadvertently making a very bad joke.

Capitalism is an arrangement and a process of people freely bidding and offering, buying and selling personally owned assets to further their personal interests by their own criteria. Consumers buy goods and services for consumption; business firms buy materials and services for production of goods to be sold to consumers. Everyone — both consumer and producer, including Mr. Cosby — *prefers* to buy any given thing at a lower price than at a higher price, of course. But the more who compete for finite supplies, the higher one must bid to get any.

Business firms compete for inputs. They are competing for productivity. The more productive a worker, the higher will competing firms bid up the price. Educated, experienced, diligent workers who are most skilled in helping to make things of relatively high value will command the highest wages. And, in their own profit-making interests, corporations have been pouring billions of dollars into remedial education in order to make workers more productive.

Firms prosper most by efficiently producing what is demanded; efficient production requires productive workers; productivity reflects largely education and experience; and productivity is rewarded. Successful firms already understand all this. Maybe Mr. Cosby, too, will learn.

Composition, Capitalism, and Comprehension

♨♨♨♨

Perhaps in all of us there is at least a small strain of the maverick, some occasional inclination to kick over the traces, and, like a free spirit, do it our own way. Those who have done their things most magnificently — the precious Shakespeares and Beethovens — have been innovators, breaking free of stultifying fetters imposed by tradition and The Establishment.

Still, the genuine sophisticate recognizes that not all heritage is a hindrance. Not all evolved rules, techniques, and criteria are products of fools who went before us and now are to be scornfully ignored.

The music critic of *The New York Times* has tried to convey this civilizing message to icons of the rock world — including Paul McCartney — who have started to experiment with classical music. The critic finds much of merit and portents of promise in an oratorio of Mr. McCartney. But he finds also "a stylistic rootlessness" stemming from formal musical innocence. It is reported that the fledgling classicist regards "his approach to composing as akin to primitive art, intuitive but unschooled. Learning to notate and studying the orchestral literature, he said, might inhibit his natural style. He also took pride in not knowing the rules of composition and therefore not being constrained by them."

The commentator reasonably regards such insouciance as silly. There is a persuasive case for learning classical music before composing it. Gaining familiarity with materials and facility with techniques can only be liberating for the person of talent. Then, having well learned the rules, he can fruitfully break them.

Music is not the only area with people who speak with seeming confidence on matters about which they know little. Economics, in particular, attracts charlatans by the carload.

An official of an organization of incessant complaint and criticism has blessed us with a discordant diatribe. The object of his scorn, sarcasm, and superciliousness is something he chooses to call "capitalism." All the weaknesses and deficiencies of individuals, all the woes and miseries of society, are immediate consequences of "capitalism." Greed and selfishness, stupidity and insensitivity, deviousness and unfairness, coercion and fraud — all are manifestations of "capitalism."

No economic arrangement will convert scarcity into plenty or transform men into angels. But masses of humanity are learning from experience that our best hope of relatively prosperous and civil communities lies in private rights to use of property, open markets, and contained government. It is thus that individual choice, initiative, and productivity will best flourish. And it is in those clumsy and divisive strategies and activities which are most *non-* or *anti*-capitalistic that we have performed worst.

There is a persuasive case for learning what capitalism is and is not before assessing it.

Mouse Wisdom: Understanding Adam Smith and the Economy

ᴓᴓᴓᴓ

Mouse Karl was in one of his sophisticated moods of insightful sneering. "You and Professor Allen," he sneered to Mouse Adam in sophisticatedly insightful manner, "like to laud Adam Smith as the great father figure of modern economics. But Smith was either extraordinarily naive or a deliberate purveyor of capitalistic propaganda. And, in extolling Smith, you and Allen also are either innocent of sense or guilty of little integrity."

"Well!" exclaimed the amiable Adam. "What inspired that outburst? Adam Smith was capable of error and inadequacy. Further, there have been giants in the history of economic analysis both before and after Smith. Still, his influence on serious economic thought has been enormous."

"That has to be a misfortune," snapped Karl, "for Smith basically misled us. He taught that we prosper most when we put ourselves into the grubby hands of business people, painting captains of commerce as paragons of prosperity and philanthropy. In actuality, capitalists are at least as greedy and self-centered as real people."

"You may not be persuaded by Smith's analyses of history, institutions, and policies," replied Adam with some impatience, "but do try to get straight what the man was saying. Smith certainly was *not* an apologist for the business community. He observed: 'People of the same trade seldom meet together, even for merriment and diversion, but the conversation ends in a conspiracy against the public, or in some contrivance to raise prices.' He bitterly complained about the common propensities in the business world to try to monopolize and collude, to conspire against workers and the public, to seek governmental protection against competition. Does this suggest that Smith wanted the businessman, any more than the king and his bureaucrats, to be the autonomous master of mankind?"

"I confess that I am confused," conceded Karl. "If businessmen are so grasping, so willing to exploit, how could Smith promote an arrangement of private property and open markets, thereby giving free play to the most unlovely characteristics of people?"

"Market processes, with efficient production and exchange," answered Adam, "do not require that we like one another and are inspired by purity of heart to cooperate with one another. Market institutions and prices provide options and incentives to use our privately-owned resources well. Our intention is to benefit ourselves. But we individually prosper by supplying valuable goods and services to others, led as by 'an invisible hand' to coordinate our activities to the benefit of all."

"I see," said Karl contritely, "that there is more sense and subtlety in Smith than I had supposed. Smith understood that men are not angels. But with appropriate ground rules of the market, we can — quite amazingly — channel acquisitive instincts and aggressive inclinations to mutual advantage and the common good."

Mouse Wisdom: Right Thinking, Good Feeling, and Power

ᘓᘓᘓᘓ

Karl, the rather surly and belligerent mouse of my office, was in his usual mood. "Professor Allen and his economist friends," he belligerently grumbled in surly manner, "are confused wimps."

His mouse friend, Adam, was pained but patient, and waited for an explanation.

"Economists are wimps," Karl went on, "because they profess to be leery of *power* some mice have over others. One must be a mouse among mice. We must *do* things to live well, and, by definition, power is the capability to get things done. But economists are confused wimps, because they worry much more about *governmental* power than about *business* power."

"No economist would deny," Adam said assuringly, "that there is work to be done in a world of scarcity. And we certainly are much more effective — more powerful, if you please — when we work together. The real questions pertain to *organization*. *How* are we to coordinate our individual efforts for *whose* purpose?"

"In broad outline," snapped the narrow-minded Karl, "the answer is apparent. We cannot expect tens of millions of mice to agree spontaneously on what to do and how to do it. A few at the top must be in charge. But those few cannot be businessmice. Daddy Warbucks types are selfish and mean-spirited. In contrast, government mice are nice, dedicated only to public service."

Adam was aghast. "You're fooling," he suggested without conviction. "All mice are interested in their own jobs and rewards. But those in business best prosper by being most productive, efficiently responding to community preferences. Those in government best prosper by subtly subsidizing inefficiency, increasing their own stature and authority while reducing the community's wealth and freedom."

"Doubtless, autocratic, arbitrary, largely unaccountable government power can be misdirected," conceded Karl. "But that means simply that we have to have genteel people shrewdly running a civilized community. As a glamorous economist once put it: '... dangerous acts can be done safely in a country which thinks rightly, which could be the way to hell if they were executed by those who feel wrongly.'"

"That surely is silly," said a somber Adam. "Sometimes we have to do dangerous things in an unfriendly world. But, by definition, dangerous acts cannot be done safely. And the danger is not lessened by bowing obsequiously to those of purported inspired genius and good feeling who possess great powers of conviction and of persuasion. Beware those who are supremely satisfied that they know — and should be allowed to impose — what is best for the rest of us.

"Big government," Adam concluded, "means power of a few imposed on the lives of many. Six thousand years of recorded human history have provided ample evidence that big concentrations of discretionary power are to be avoided where possible and severely contained where unavoidable."

"The World's Most Materialistic Nation"

✍✍✍✍

Many have much difficulty accepting a world of possibilities which are limited and costly. They look for reward and refinement obtained without pain and price. When choices must be made and pains borne and prices paid, they blame, not ubiquitous scarcity, but materialistic society.

A Los Angeles newspaper has a popular columnist who specializes in dry humor and wry wisdom. He is amusing when innocuous, but when trying to be analytical and philosophical he can be as misleading as the editorial writers of his paper.

The columnist visited a coastal neighborhood of Los Angeles. He had a "pleasant" lunch in a cafe which is "an ornament." And the people parading along the boardwalk were "wonderful." But these "wonderful" people evidently are getting "the kind of atmosphere they deserve." If so, they don't deserve much. For the cafe is an oasis in a desert of sleaze. "... the end of the continent," he writes, "the end, actually, of the Western World" has become "a cheap bazaar, a penny-grubbing row of hustlers." "Perhaps it's only fitting," he concludes, "that the West Coast of the world's most materialistic nation should be a store-front."

"... the world's most materialistic nation ...." Nonsense. People, unfortunately, are people. What they reflect largely are the common human qualities of greed and gaucherie. They differ little among themselves in such unsavory respects, although the relatively wealthy can better camouflage such characteristics. If — contrary to fact — we could measure degrees of "materialism," we would not find one nation significantly more materialistic than all the others.

Minimal fulfillment of material wants is not a sufficient basis for advancement of the arts and sciences, but it is necessary. Primitive, impoverished communities do not produce much of the mind or reveal much of the soul. Of necessity, they must be wholly materialistic almost constantly merely to survive. You may rejoice in concert halls and art museums. But the works performed or displayed there are not manna from heaven or conjured only from delicate emotions. They stem from a particular use of scarce resources. They are costly and must be paid for. They are a luxury and can be afforded by only those societies of well-directed materialism, people who need not devote all their efforts and available resources to satisfying elemental wants and requirements.

Do not scorn producers, including those who bring demanders and suppliers together in the market. Do not further corrupt parasitic flower-children by telling them that they are precious and fetching in their uselessness. And do not subversively and ridiculously falsify the record by blaming America first and capitalism alone.

It is not that the rest of the world is less materialistic than we are; rather, it is commonly less efficient in its materialism.

On Herds and Free People

ﾟﾟﾟﾟ

The massive but jerry-built mansion of communism is ingloriously collapsing. Its failure — in both theory and action — is almost embarrassing in its abruptness and totality. But a hard-core band of American intellectualoids — professors and journalists, for the most part — will not abandon the sinking ship of collectivism. They suffer form a commissar complex. Watch them twist and squirm as the vicious idiocy of a centralized-command society becomes evident.

One last line of defense in the fiasco is that "pure" communism really is perfectly splendid, but the clumsy Soviets and their crude little friends simply bungled the job, so we should continue to try it and finally get it right. A second defense is to renew the attack on the open, individualistic society of democratic capitalism, for it, too, has failed to generate utopia.

The pervasive, overbearing state has had its opportunities for thousands of years — and its performance has been abysmal. The essence of communism, as Karl Marx boasted, is to cultivate an alleged herd-like instinct of humans, to mold inherently compliant people into a homogeneous class and mass. Discipline is to be imposed from on high, with activity directed by publicly unaccountable bureaucrats armed with five-year plans. Supposedly, this kind of command regime provides the essential core of efficiency.

But any civilized concept of efficiency — political as well as economic — calls for processes and production in accordance with *personal* desires and preferences of *individual* members of the community. Private property, lamented Marx, fatally distracts and scatters the subservient herd. And, of course, it will not do in the smothering Brave New World for individuals to be free to pursue their own various ends, using their own resources in ways consistent with their own aspirations and criteria.

The critical claim is correct that even robust capitalism will not restore the Garden of Eden. With *either* capitalism or communism, this will remain a world of scarcity and thus of conflict. But the record of capitalism in alleviating scarcity, in facilitating best possible adjustment to unavoidable limits, has been accountably satisfying.

Even Marx lavishly praised the remarkable productiveness of capitalism.

Further, capitalism has performed best when it has been constrained least, with minimal dilutions and distortions by governmental directives, penalties, subsidizations, and discriminations. The purported problems of capitalism stem mainly from stubbornly persistent efforts — by both its avowed enemies and its unconscious friends — to subvert and transform capitalism.

The lovers of state power and planning — and of herd-like communities — fatally misconstrue and conveniently misrepresent the nature of people and their past and their potentiality.

Making of Public Policy

Congress, Ethics, and Rules

✄✄✄✄

"The rich are very different from you and me." "Yes," wrote Ernest
Hemingway, "they have more money."

But what of public officials? Are they different from you and
me? Many believe that government types, unlike the rest of us, should
always put the community's interest before their own.

So when government representatives do not act altruistically, a
lack of ethics is often blamed. Ethical behavior is no less important in
personal and commercial relationships than in government. Honesty,
tolerance, dependability, responsibility   —   such ethical attributes
facilitate interaction of individuals in directing competitive behavior to
productive ends.

But even if all were always ethical, individuals would still have
to face scarcity, make choices, and bear costs. And when doing so, they
would not selflessly sacrifice themselves to help others or, at the other
extreme, selfishly promote their interests by destroying others. Neither
full-blown altruism or greed would dominate activity in a world of high
ethics. Here, individuals act with a regard for both others and
themselves. By following legitimate self-interest, they utilize their
productive resources to promote best the well-being of others.

In effect, that is what the marketplace does well. Its rules of
conduct direct individuals to promote others' interests   —   in order to
promote their own. To obtain more, one efficiently produces what
others want.

But people are not angels. Unethical behavior stains the
marketplace, as it blemishes personal relationships and government.
Compared with the marketplace, however, government lacks effective
rules of the game to direct self-interest to the common benefit.

These rules are absent or weak for a number of reasons. First,
government officials are often unable to *identify* community
preferences. The community cannot easily communicate to government.
Most voters rationally remain ignorant about particular issues, for
becoming well informed is a costly process with only the small benefit

of casting a vote more intelligently — and the vote is for a candidate who represents a large package of diverse issues.

Second, government people typically lack effective *incentive* to satisfy community preferences, for, unlike producers in the market, they do not increase their own wealth by efficiently investing resources they control.

And third, government officials predictably give disproportionate weight to *special interest groups* that lobby forcefully for actions which bestow handsome benefits on them but spread costs inconspicuously among the community.

So even if officials were always ethical, they would still indulge vigorous special interests at the expense of nebulous community preferences. The fundamental problem of government is not so much inadequate ethics as of deficient rules, which provide inadequate information, faulty guidance, and ineffectual constraints for government.

Thomas Jefferson and Leviathan

✍✍✍✍

Several years ago, we were treated to a treatise entitled, "The Imperial *Presidency.*" But we may fear also the constitutionally ill-defined *judiciary,* which ill defines the Constitution. And for some, there is no imperialism like *Congressional* imperialism — unless it be that of the *administrative bureaucracy.*

Government is rule-making power. By decreeing rules, government stipulates who may do what in what ways, it sequesters wealth to enforce the preferences of those in command of political power — and it provides massive opportunity to the political elite for personal aggrandizement. The various roles and activities commingle and coagulate into one mass of self-serving and self-generating power.

The power of government — the power to forbid and to channel community activities, the power to reward and to penalize, the power to requisition and utilize great resources — is enormously valuable. What is valuable will be ardently sought, and what is sought will be sold at some price. Precisely what is bought and sold, and the nature and size of the price, are determined by the ground rules of the community. But in any society, there will be mighty efforts to obtain political power. And those very efforts work strongly to increase and centralize the power.

The ingenious efforts of our constitutional founding fathers two hundred years ago have had a unique degree of success in perpetuating our liberties. But even the most sophisticated structuring of government may be doomed to progressive deterioration and ultimate failure before the unrelenting tides of aggressive greed.

Thomas Jefferson fought the magnificent fight for freedom, but he was not naive. "The natural progress of things is for liberty to yield and government to gain ground," he observed. He saw that "one of the most profound preferences in human nature" leads to "appropriating wealth produced by the labor of others, rather than producing it by one's own labor." And the appropriating is done largely through government: "... the stronger the government, the weaker the producer," he warns us, "the less consideration need be given [the producer] and the more might be taken away from him."

The most basic political question is not the relative degrees of imperialism among the presidency, the courts, the legislature, and the bureaucracy. The problem is *governmental* imperialism. Maintaining the appearance and even the reality of a steady *balance* of power among the various divisions and agencies of government will not maintain freedom if the *amount* and *pervasiveness* of government power increases fast enough long enough. Leviathan is Leviathan, and it can continue to engulf and thoroughly dominate the individual and his private associations, whether the honcho of the state is called President, Justice, Congressman, or Commissioner.

Time, Thought, and the Making of Policy

♪♪♪♪

Much of public policy inevitably is economic policy. But it would be remarkably innocent to suppose that many economists in government devote their major energies to imaginative meditation on the massive problems of the universe or to construction of elaborate analytic models.

Government life is not the contemplative life of the logical and independent mind, with scholars of maturity and continuing accomplishment systematically bringing their accumulated wisdom and developed expertise to bear on the policy issues of today and the shrewdly anticipated problems of tomorrow.

Commonly, government economists are quick-draw specialists, shooting from the hip and putting out fires. Not only are they pressured to come up with answers to problems when no well-founded answers exist, but they have to do so almost instantaneously, for there is no time for contemplation, research, deduction, and precise writing. Crises must be dealt with right now, so gather a few data and prepare a memo by tomorrow morning — if not by this afternoon.

An eminent economist serving in the Defense Department found that "there is never an opportunity to study a problem in the sense that an academic wants to study a problem .... The decision has to be made quite often within ... minutes. ... In the academic world, you think now and decide never; ... in the government, it's just exactly the other way around."

In his first week on the job, a senior staff member of the Council of Economic Advisers was instructed by the Council's chairman to prepare a memo on the balance of payments impact of a dock strike. He had six hours for the job — including typing time. The memo, by the way, was to be provided to government attorneys who were to seek a Taft-Hartley injunction in court the next morning. The legally specified basis for the injunction was demonstration of a national emergency. So, first, the Administration made the decision to claim an emergency, in order to obtain the injunction, and, then, economists were to provide justifying data and analysis.

This incident was related to the director of an "analysis" office in a major department, who responded: "We have that all the time. ...

[The current Secretary] never gets around to anything until Monday for Tuesday morning, and so people work frantically all day and literally often all night to have it ready for Tuesday morning. ... So we had to pull this thing together, rewrite some, edit it, get it typed, reproduced in umpteen copies, because everything has to be in umpteen copies. We had about 95 pages in six hours.... I had the whole staff working on it. Well, we did it, but you're not very proud of it. ... I can cite frantic things ... papers fell all over the floor, and we were all crawling on the floor getting our particular bits .... It is really incredible, you just can't believe it ... it was laughable ... really wild ... it is appalling, and ... sometimes these papers ... are the basis for policies and decisions...."

Maybe laughable, certainly appalling. But so it often goes in government: decide now and think never.

Thought and Influence

✍✍✍✍

There was a peculiar letter recently in *The Wall Street Journal*. Presumably, it is meant to be taken seriously, for one simply does not write non-serious letters to the *Journal*.

The letter claims that there are two Milton Friedmans. One Friedman is the Nobel Prize-winner, and the letter describes him as "a brilliant theoretician" who "peddles only pure reason." But the other Friedman "refuses to stay in his think tank" and "peddles dope" to "economically immature politicians." The alleged dope includes criticism of the Federal Reserve and condemnation of minimum wage laws — criticisms and condemnation in which Dr. Friedman is joined by an enormous proportion of economists.

The cutesy letter is, indeed, peculiar in professional substance — but quite common in the convictions of the community.

According to common conviction, it is alright for you to think — even to think insightfully, innovatively, and profoundly — so long as your ideas have no consequences. We will "praise and honor" the thinker, says the letter-writer, so long as we can keep his "grubby hands off our economy." Feel free to do your intellectual thing so long as we are free to keep you quiet and ignored.

It is alright for you to generate conclusions logically and support them empirically so long as you do not effectively promote them, always giving equal weight in your discussion to alternative views which do not meet the market test of thought. The criterion of teaching is to be balance in presentation, not correctness in analysis.

Such schizophrenia and perversity is widespread.

It is alright to earn much money so long as taxation and regulation keep your consumption and your contributions to political campaigns not much greater than mine.

Productivity is alright, even if grubby, so long as we are not obliged to link performance with pay.

It is alright to accumulate some appreciable wealth so long as you cannot bequeath much of it to your children.

It is alright to be competent and accomplished so long as we have quotas on hiring and on college admissions so that the relatively incompetent and unaccomplished will not be handicapped.

It is alright to advocate — indeed, to praise — competition, so long as I can use government taxes and constraints and subsidizations to promote my monopoly.

Free trade is alright, so long as it is fair, and fair trade requires protecting me from those — both domestic and foreign — who can make a better product or produce at smaller cost or sell at lower price.

The open market is alright so long as government puts a lid over prices of things I buy — such as apartments and foreign currency — and a floor under things I sell — such as farm goods and labor services.

Many among us, despite protestation of personal purity, do not truly trust either the mind or the market. Sense is alright so long as we can dominate it will silliness.

Laws of the Few and of the Many

ॐॐॐॐ

Every day I grow older. So does the American population. At the turn of the century, people 65 years and over made up only 4 percent of the total population; by 1930 they were over 5 percent; in 1970, nearly 10 percent; now, close to 13 percent — and the trend will doubtless continue.

As the upward surge in the proportion of the elderly gathered strength in the 1930s, retirement and medical-aid legislation began a governmental subsidization of the elderly which some find troublesome. We will have fewer and fewer active workers in the future supporting each retiree.

This is a real issue. But does it follow that the problem of helping the old will grow along with the ratio of the old to the whole population? Farmers did not find it so when changing in the opposite direction. A century ago, people in agriculture made up 95 percent of the country. That ratio steadily fell, and now the agrarian sector is only about 2 percent. As the proportion fell, the farm bloc gradually increased its political power but recently has begun to lose it back.

There seems to be a Law of the Few. When a special interest group is very large relative to the entire community, there are not many to subsidize it. As the group becomes relatively smaller, but is still sizable, it can adequately coalesce into a potent lobbying bloc: Goals can become better defined and focused among fewer people, organizational costs are reduced, and benefits of collective action become more concentrated.

Economist Richard B. McKenzie finds a corresponding Law of the Many. A very small class of citizens may attract little political attention; then, as it increases over time relative to the entire community, it gains political muscle, especially if the people can organize well as a pressure group; but eventually, the bloc becomes so large that its demands on the rest of society become onerous, and it becomes so diverse that the difficulties and costs of organization dilute political effectiveness.

As farmers reached a peak of power when declining as a proportion of the population and then weakened as they continued to fall in relative numbers, so have the elderly gained in influence as they grew to an optimal proportion of society; and recently they have shown signs of weakening power as they grow to still greater proportions.

Professor McKenzie finds much evidence consistent with this application of the Law of the Many. Annual real net benefits per capita for the elderly have been about constant, or even fallen a bit, since 1982. During the 1980s, elderly benefits decreased significantly relative to the general economy and to the rest of government spending. Indeed, the rate of increase of elderly benefits per person began to fall in the early 1950s.

So the elderly continue to expand in numbers and as a share of total population. But that very expansion has contributed to a weakening of political influence. And politicians do not humor weakness with ever-increasing benefits.

Politicians and Progress

Sociology and psychology are fields infested with land mines even for specialists. Amateurs should cultivate the pride of humility. Still, we cannot hope to understand how the world works and to help it work better unless we have some well-founded notions of why people persist in acting like people.

The *Los Angeles Times* has presented a long feature on a member of the California legislature who may be "the nation's most influential black female elected official." It is a striking profile, disturbing in some respects.

The woman is imposing, respected and dreaded by both foes and friends. Evidently, she is a woman of inner strength as well as outward abrasiveness, of outward assurance as well as inner misgivings, of social commitment as well as alienation from the world she wants to impress and reform. She is characterized as a Machiavellian politician who largely disdains diplomacy with opponents and civility with her own associates. She seems to have difficulty distinguishing belligerent boorishness from tough-mindedness.

Her mode of behavior is mainly conspicuous physical activity, energized by barely disciplined emotion — rallies, marches, confrontations — all of which she finds to be "exciting, exciting, exciting." But her agenda consists of little more than hopes and visions; her strategy is confined mainly to randomly selected, immediate coups. And this, she seems belatedly to suspect, is not a basis of long-evolving progress.

Excitement of the moment cannot be indefinitely sustained in the ranks, and the beleaguered opposition learns to weather the loud aggressiveness. The irrational high hopes, unabetted by coherent conception of social construction, begin to wither, with expended euphoria leaving frustration, embitterment, and war-weariness. The initial victories are real but severely limited, and the enemy feels confirmed in his long-standing wonderments about the competence and commitment of the rag-tag troops — doubts which are increasingly shared by the activists themselves.

The black woman legislator shares one problem common to all politicians: there is little time — or inclination — for thought and deduction, little energy for research and analysis, little feel for intellectual persuasion. Harried and preoccupied with crises of the moment, the politician begins with analytic capital which is inadequate for the job and then becomes increasingly outmoded and deteriorated.

Racial-minority politicians have peculiar problems in moving from preoccupation with tactics of confrontation to strategies of growth. How, indeed, are we to make significant, continuing progress in melding into a civil, prospering society people of greatly different heritages, preparations, mores, and aspirations?

Whatever may be said in support of a period of belligerent eruption, beyond a point quite quickly reached, profane posturing must give way to productive performance.

Lower Education: Schools and Sense

Education and Entrepreneurs

ॐॐॐॐ

Can we make public schools work?

Teachers and administrators typically tell us te give them more money and make classes smaller. Yet real spending per pupil has increased, classes have gotten smaller, and student performance has deteriorated and stagnated.

Others advocate deregulation. Free schools from stifling government regulators, they say, and each school will find its own best method of education. The proposal has some sense. After a nationwide study, John E. Chubb of the Brookings Institution concludes: "The public education system functions naturally and routinely ... to burden schools with excessive bureaucracy, to discourage effective school organization, and to stifle student achievement. Efforts to improve schools are therefore doomed unless they eliminate or sharply curtail the influence of the institutions that cause the schools' problems in the first place."

But deregulation, by itself, is no solution. Making schools unaccountable to government still leaves them unanswerable to the communities they serve. How, then, to make schools answerable?

Mr. Chubb and colleague Terry M. Moe propose "a new system of public education that will not be governed directly by politics but will be controlled indirectly through markets — through school competition and parental choice."

Offering similar advice for schools in North Carolina is John Hood of the John Locke Foundation. Mr. Hood observes that schools can be freed from stifling bureaucratic control and at the same time be made directly accountable to the communities they serve. This can be done by making schools "entrepreneurial" institutions.

Mr. Hood observes that we rely on entrepreneurs to produce most of what we buy. These are people who risk their wealth in an

effort to satisfy community preferences. If they correctly anticipate and
efficiently satisfy those preferences, the community rewards them with
profits. But if they fail — as many do — the community penalizes them
with losses.

How different are public schools with their guaranteed
customers? Schools do not flourish or fail according to their success in
producing services communities prefer. Instead, schools satisfy their
own bureaucracies, resist threatening changes in organization and

Indexes of Real Public School Spending Per Student, Scholastic Aptitude Test Scores, and Student-Teacher Ratio, 1963-1990

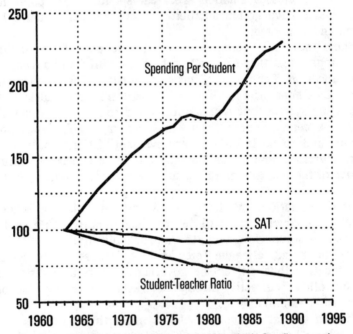

Note: Data are for all elementary and secondary public schools. Spending-per-student
is adjusted for inflation by using the consumer price index. Scholastic Aptitude Test
(SAT) scores are the combined scores for verbal and math tests.

Sources: The *Condition of Education, 1990*, U.S. Dept. of Education; *Digest of
Education Statistics*, 1990, U.S. Dept. of Education; *College-Bound Seniors: The Class
of 1990*, The College Board.

technology, pay bad workers as much as good ones, and protect shirkers with tenure.

But public schools could be innovative, efficient, and accountable — if, that is, they functioned like entrepreneurial organizations. Instead of directly financing existing schools, government could let parents direct the funds to the schools they choose. A public school would then obtain revenue only by satisfying customers.

"No matter how interesting or promising a particular entrepreneurial school might be to elected officials or the politically powerful," explains Mr. Hood, "it would thrive or fail solely on the basis of customer selection. If parents did not choose to send their children to the school, it would cease to be."

Smoking and Schooling

৶৶৶৶

Nicotine is as addictive as heroin or cocaine, says the American Lung Association. And the Surgeon General's 1988 report on smoking concludes that people persist in lighting up despite known health risks because tobacco is so addictive.

So how to give up smoking? A common answer is medical treatment. Presumably, smoking is a *disease* requiring a *medical cure.*

But Stanton Peele, a psychologist and health-care researcher, disputes this conclusion in a *Reason* magazine essay. He cites a national survey by the Centers for Disease Control, which discovered that people are most likely to quit smoking *on their own.* Of smokers who tried to quit in the previous decade, more than 47 percent who tried on their own were successful. But fewer than 24 percent who relied on treatment succeeded.

"Along with a desire to stop smoking," observes Mr. Peele, "the most important ingredient in quitting seems to be the belief that you *can* succeed, that you can live and function without cigarettes." But by focusing on smoking as a disease requiring medical treatment, programs undermine individuals' responsibility for their smoking. The message is that people can *not* quit smoking by themselves. No wonder those in treatment programs are less successful than those who try to quit smoking by accepting responsibility for their behavior.

The lesson applies also to schools. Students, too, are more likely to succeed when they realize they are responsible for their personal performance. Yet, for years, many educators in one way or another have repudiated or unwittingly undermined individual responsibility in the classroom. As treatment programs have unintentionally told smokers they cannot succeed on their own, so also have many schools told students they cannot achieve on their own. Instead, societal diseases like poverty, broken families, drugs, and racial discrimination are blamed for a lack of student achievement.

One result is a decrease in student performance. An associated result has been serious erosion of academic standards. If responsibility for student achievement falls on society at large, not on students, then standards of individual performance make little sense. Indeed, educators who require their students to satisfy academic standards have been called oppressive, insensitive, and elitist.

This view is patronizing and pernicious. Patronizing because it assumes that students cannot succeed on their own. And pernicious because it robs many of an education.

Fortunately, some schools began reinstituting standards during the '80s. Student performance then began to pick up noticeably, especially among black high school students.

Their achievement shows that individuals behave differently when they know they are responsible for their successes and failures. They are then more likely to succeed when trying to quit smoking. And they are more likely to learn in school.

Economics Courses, Comprehension, and Exams

∅∅∅∅

A national sample of high school students has done very badly on an economics test consisting of multiple-choice questions. Some academic types and other pillars of the community have been properly horrified, and there have been renewed calls for more mandated economics education lest the Republic crumble.

I really am not in favor of ignorance: education in general, including education in economics, has its attractiveness. But how important is it for high school kids to have exposure to formal economics — even if, uncommonly, the exposure is substantial, the reading materials excellent, the teachers committed and competent, and the subject matter is genuine economics rather than consumer tips, business education, or ill-defined "social studies"?

No society has owed — or is ever likely to owe — its growth and prosperity to sophistication of its citizens in nominal economics training. One's personal wealth will not be increased by learning marketplace tricks in an economics course, for such tricks are not taught there. Even business decisionmakers use little of the trappings of overt economic analysis: the "economics" they use comes readily to mind through common sense, jungle instinct, and experience, not requiring the taking of a course. If, on rare occasions, the fruits of sophisticated and stylized economics are to be plucked, a professional economist can be hired, as accountants, statisticians, and lawyers are hired for their specialized, arcane services.

Still, education for the sake of education, for the sake of intellectual and cultural refinement — if designed appropriately and carried out effectively — is a worthy endeavor. It is appropriate that the elders of the tribe see to it that the braves learn something of the institutions and ways and policies of the world even if such cultivation teaches little of the grubby mechanics of holding a job, consuming and investing shrewdly, or running a business.

But *is* economics education designed appropriately and carried out effectively? It appears that commonly high school courses in so-called economics have been designed by analytic hacks, taught by bewildered innocents, and in content bear hardly a family resemblance to genuine economics. And now, the *testing* of students' economics competence presents additional problems.

The recent high-school test — quite predictably — is very big on selected *words* of economic language and very light on carrying the *tune* of economic analysis. It focuses on vocabulary and definitions and summary relationships, conclusions, and characterizations. But to memorize a list of foreign words does not by itself mean operational mastery of the language. Economics is basically "a way of thinking," "a technique of the mind." Traditional high school classes are not likely to go far in developing such facility. And standardized multiple-choice exams are not likely to go far in usefully testing it.

Mouse Wisdom: Television Education with Commercials

✍✍✍✍

Sensitive Mouse Karl was resplendent but outraged in his rodent rectitude. "Look at this outrage," he calmly screamed.

Mouse Adam was somewhat shaken by the outburst of sophisticated agitation. "Is Western Civilization in peril?" he asked.

"Yes, now that you mention it," cried Karl. "A business organization is corrupting our perfectly splendid educational system. It is offering junior and senior high schools expensive communications equipment. Each school is given $50,000 worth of television monitors, satellite dishes, and video-cassette recorders. And it provides a daily ten-minute program of news headlines, background material on major issues, week-long series of significant analyses, miscellaneous facts, and quizzes."

"That sounds great," mused a bemused Adam, "if the program is well done. So how is this a dastardly scheme of subversion?"

"Oh, the program has been generally well received by both students and teachers," Karl grudgingly acknowledged. "But the idea is fatally flawed in its essence. First, every student is to watch the program. That makes the audience captive, and in this Land of the Free schools are not to *require* students to do *anything*. Second — and here I nearly swoon," nearly swooned Karl, "the ten minutes of good substance is polluted by an additional two minutes of (if I must use the word) *commercials!*"

"Gracious," groaned Adam in mock horror. "You mean all this equipment and programming is not free? The suppliers have to be compensated?"

"Of course, it has to be paid for," grumped Karl. "But no one should *profit* from the arrangement. It ought to be unconstitutional for public schools to sell audiences to advertisers. Such grubbiness is a poor example for sensitive young scholars."

"I confess," confessed Adam, "that I had not realized that today's school kids are such delicate flowers and that today's schools are such pristine centers of sanctity and decorum. On the contrary, children are now raised on TV commercials, and another two minutes per day of them will not be fatal. Indeed, the ratio of substance to commercials is much greater in this school program than the ratio in regular television. And the schools certainly can use outside professional help in teaching current events and recent history."

"Then why is it," asked a confused Karl, "that conspicuous elements of the educational establishment do not wish to participate in this TV venture?"

"Could it possibly be," softly suggested Adam, "that school administrators and spokesmen of teachers' unions are fearful — not of corruption of students by commercials — but of competition from outsiders? They may be unsettled by imagination, initiative, and innovation in the classroom. Or do they find advertising — and capitalism in general — to be crass and coarse? Perhaps they are repelled by markets and profits."

"To such questions, the correct answer," answered Karl, "probably is: all of the above."

Higher Education: The Crisis of the Campus

Of Bruins and Humbugs

ℒℒℒℒ

Public universities in California have been recently assaulted and subverted by aggressive know-nothing intellectual ragamuffins.

Consider shenanigans involving departments in two schools. At a conspicuous university in the southern part of the state — a neighbor of Big Bear Mountain, it can here be delicately given the *nom de plume* of Bruin U — mobs and politicians loudly sought to convert a Chicano Studies *program* into a Chicana/o *department*. At a less conspicuous school in the northern part of the state — call it Humbug U — administrators have slyly suppressed the systematic study of economics, obliterating the Department of Economics.

Both efforts — expansion of one program at Bruin and contraction of another at Humbug — have largely succeeded. And the successes have dismayingly wounded an already weakened state university system.

There has long been sporadic pressure for a Chicano department at Bruin U. But the demand has been more political than professional. Resources and learning opportunities have been available for years, with a great variety of courses in both a Chicano Studies program and a Latin American Studies program. Degrees are offered in both. But all this, along with the lure of instructors handing out ridiculously high course grades, attracted only a minute number of majors. Last spring, an element of agitators decided that the time was ripe — when university finances were in desperate straits — to make the grandstanding push for departmental status and budget commensurate with the bloated grades.

Along with mob hooliganism, including a trashing of the Faculty Center, the key offensive tactic was a hunger strike on campus. Nine sensitive and heroic souls — a faculty member, five Bruin customers, and three outsiders — offered their bods in promotion of the life of the mind.

On the fourth day of the fast, I spent half an hour talking with five or six of the supportive Chicano students congregated on the selected hallowed portion of the university grounds. They were entirely pleasant. And they were wholly uninformed on, and not much interested in, the various questions I asked:

• What is the substantive content of the departmental proposal? How many courses in what sub-areas would be offered, given by how many professors, with what degree requirements?

• Is this department, like all others at Bruin U, to be a research, as well as teaching, unit, offering graduate degrees?

• Would the department duplicate, with its own specially hired faculty, courses now available — e.g., International Economics — in other departments?

• To what extent is the focus and thrust to pertain to Mexico and how much to the Chicano experience in the United States? Is the major underlying purpose to provide specialized, sophisticated education to Chicanos or to provide general, elemental introduction to non-Chicanos? Is the essential idea to enable young Chicanos to "find themselves" and revel in their culture or is it largely to equip them to be productive in the larger society and thereby prosper?

• Is this single department to be the intellectual and cultural counterpart (and counterweight) of all the rest of the huge campus — and, if so, doesn't that imply that it must be an interdisciplinary program and not a conventional, tightly defined department?

• Can there reasonably be a Chicano department without introducing also departments for blacks, Asians, Jews, women, homosexuals (and straights) — and perhaps one for white, male Protestants?

The budding scholars acknowledged their innocence on all such issues of purpose and procedure, but insisted that it was somehow vitally important to have their own "autonomous" department. They did not reply to my observation that evidently they wanted simply to gain departmental administrative status and only then would they begin to wonder about what to do with it.

It has been embarrassingly apparent from the outset — and later it was made explicit — that the Chicano movement and its political and community support has nothing in essence to do with scholarship, learning, teaching, research, and analysis: it is wholly about domineering, getting a slice of the action, getting on the 6 o'clock news, and controlling some wealth created mainly by others. It has nothing to do with constructively joining forces, with assimilation or melding into a broader, more encompassing community of scholars; it is, instead, calculated invasion and manipulation, a taking-over and a casting-out of an institution and its purposes, strategies, standards, and ethos which have, by and large, served society very well for a long time.

*****

An eminent legal scholar was asked what is the best undergraduate background for law school. He replied that the major field was less important than certain personal qualities and characteristics: if the student can read and write effectively and will work very hard, he can do well in study of the law.

But, the scholar continued, the undergraduate major is not a trivial matter, and the most appropriate specialization is economics. The major reason for the attractiveness of study of economics as background for study of law is not *subject-matter* — although economics and law mesh well in substance. More important is *methodology*, the technique of logical thought. Economics majors are used to dealing systematically with formal models of definition and relation; they are oriented toward rigorous deduction and empirical testing; they are, in short, problem-solvers.

For years, ol' Humbug U has belittled and suppressed the study of economics. Now, they have effectively suspended the major in economics, abolished other campus programs in economics, and reduced the economics faculty essentially to two teaching positions.

The school has severe budgetary problems, to be sure, but while trashing economics, it has introduced *174 new* courses in the last two years, including "Sex, sexuality, and power," "Eating disorders," "Lesbian studies," "Tap dance," "Native American women literature," "Religion and Feminism," and "Inspiring grass roots empowerment."

More courses are offered in Psychology than in Economics, History and Political Science combined. There are four times more courses in Sociology than in Economics, along with some three times as many in Journalism and in Speech Communication. More are given in Native American Studies, in Ethnic Studies, and in Recreational Studies than in Economics, and as many in Women's Studies as in Economics. There are more in Music and in Physical Education than in Mathematics, Chemistry, Physics, and Economics together.

Certainly, there is more to life — even the life of the mind — than elegant solving of well-specified puzzles. But the historian, political scientist, sociologist, anthropologist, or litterateur who is innocent of the elements of economic analysis is much less useful than he could be, and upon occasion will naively do harm.

Similarly, there is more to public policy and community survival in an unfriendly world than economics narrowly conceived. But we will mislead ourselves, divert and dilute our efforts, and waste our resources if we do not consistently and pervasively think in terms of such economics concepts as scarcity, alternatives, choices, costs, and productivity. If we are to save ourselves and prosper, it will be through the hard-headed "economic way of thinking," not by ethereal navel-contemplation and mushy-minded lurches in incoherent efforts simply to be sensitive and do good. One might suppose that university administrators would have some comprehension of all this. But evidently it is far too subtle for the petty and provincial paper-shufflers at Humbug U.

Education and intellectual professionalism are activities and competencies of some sophistication. Their promotion and attainment require and reflect a degree of refined acuteness. They are not likely to be developed effectively through the treacherous mischief of callow mobs, or conniving politicians, or contemptuous or cowardly administrators. Bruin U and Humbug U have been raped — and many there have enjoyed it.

The Crisis of the Campus

⌀⌀⌀⌀

I am a grumpy professor at a prestigious university. I am grumpy because I am a professor. For I do very little teaching; instead, I merely conduct classes. More accurately, while conducting classes, I profess much profundity — but not much is learned. And what little is learned is largely confined, by choice of the customers, to immediate, nitty-gritty concerns of the final exam.

The intellectual returns from student investment cannot be great when the investment is not great. And there is not likely to be great investment by those who are uncommitted, unorganized, undisciplined, unprepared, and unconscious, who have no professional pride and no conception of competence and accomplishment.

The problem is not only that most children of the campus — there *are* a few blessed exceptions — do not know much and cannot do much. In addition, most are blissfully unaware of how little they know and can do; they are not effectively engaged in the subtle and rigorous process of learning and have little notion of what is entailed in learning; and they have neither found nor had impressed upon them effective incentive to try to discover what to do in trying to learn. They are young even for their tender years.

Such dour assessment reflects a mountain of discouraging evidence. A few anecdotes illustrate:

• There was the freshman who allowed as how she would like to be a biologist, for, in her only biology class (in a lousy high school), she received a grade of D.

• There was the senior who had a part-time job as receptionist in an engineering firm, and concluded that it would be neat to be an engineer — although she found it impossible to grasp the concept of the slope of a straight line.

• There was the upper-division customer in a history-of-economic-theory class who asked the instructor during the final exam if we are living in the 20th century.

• There was the large proportion of another history class who agreed that Aristotle elaborated received Christian doctrine — 300 years before Jesus.

• A student in academic difficulty explained his failure to copy some key material from the blackboard by saying that he did not understand the point of the material — "and I never take down things I don't understand."

• More than one-third of a principles-of-economics class agreed that "there is no fundamental economic difference between communism and capitalism because both types of economies have capital goods and markets and economic managers."

• Nearly half of a basic economic theory class asserted that we live in a world of scarcity "because business is run for profit" or "because property is privately owned."

These genial young people hardly try to conceptualize, synthesize, and generalize; they have gained virtually no erudition or perspective; they are embarrassingly inarticulate and illiterate; they have no developed wisdom or insightfulness or sense of the wholeness and evolution of any part of their world; they are utterly lacking in analytic intuition, feel for causal relations, and intellectual flair.

An eminent colleague has publicly stated that "the *majority* of students cannot think or write or study at the college level. Neither will they learn. Most will graduate with a C, C+, or B- grade average. But they are *totally uneducated*. And most of them don't know it, having picked up no idea of what an education might be. The whole thing is scandalous."

Scandalous, indeed. But, in this crisis of the campus, do not look for much voluntary reform from college administrators and faculty, who commonly acquiesce in and even prosper from the scandal.

University Diversity and the Costs of Affirmative Action

ॐॐॐॐ

Not all university deans are all bad, even when awake. I once had a genteel discussion with the dean of a professional school. We talked about achieving sanctified "diversity" through "affirmative action" in the hiring of faculty.

The dean was pleased by his school having hired several racial-minority professors, and he said that he takes Affirmative Action "very seriously." At the same time, he held that the recruits were excellent by traditional academic/professional standards. I expressed gratification from the good fortune of the school in satisfying criteria both of minority status and of quality. The dean evinced some wonderment of why there need be any problem in such simultaneous satisfying of criteria.

But a potential problem inheres in use of dual criteria: *If* each criterion invariably yielded common guidance — if both indicators always pointed in the same direction — there would be no occasion to use both. Whether the potential problem becomes manifest is a case-by-case matter of how good one's fortune is. The rationale of Affirmative Action is that too few minority candidates rank sufficiently high on the scale of demonstrated or predictable competence, so non-professional considerations are sometimes required to offset professional deficiencies.

To "take Affirmative Action seriously" is to assign weight to the criterion of ethnicity or sex or religion or whatever. To assign such weight is to be willing to bear some amount of alternative cost — to be willing to trade-off some traditional professional excellence — in satisfying the conventionally extraneous criterion of minority favoritism.

If a university hires a minority individual because he is the best candidate, then no "affirmative action" was required. If that person would not otherwise have been hired on grounds of professional attractiveness, then there is waste and injury. Not only is there injury to the forsaken victim of the discrimination, but an inferior product will be supplied to the customers of the school. Even the coddled hiree may consider it a partially Pyrrhic victory as he labors under a cloud, while the most able of the minority staff are inappropriately tarred with the brush of suspicion and resentment.

Minority communities stand in need of genuine successes — successes beyond suspicion and reproach, unambiguous instances in substantial numbers of conspicuous accomplishment and warranted stature. Ignoring, much less subsidizing, mediocrity, winking at inadequate performance, will strengthen prejudice and invite scorn, delaying evolvement of practical equality of treatment and opportunity.

It has been contended that this is not properly the end of the story. Arguments have been made that traditional considerations of scholarly competence should be *supplemented* by additional sorts of measurement, especially in the interest of having variety of faculty background. But the great bulk of the campus curriculum calls for no idiosyncratic faculty experience. There is no such subject as "black statistics"; one need not be a victim of cancer to be an analyst of causes, diagnosis, and treatment of cancer; and it is not necessary to be unemployed to know much about determination of national income and production.

Indeed, some sorts of personal background and commitment to causes are a handicap of distraction and bias, not an asset, in gaining and conveying a balanced analytic understanding of the subject. The notion that there is something called "black law" or "women's law" which can be well taught only by blacks or women is persuasive only to those who prefer propaganda to dispassionate pedagogy.

Others hold that evaluation of scholarship is to be, not supplemented, but *eliminated*. There *are* qualities, characteristics, competencies, and accomplishments which can hardly be mechanically measured to the fourth decimal place, so some find it convenient to disdain sophisticated assessment and call for reliance on little other than random selections to fill quotas.

It may be that, in some cosmic weighing of all considerations, it is proper to be ready to bear (by whom?) some amount (how much?) of some sorts (what kinds?) of costs in the interest of greater minority representation than would obtain through traditional professional recruiting. I respect diversity of preferences and differences in willingness to bear costs. But I shall not applaud any attempt to suggest that there *are* no costs in Affirmative Action — or that the costs are surely smaller than associated gains.

*****

A university is to be an institution through which very able and thoroughly committed people preserve, enhance, and disseminate accumulated knowledge and acquired techniques of thought. All those who are prepared, in aptitude, attitude, and accomplishment, to participate effectively in the life of the mind are welcome, for there is sophisticated work to be done. But that work is diverted and resources are wasted by campus politicians among the faculty and the administrators (and by students who find brash promotion of Good Causes more fun than laborious study). It is such professional charlatans and intellectual wimps who prattle about university "greatness through diversity."

Much diversity is inherent in a university. The very word — uni-versity — suggests a fruitful bringing together of diverse elements and activities. But the latest cause of campus agitators is for still more diversity.

The agitation typically is incoherent at any level above sloganeering. Everyone with legitimate business on a university campus agrees that it is totally reprehensible to *deny* faculty employment (or student admission) on grounds of race and sex and nationality — or on grounds of religion, as was done in an earlier day. Should it be more acceptable to *favor* people on such grounds?

Presumably, there are *some* sorts of gross gains from diversity itself. It is possible that a campus will be more attractive in *some* respects in being populated by women as well as men; by including pink, black, brown, yellow, and red skins; by having Christians, Jews, Muslims, atheists, and Druids; and perhaps by fat and thin, tall and short people. But *professional excellence* has nothing to do with such extraneous criteria. And it is already shamefully the case that criteria and standards of competence have often been diluted and even discarded, subverting the university in the specious name of diversity.

It is not at all to be expected that we will be blessed with the coincidence that in maximizing diversity we will maximize quality. A choice is required. If we are to be faithful to our trust, we shall seek the professionally *best* faculty and students, not a variously *diverse* group. In the process of obtaining the best, appropriate diversity will take care of itself. But if we consciously and insistently seek diversity for its own sake, quality will be a casualty.

Minority Students and Educational Mismatches

✍✍✍✍

Thomas Sowell is a leading economist, black, and a friend of mine. Not many meet all those criteria.

In 1972, Dr. Sowell published a book, *Black Education: Myths and Tragedies*. Part of the book recounted the foolishness and perniciousness of "the black policies" of some conspicuous universities.

We are not able to select only the very best — the most capable and committed — young people for college education. But we can do better than we have done. We might then find an increased proportion of the campus clientele consisting of black and other minority students. At any rate, the critical criterion in selecting students is intellectual competence and professional capacity; the central strategy in recruiting is to identify and properly prepare those with the most promising qualities and characteristics.

Such identification and preparation presents imposing problems. But in some admissions procedures, there has been no effort to find, and admit only, the very best. While the best would be permitted to enroll, fawning attention and scholarship aid was focused on the less promising. It was supposed that mediocre minority students would be most likely to return to their communities and be more readily accepted there. It was supposed, further, that those minority young people who, through innate competence and prodigious effort, had prepared themselves well for college required little aid, no matter the degree of their economic poverty, and had alienated themselves from their neighborhoods by assimilating so well into middle-class mores and standards.

Only a few decried the waste inherent in subsidizing mediocrity and predicted the embitterment and rebellion of all campus elements as a result of such discriminatory investment and misguidance. In a *Fortune* magazine essay, Dr. Sowell has found the predictable fiasco to have materialized.

Much of campus difficulties stems from a continuing administrative "body-count" mentality. It is more chic now than before to enroll good minority students, to be sure. Indeed, it is sought to enroll more than the pool of adequately able students contains. So the best schools dip lower and admit those who could gain from experience at less sophisticated schools but who are "mismatched" in schools with superior students. Good minority students who would do well in competition with other equally good students, become resentful and recalcitrant in competition with still better students.

The problem is not confined to the most elite schools. When they siphon out of the talent pool students who would be more comfortable and productive in second-tier institutions, then these latter schools raid the pool of students who should be in third-tier colleges. The frustrating mismatch of students and schools is thus generated at all levels.

We will make more progress, in an atmosphere of greater decorum, when substantive minority education rather than numerical minority representation becomes the controlling objective of colleges.

Poets of the Media:
News and Views

Thought and Talk

&&&&

For many, the mouth is the most important part of the head. This is especially discouraging and disconcerting on the university campus and in broadcast journalism. Scholars and commentators both are in the thought-and-words business, with thought intended to precede words.

One of the fundamental functions of the academic faculty is to impress upon young scholars that, first, college kids initially know and can do little; second, that they can accomplish much by commitment to laborious, unglamorous effort in the vineyards; and, finally, that the rest of the community has little reason to take them seriously by refined criteria until they are well on their way to fulfilling substantial potential.

It is unwise to greet incoming freshmen by holding their hands and telling them that they are precious. The proper introductory word to the troops is: Seek ever so hard to develop professionalism, and do not disgrace yourselves and waste resources by trying to wheedle great returns from puny investment.

Unsurprisingly, few of the college clientele well receive and fully accept the harsh message of attaining professionalism through effective investment. But they are boys and girls. How about the men and women in television news? Surely, they are committed to producing and selling a product of sophistication.

Well, how sophisticated can be a reading of little more than headlines? Some stations try occasionally to camouflage superficiality by offering "commentary." And the commentators sometimes stress their seriousness by removing the coat and loosening the tie or squinting the eyes and furrowing the brow. But what they present is intellectual garbage — little but bias and bombast, with no theory, no deductive line of thought, no measurement, no testing of hypotheses. And sometimes they let the cat escape the bag, acknowledging that they are peddlers of garbage. After all, one news director tell us, "commentary is by its very definition not supposed to be objective ...!"

All this nonsense is predictably associated with the *political*-type prattling which is virtually the sole content of TV news commentary, given by innocent people of no analytic credentials. But there is more to hard news than antics in city hall, the state capital, and the Washington Beltway, and there is more to commentary than the poetry of politics.

To express an opinion calls for the bearing of a responsibility — a responsibility of dispassion, rigor of thought, and systematic survey of relevant information. So we might expect senior people in the broadcast thought-and-words business to have some awareness of the usefulness of the basic analytics and applied logic of the accomplished *economist*.

Alas, happy-talkers of the TV news set evince the sophistication of college freshmen with respect to what are the purposes and products of economics and what economists can — and cannot — do. Television commentary is mainly talk with little thought.

All-Talk, No-Thought Radio

∅∅∅∅

One thing worse than *no* education in economics is *bad* education in economics. And bad education is to be found in many places in addition to classrooms. One source of terrible tutoring is the typical radio talk show.

With few notable exceptions, the circus ring-master of the interview and call-in programs is a crude, cocky, cheap-shot poseur of erudition and shrewdness who loves to domineer and delude. He — or an Amazonian she — has an audience of innocents who are poorly prepared to protect themselves from professional charlatans and are seduced into supposing that they are participating in an intellectual exercise.

The representative talk show is ridiculous, if not reprehensible. It is unstructured, unfocused, diverted into dead-ends by questionable questions, with occasional relevant suggestions never followed up and productively pursued, requiring herky-jerky shooting from the hip by frustrated guests. In the incoherent format, the blind lead the sighted willy-nilly into alien territory and thickets of trivia while appalling the visiting analyst with uncongenial and unsophisticated shenanigans.

Genuine and seminal thought — posing pertinent questions and deducing useful answers, fruitfully applying theory and drawing on evidence, systematically and dispassionately diagnosing and prescribing — is not conducted with a format of 20-second responses to disconnected questions, and with commercial breaks, promotions, and traffic reports absorbing more time than the substantive discussion.

A fellow economist and I were recently guests on such a show to discuss the current and prospective state of the economy. We were given no opportunity to give prepared opening statements or summary conclusions. Together, we had 20 minutes actually on the air on a program spread over more than 80 minutes. And the twenty minutes divided between us — all in response to naive questions and inane comments — could not be used effectively.

What bits of wisdom and nuggets of information did the audience hear? Well, the head of an automobile company was quoted approvingly as saying that the current situation is the worst since the Great Depression of the 1930s — a contention manifestly untrue. It was suggested that the Depression was a result of the inactivity of President Herbert Hoover — a contention manifestly untrue. It was contended that the savings-and-loan fiasco is the result simply of financial deregulation and thievery — a contention manifestly untrue. Indeed, the untruths and distortions and misplaced charges and poorly founded generalizations piled up as high as an elephant's eye.

Hope springs eternal. My friend and I went onto the show to help the cause of comprehension. Instead, the professors inadvertently became participants in prostitution. So much for all-talk, no-thought radio.

On Beastliness: The Media and The Public

✍✍✍✍

We all are tempted upon occasion to feel that "the public is a great beast." When we are on the losing side of an election or observe the latest rock-and-roll folk heroes, we spit — preferably downwind — and castigate the uncouth masses.

Still, the public is surprisingly unbeastly. Its sense is greater and its sanity is firmer than are easily accounted for. The twentieth century does provide ample illustration of how even sophisticated societies can be subverted and manipulated for evil purposes by totalitarian authority. But communities characterized by sufficiently free markets of ideas continue to exhibit much shrewdness and non-hysterical judgment.

The media are inevitably conspicuous in the market of ideas. Unhappily, their strategies of participation in the market do not always warrant applause. Their concern commonly is not competition of *ideas,* but competition *within the media.* With each purveyor of supposed news and views seeking to monopolize the market, ideas and their effective presentation are generally diluted and distorted, if not demolished. After the news program has provided happy talk about sports, weather, psychology, shopping hints, and stories on the day's robberies and rapes, there is no time for ideas.

Consider a sample of my own experience. A major, network-affiliated, radio news station interviewed me on the sizable subject of federal tax reform. The recorded conversation lasted ten minutes. The excerpt of my remarks actually broadcast was fifty-four seconds. I was in good voice, and each moment was golden — but fifty-four seconds were not enough to do much justice to the subject.

Then there was the panel discussion broadcast by a major, network-affiliated television station on the sizable subject of minority college admissions. The discussion lasted sixteen minutes, a non-trivial amount of time for a well-conducted interview of one person. But there were *four* members of the panel and *two* moderators — six people incoherently sharing sixteen superficial minutes. In that jumble, good sense was not well served.

But the radio and television programming came out better than the antics of a major news service. I was one of four testifying before a committee of the California Assembly. The other three supported the socialistic nonsense under consideration; I was the only one who defended truth and light. But the reporter of the wire service interviewed each of the others for her story, and pointedly shunned me. The clients of the service never learned that there is at least one sane Californian.

It is remarkable that the public has so well survived a diet of mush prepared and served by cutesy, subversive bush-leaguers. The public is not a mean and mindless beast. But it is often treated by the media as if it were.

Mainly Microeconomics:
Analysis of Relative Prices
and Resource Allocation

ᙏᙏᙏᙏᙏᙏ

Introduction

In a world of scarcity, choices among available alternatives must be made. So priorities must be established, production must be organized, and bearing of costs is unavoidable. How are consumption, saving, and production plans to be made and implemented? Who makes and implements, through what processes, and on the basis of what objectives and criteria?

A few of the many considerations involved in the administration of scarce resources can be illustrated with the diagram below. The figure presents a "production-possibilities" curve, measuring output of guns horizontally and butter vertically. Given current technologies and resources, the economy's maximum production of guns alone is OA units; if nothing but butter is produced, OB is the maximum output; if some of both are produced, maximum combined outputs — such as at points C and D — are production possibilities. The line from A to B, here bulging out a bit from the origin, is the *boundary* of production possibilities: We do not have the resources to go beyond the boundary to some such point as E. That there *is* a boundary of production possibilities reflects the existence of scarcity.

Production Possibilities:
Feasible and Infeasible, Efficient and Inefficient

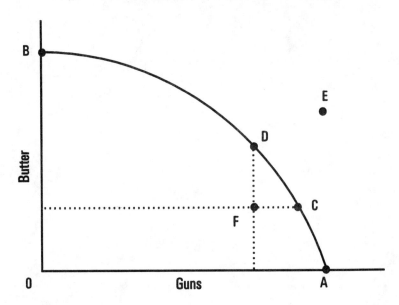

Since the curve shows the alternative *maximum* combinations of guns and butter, it is a curve of *technological efficiency*. Of course, we may produce *less* than the maximum, locating ourselves inside the boundary, as at point F. F is a combination of *technological inefficiency:* We could continue to produce the amount of guns measured by the horizontal distance to F while increasing output of butter vertically to D (or continue to produce butter in amount up to F, while increasing guns horizontally to C).

We are productively efficient when, with a given output of one good, we cannot produce more of the other. To produce more of the other, we would have to reduce output of the one: In moving from point C to D, we increase butter, but with the *cost* of decreasing guns. And as we move further up the curve, there is an *increasing* horizontal amount of guns foregone to release resources to produce a given increase in butter.

Which of the infinite possible combinations of production is "best?" This is a matter of choice. *Whose* choice? And *how* is the preference manifested? In a predominantly "open," "private property" community, the controlling preference is that of the members of the community, and they register their choices (and provide guidance and incentive to producers) by voting with dollars in the market. In such a society, *economic* efficiency subsumes technological efficiency and involves also the stipulation that we produce at the particular point on the production possibilities curve which the people in the market deem to be preferred.

Every society, from dictatorial to democratic, values technological efficiency: produce a given output with minimum physical cost, and maximize output with a given cost, with full use of resources. We want to be on the production possibilities curve; more broadly, we want *economic* efficiency by being at the most preferred point on the curve.

We are now necessarily talking about more than just mundane "producing" and "consuming," more than dreary details of market procedure and "business administration." To think broadly and fundamentally about the economy is to think of the entire society and its members. Adam Smith and Karl Marx agreed that how individuals look at the world and form their attitudes and aspirations are determined largely by how they earn their daily bread.

More than considerations of psychology are involved. The essence of the processes of the economy is critically intertwined with the structure of the society. The ground rules of the one must be compatible with the orientation of the other. The classic problem of "order" has been how to establish or nurture institutions and practices and attitudes which will enable self-centered, acquisitive, and would-be autonomous individuals to live civilly and productively as a community.

Many have supposed that order must be achieved at the expense of liberty. Some person or small group must be in charge, to whip the boys into line: We must impose a prison or a zoo to avoid anarchy. We have been told

that individual liberty must be severely curtailed to achieve national honor —
and to have the trains run on time.

A few thinkers have provided a different approach to the problem of
order. Among others, Adam Smith took men as they are but envisioned a set
of fundamental rules and general procedures — private rights to use of
property — which would not only indicate options and constraints, but would
permit and encourage personally inspired activity to serve (without intent) the
general community interest. We can hardly expect to extinguish self-interest,
but we can establish rules of the game which will channel strivings for
personal gain to the common good.

This is a *market* mechanism. In an individualistic community,
individuals can bid and offer, save and invest and produce, as they please, in
the use of their own resources for their ends but to mutual advantage. They
pay one another to obtain what they want and sell their own products and
services to gain income. One prospers much when what he offers for sale is
highly valued by others. The community in general prospers when people are
useful to each other. Producers typically make themselves useful in
anticipation of reward, uninspired by self-sacrificing altruism. Seeking
reward may be grubby, but it is a stronger, more reliable reed on which to
lean than relying on the kindness of strangers.

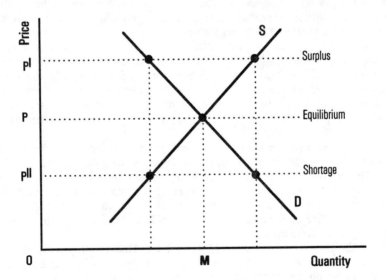

Demand and Supply: Equilibrium, Surplus, Shortage

Market activity not only generates prices — prices both of commodities and of productive services — but it tends strongly to generate *equilibrium* prices. Equilibrium prices "clear the market," equating amounts demanded with quantities offered for sale. The diagram is a simple format combining a downward-sloping demand curve with an upward-sloping supply curve for a commodity. At price OP, buyers want to buy and sellers also want to sell OM units: there are no frustrations of sellers wanting to sell more than buyers want to buy, as when the price is too high at OP', nor is there buyer frustration from quantity demanded being greater than quantity supplied with the price too low at OP".

If price is above or below the equilibrium level, free market activity would move it toward equilibrium: Frustrated would-be sellers would bid the price down from OP', and disappointed buyers would bid it up from OP". But markets are not always free and open. Government pegs many prices at non-clearing levels. Price floors thus generate "surpluses" of agricultural goods and of labor (minimum wages); price ceilings generate "shortages" or apartments (rent control) and of gasoline and of foreign exchange in international money markets.

Can we have efficiency with freedom? To organize an individualistic society's economic activity, we require more than technological, engineering knowledge. We must have, in addition, economic values. Those values are manifested as prices stemming from activity in the market by all the members of the community. Efficiency requires, and freedom yields, market-determined and market-clearing prices. We cannot have efficiency without freedom. Because for us economic efficiency is defined in terms of well serving personal preferences, and a productive result is attained through rewarding personal performances.

Economics, Economic Order, and Economies

The Classical Economists

ᴓᴓᴓᴓ

The modern period of economic theory began less than 250 years ago. For a century or so, that history was dominated by the "classical" school. The great father figure of the classicists was Adam Smith. Smith and his intellectual kin were an impressive group. Consider some of their qualities and characteristics.

Foremost was *integrity*. They exhibited boldness and candor in acknowledging issues and facing up to analytic complications. Their ingenious treatment was rarely definitive in substance and often primitive in technique. But the first step in resolving a problem of analysis or a dilemma of policy is forthrightly to confront the question.

Confronting questions effectively requires non-romantic *realism*. The classical writers took people as they are and the world as it is. What people are is acquisitive and aggressive. What the world is reflects resource scarcity, consequent conflict, and unavoidable choice-making and cost-bearing.

Such attitude and orientation leads to nitty-gritty *empiricism* of observing, measuring, assessing, and prescribing. What are the real-world institutional arrangements, market procedures, and policy parameters which will best conduce a coordinated, prospering society of people who ungenteelly strive to fulfill grubby aspirations?

Theory, then, is to be pursued, not for sheer elegance in abstract thought, but for fruitful elucidation of problems and prospects of a hard world. The classical writers were *analysts*, not ideologues. They made painfully clear the bases of class conflict and social disharmony; they were vigorously critical of common characteristics of all social segments, decidedly including business types; they castigated alike the rapacity and venality of the commercial and governmental establishment and the ignorant irresponsibility of the poor.

They were intellectual *innovators* and *reformers*. They wanted to enhance the wealth of the community and the status of workers. But they were dubious of the efficacy and even of the motivation of most efforts to do good. Little good was likely to come from meddling government or monopolizing business. They slashed at such institutions as imperialism and slavery; they repudiated such policy orientation as transfer of wealth rather than production and exchange of goods; they ridiculed the dominant social classes of landed aristocracy, rising capitalists, and entrenched political powers.

Adam Smith and the other classicists assuredly were not contented apologists for the status quo. They devastatingly challenged long-established philosophies. But they offered no easy utopia, no naive optimism: the open-market, private-property, competitive economy provides the best of possible worlds — but the best will not be very good.

It is a considerable pity that not all of today's economists have well-learned what the classical economists taught.

Grubbiness and Sense in a Hard World

ØØØØ

In this world of scarcity of resources and frailty of character, we live subject to constraints and inhibitions imposed by precepts of law and social values and personal morality. Options are limited, and frustrate preferences. People evince a powerful, pervasive propensity to seek additional alternatives and to exploit known options to improve their lot. We try to make do best within the parameters of our possibilities.

Those parameters — those constraints of technology, resources, institutions, and principles — vary greatly around the world and over time. Some of us were born relatively free. Obviously, a high degree of freedom is not inevitable for all, nor will it surely survive forever for any. For freedom to have concrete significance for real people in a real world, it must be used. It must be made operational in the actual, grubby marketplace.

So how are we to organize our activities in order to minimize and ameliorate outrage and injury while seeking to prosper? Most of us *do* agree that organization is required. Brutal anarchy is not a society at all — and all anarchy is brutal. The essence of practical freedom is that each person have a very wide range of well established and protected choices in using resources owned by him in ways which will best serve his own purposes by his own criteria.

This is the essence, not only of freedom, but also of efficiency. An efficient economy does not require state-owned resources or centrally imposed five-year plans. Nor does it require that each of the many buyers and sellers in the marketplace be aware of the "big picture" of our massive, intricate economy. Nor does it call for each citizen to try to serve his own notion of "national purpose," sacrificing personal well-being and eschewing individual rationality for presumed ends of "public policy."

Efficiency calls, instead, for each of the millions of free men in free markets to handle his own limited affairs well. This is not anarchy. For handling one's affairs well requires sensible response to information generated by interlocking market activity. The market tells us of consumer preferences and producer costs; it provides procedures and mechanisms for organizing production, offering goods and services for exchange, and consummating transactions; it rewards best those who make themselves most valuable to others, offering great incentive to be most useful.

Some find repulsive this picture of induced social coordination of acquisitive, would-be autonomous characters. They prefer to look upon people as driven by wholly unselfish motives, moved by the goodness of their ruby hearts, yielding spontaneous cooperation. Alas, they massively misconstrue the real nature of people, and they describe, not the world, but heaven.

Government, Markets, and the Community

♨♨♨♨

Little of the political world is sophisticated. There is deviousness, to be sure, but not subtlety. For the essence of politics is power to control people and resources, with the power exercised unilaterally from on high. In this one-way application of authority, gains of the beneficiaries are accompanied by losses of the unfavored. It is not even a *zero*-sum game, for the governmental shenanigans diminish our productivity as well as our civility, and the aggregate community is a net loser.

All this is vastly different from the open market, where power is diffused. Market power is diffused by existence of *alternatives* and also by the *reciprocal* nature of personal interactions.

Both buyers and sellers have *alternatives* even when confronted by the largest of corporations: the consumer can choose *not* to buy from General Motors, and the worker and the investor can choose *not* to work for or invest in General Motors. There are many other suppliers, employers, and opportunities. And when transactions *are* made, *all* parties involved gain from the interaction. Market activity is a *positive*-sum game, yielding net benefits to be shared by the participants.

But even after six thousand years of recorded oppression and waste by political masters, we find government described in terms of warmhearted benevolence, as an altruistic agency which — out of the purity of its bureaucratic heart — cures ills and rights wrongs, and thereby binds us together in good fellowship. Such foolish rhetoric cannot resemble reality. For opinions widely differ on the nature and the ranking of the ills to be cured and the wrongs to be righted; and even with some degree of consensus on objectives, there will be offered numerous, often incompatible, strategies and tactics of implementation.

Major reliance on government does not magically eliminate community frictions. A policy can be rammed home with the police power of the state, but imposition of policy does not imply universal gains. Indeed, characteristically, the nature of government objectives and processes is such that policies impose net costs on some while bestowing net benefits on others. Government taxes, subsidies, penalties, mandates, prohibitions, allocations, redistributions — the inevitable tools and tactics — divide and impoverish us.

The consequence of uncoerced *market* activity is *mutual* benefit: a free man will not participate in a transaction which, in his own view, makes him worse off. In the political market, there is no magnificent department store where the merchandise can be examined; there are no warranties, no money-back guarantees, no changes of mind allowed; there are no protections against shoddy workmanship or false advertising. In the political market, there is no provision of variety and substitution: you cannot choose portions of programs of various candidates — you are stuck with a mayor or a senator for his term of office, and can only hope he will represent your view more or less closely most of the time. And you are stuck with monopoly suppliers of government goods: government does not provide alternative fire and police and education and garbage-collection services. But in the economic market, you can fashion your consumption in close accordance with your preferences — and quickly change your consumption as your preferences change — by shopping among many competing sellers.

While divisive, wasteful government is hailed as the great benefactor, the efficiently coordinating market is typically maligned in terms of insensitivity and selfishness and unfairness. We pay dearly for such monumental perversity.

On Letting an Economy Take Its Course

ﾟﾟﾟﾟ

Have interest rates been, or will interest rates be, "too high"? Can anyone know?

What can be meant by interest rates being too high? Any market-determined price is determined by the market. Any market variable is part of a massive, ever-changing constellation of interconnected variables. The variables are real and financial, personal and group, institutional and natural. As the expression goes, "everything depends on everything else," where "everything" ranges from attitudes to automation.

We cannot diddle with one variable — whether interest rates or government spending, the amount of money, exchange rates, farm prices — and expect everything else to remain the same. So we cannot peg one variable at a time, setting it at some level somehow deemed desirable. And what is deemed desirable will itself change as other things are affected. What interest rates should be, what the pattern of relative prices should be, what the levels of saving and investment should be — none can be sensibly specified in isolation, without regard for all the other ingredients of the economy and of society generally.

The optimal value of any one variable is affected by the context. But the context consists of all those innumerable other variables which also have to be defined and specified. So we cannot go far in identifying optimal values of *particular* variables without simultaneously identifying the values of *all* variables. And such specifying would not be definitively done once and for all. The world is a changing place, and the constellation of values would have to be constantly altered. The mighty mind is wearied simply by contemplation of the monumental magnitude of the convoluted chore.

All our wit and wisdom, all our compassion and calculation, will not tell us just what are the interrelated values — the levels and the rates of change of variables — which together will place us as close as possible to bliss. There are too many people, and the people are too changeable and complex, for any one of us to be able to envision perfection for the rest of us. There are too many resources and production techniques, and the resources and techniques are too changeable and complex, for any one of us to be able to tell the rest of us how to get to perfection even if perfection could be described and defined.

Happily, we do not require direction or decree by a Solomon or a Caesar. The best we can hope to do — and it is a reasonable hope — is to establish a clear, consistent, basically constant context of minimum constraints and maximum alternatives. A well-contained government, widely held private rights to use of property, open competition, stable money — such are the basic ingredients of a free and prosperous community. In the workings of such a community, solutions of specific concerns like interest rates will readily evolve without a central plan or dictate.

Demand: Preferences and Choices

Needs and Preferences, Decrees and Market Bids

ᔕᔕᔕᔕ

Marxists and poets speak of "needs." But, in economics, "need" is a non-word. Economics can say much which is useful about *desires*, *preferences*, and *demands*. But "*need*" presumably is a moral, psychological, or physical imperative which brooks no compromise or adjustment — or analysis. If we "*need*" something, we *must* have it: There is literally no alternative of either substitution or abstinence.

But the assertion of absolute economic "need" — in contrast to desire, preference, and demand — is nonsense. What do we do if I "need" a certain amount of something and you also "need" a particular minimum amount and both our "needs" cannot be satisfied? It actually is the condition of this world of scarcity that we have conflicting claims which must be somehow resolved. It does no good for each of us stubbornly to stamp a foot, spit downwind, and proclaim inalienable "needs" which in the aggregate *cannot* be fully satisfied. Scarcity, by its nature, gives rise to competition, to conflict, to the necessity of *rationing* in some manner the things we desire.

Do we ration goods among competing claimants through fighting and force? That is suicidal anarchy. Do we ration through governmental directive? That is stultifying repression. Do we ration through market processes? That is efficient freedom.

But the message of efficient freedom is unattractive for some. If one advocates allocation through a market procedure which makes relative preferences manifest and effective, there will be a clergyman who will ask, where in your analysis is the variable representing gentle compassion, and there will be a journalist who will protest that you lack humane values.

If distribution by central authority for the purpose of better satisfying "needs" were desirable in the case of medical care or concert tickets, it is difficult to see why the same system should not be used in distributing the *entire* social output, regardless of differing productivities of workers and differing preferences of consumers. Few of our self-styled benefactors go that far. (Nor do the Russians go that far in practice.) What they enthusiastically champion case-by-case, even the naive and the vicious recognize in the aggregate as in some sense ridiculous — both unfeasible and unappealing.

Obviously, the world is complicated and frustrating. To make do well, we must analyze cogently and act effectively on the basis of the analysis. We must have intellectual guidance — an analytical orientation, a set of criteria and techniques of deduction and of testing, in short, a theory. Otherwise, everything is a special case, and we are directed by whim and instinct and emotion, not by coherent principle. And the conflicts of competition, stemming inevitably from our condition of scarcity, are resolved by decrees from a ruling bureaucracy, not through individual marketplace bidding on the basis of personal preferences.

The Law of Demand and the Message of the Market

Occasionally, I have occasion to go from here to there. With time constraints which are severe, I go by big, iron bird, despite the fact that travel in the cattle-car section of the plane is pretty primitive.

The head of a major airline has made a statement which does not assuage my distaste for commercial flying. On the matter of pricing, he said, anyone who has to get to Detroit will fly there, whether the fare is $150 or $250 or $350. The remark is reminiscent of the old Robber Baron motto: "The public be damned." And aside from it being a public relations *faux pas*, it is lousy economics.

For *some* people in *some* circumstances, the amount of travel to Detroit will not be affected by price within the range of $150 to $350. But for *most* people in *most* circumstances, the amount of travel demanded will be determined largely by price within that range. And for *everyone* — and for every *commodity* — the amount demanded will be reduced by a *sufficiently* higher price.

The Law of Demand says that the *price* of a good and the *amount* people are willing to buy are inversely related. Starting with today's price, the price can be raised enough to induce people to buy less; and price can be lowered enough to increase the amount demanded.

The Law of Demand holds for labor services as well as for airline travel. Does anyone this side of Mortimer Snerd really suppose that employers will hire as many workers at $4.25 an hour as they would at $3.35? Surely not. And yet, a majority of Congress voted to increase the minimum wage, and the President went along, while insisting that employment would not be affected.

The Law of Demand holds for gasoline. During the OPEC cartel shenanigans of the 1970's, many people with a public forum asserted that letting gas prices rise would not induce the community to cut consumption to match available supplies. They were wrong, of course, as events eventually demonstrated what reason predicted.

The Law of Demand holds for apartments and water and medical care. With all these products, a market-determined price will clear the market, equating amounts demanded with amounts available. A market-clearing price next year may be higher than today's market-clearing price. And if government controls prevent price from rising, then we will have imposed upon ourselves a shortage. At the old, frozen price, people will continue to demand as much as before, while the market is telling us to demand less.

In their own interests, people will listen to the market, and adjust to it, if Big Brother does not block the message. The Law of Demand is bigger than all of us: there are no exceptions to the law, and we cannot repeal it. But with price controls, we can frustrate its beneficial operation — and with bad pricing policies, which ignore the law, business firms can lose wealth.

Tunnel Vision, Tunnel Use, and Advance of Theory

⌾⌾⌾⌾

The notions of demand and supply, when appropriately used, can help in explaining the world. But they are not perfectly self-evident notions, and their fruitful use is not perfectly simple.

Consider what have been called two "laws" of demand. The first law says that, at a given moment, less of a good will be bought at sufficiently higher prices than at lower prices. The second law says that the full impact of, or the total adjustment to, a higher price takes time.

No economist denies the validity of the first Law: right now, when you must pay more for gasoline, you will choose to buy less gas.

The second law of demand seems to be a straightforward extension of the first. Adjustments are involved in reducing the amount demanded of a good in the face of a price increase, and not all adjustments are fully made instantaneously. When gas prices rose sharply in the 1970's, people cut back consumption in various ways, but some ways took more time than others. Shorter but less scenic routes had to be discovered; car pools had to be organized; shopping schedules had to be rearranged; travel habits had to shift from private automobiles to buses and motor scooters; more fuel-efficient cars had to be designed, built, and sold.

Is the so-called second law of demand really a "law," being invariably true? It is abstractly plausible and consistent with much evidence. But Timothy Hau, of the University of Hong Kong, may have found an exceptional case.

When the toll for private car and taxi use of a Hong Kong tunnel was doubled in mid-1984, automobile use of the tunnel immediately fell appreciably, and at the end of 1986, it remained smaller than it had been before the toll increase. This is consistent with the first law. But all of the reduction in purchase of tunnel use took place in the first month; after that, use of the tunnel gradually crept up. And this does not support the second law.

Perhaps it turned out that knowledge was initially so inadequate that the first step of adjustment to the toll increase was quickly deemed to be exaggerated. In particular, use of the harbor ferry, which immediately rose greatly and then trended back down, turned out to be less attractive than originally anticipated. So proper statement of the law must specify an adequate degree of knowledge of alternatives, lest the process of adjustment to the price increase be aborted and partially reversed.

Or perhaps the second "law" cannot be reasonably salvaged. It may not be a "law" at all, but only a suggestive first approximation. But a generalization can have less than perfect predictive power and still be useful.

At any rate, all this suggests the way of analytic progress. Analysis requires theory. But the theory must perform: it must pay off in helping to explain phenomena. If the applied theory does not well enough account for the thing to be explained, the world will go on, but the theory is to be adjusted.

Biological Variety and Economic Choice

✍✍✍✍

Variety may be the spice of life; at the same time, certainty has its satisfactions, and conformity has its comforts. It has been wisely observed that the secret of civilized society is to meld change with stability, variation with standardization, diversity with uniformity, uniqueness with predictability.

Each of us observes, experiences, and assesses the world with different combinations of hopes, criteria, standards, and sensibilities. In the complex equation of society, who is to determine which elements are to be constants and which are to be variables?

Few of us thirst for the role of community architect, specifying the places and degrees of variety and of system in the social scheme. But some sensitive souls are willing to assume the burden. One is a Harvard biologist.

Evolutionary biologists, he tells us, "relish diversity." Nothing "could possibly be more magnificent than the fact that beetle anatomy presents itself in more that half a million separate packages called species." He acknowledges, grudgingly, that engineering considerations of efficiency call for a degree of imposed universality in large, utilitarian projects. But in relatively limited and local contexts, he is steadfastly "a watchdog for the preservation of...fragile variety and an implacable foe of standardization and homogenization."

This watchdog snarls in particular at the McDonald's fast food chain. Informal eateries, after all, are places of "immediate and daily use that cry out for local distinction and its attendant sense of community." The scholar professes "an abiding respect for...institutions that have prevailed and prospered with integrity in an unending sea of change...." And yet, he likens the prospering McDonald's to "a horde of rats" wiping out all "endemic" weaker creatures.

Good biologists evidently can be lousy economists, as is made clear by Richard B. Coffman in *The Margin* magazine. "McDonald's golden arches are everywhere," Mr. Coffman rightly observes, not because of ratlike predation, but "because consumers want them everywhere." Consumer tastes and preferences, along with considerations of production and costs, lead free men in free markets to use resources in ways most valued.

In a very small community, uniqueness may not provide variety. It may have a diner like no other in the world, but it is the only diner in town. A visitor could be intrigued by the peculiar establishment, but residents might prefer a McDonald's. In larger communities, there is variety, even if many of the alternatives — alternatives of eateries, movies, magazines, automobiles, clothing — are available all over the country.

Many market votes have been cast for McDonald's. We can be grateful that Harvard biologists do not have the prerogative of canceling those votes and denying far-flung communities the products they are willing to pay for.

Choices, Advertising, and Freedom

✐✐✐✐

It is sometimes said that the private-property, free-market economy is subject to "consumer sovereignty" — consumers reveal their preferences by "voting" with their dollars for what they want.

J.K. Galbraith, the social philosopher, denies that consumers are sovereign. He is here more nearly correct than he usually is — but for wrong reasons.

There is no dominating consumer sovereignty, economist Harold Demsetz points out. Exchanges will be made when they appear advantageous to *all* parties involved. Neither producer nor consumer, neither one trader nor another, imposes his will on the other. *Each* has only the right to offer for sale or to purchase. Exchange is not coercion; it is not imposed on others. No trade takes place if consumers are unwilling to bid prices deemed adequate by potential sellers. Similarly, producers make no sales if they are unwilling to sell at prices as low as those offered by potential buyers. Buyers who demand Cadillacs at a price of $1 will be disappointed; so will suppliers who ask $1 million. Neither buyer nor seller is sovereign.

But Galbraith discards the notion of consumer sovereignty on the peculiar ground that consumer wants have been molded by advertising. This results in something approaching *producer* sovereignty: producers supposedly make what they happen to please and convince consumers that that is what consumers want.

Now, at any given moment, people *are* characterized by certain preferences. And we can have some interest in how those wants came into being.

Wants are shaped — but by many forces in addition to advertising. Not only Madison Avenue, but also Washington, D.C., the Church, Mother, Schools, and Galbraith himself are among the forces which form wants. Our beliefs and tastes *are* to a large extent learned: civilization itself is, in considerable measure, a matter of teaching and learning beliefs and tastes. But it is *not* clear that *business firms* have a unique advantage in want-creating activity. Washington enjoys free press and TV coverage and is immune from anti-fraud laws. Professors are protected by academic freedom. Clergymen can offer, with impunity, everlasting life. Most of what I know I learned at my mother's knee and other low joints. But *business* people are constrained by innumerable provisions of law.

Galbraith fears that people are persuaded of their supposed wants. And we are to ignore these wants because they are not "natural" or "inborn."

But freedom surely means more than the right to exercise only the elemental instincts of untutored "noble savages." Freedom must mean the right to *choose* among offerings. If choice is to be meaningful, a free society must rely on a free flow of communication

— information and persuasion — from those who *compete* for the favor of adults. There must be *competition* to provide *alternatives*.

Give me options — and then stand aside while I make my own choices.

The Rationale of Trade

Trade and Mutual Gain

ㄆㄆㄆㄆ

Everyone in every society does it. They always have. But until less than 200 years ago, no one could explain why it is done — and Senator Snort and most editorial writers still do not understand.

The activity in question is trade, of course. Why do people do so much buying and selling? Presumably, they do not exchange just for the giddy fun of the activity. Instead, they swap in order to gain. Gain what? Well, after the trade, the trader considers himself to be better off, on balance, because he values more what he gets than what he gives up.

But if one participant is willing to trade away something he deems of lesser worth in order to obtain something of greater worth, surely that is the case for the other participant, as well. Each trader considers himself to have gained from the exchange. Otherwise, there would be no trade: If either person thought that he would lose from the transaction, he would not play the game.

So there are mutual gains from trade. Mr. A feels that Mr. A is made better off by the trade; Mr. B feels that Mr. B is made better off. Mr. A may believe that B is a fool to make the swap; Mr. B may be confident that A had been suckered; and Mr. C — an interested observer — may consider both of them to be strange, for no civilized person would want either of the goods being exchanged.

No matter. Each person is the appropriate, relevant judge of his own condition. If it is the personal, subjective estimation of Mr. A that he has gained by the trade, then he has gained — no matter what the preferences and assessments of others may be. And Mr. B is the pertinent judge of Mr. B's market options and actions.

Is all this obvious? It is pretty apparent once we see it. But Aristotle did not see it. Nor did Saint Thomas Aquinas. Nor even Adam Smith. And for centuries, public policy was directed on the supposition that what one party to a trade gains must have been lost by the other. The concept of *mutual* gains, with all immediate participants being made better off, is one of some subtlety.

Comprehension of the notion of mutual gains is significant as well as subtle. Such comprehension provides orientation in confronting the world.

If one believes — as have a great many over the ages — that all the gain from an exchange goes to one trader, with that gain matched by loss suffered by the other trader, then the world is one of bitter conflict, a war of each against all others. But if it is understood that both parties gain from appropriate trade, then the world is seen as one of possible coordination to the benefit of all.

At best, we still will inhabit a world of scarcity — and thus a world of strain, frustration, and conflict. But we can best adapt to scarcity, making the world less hard and hateful than it otherwise would be, by trading to mutual benefit.

Mouse Wisdom: Quick Paws and Twisted Ethics

✍✍✍✍

"Unethical!" exclaimed Mouse Karl to his friend Mouse Adam. "They take the money and run and give nothing in return!"

"Calm down," admonished Adam. "Who are *they*, and what did *they* do?"

"*They* are the big company that made the fancy shoes you have on," answered Karl.

"The Quick Paw Company?" asked Adam, looking at his new sneakers. "It makes all kinds of athletic shoes and is the top producer of whiskerball boots."

"Yes," complained Karl. "That's part of the problem. Quick Paw has one of the biggest shares of the athletic shoe market. It makes its products elsewhere and then sells millions of dollars worth of them right here in our community. For our buying all those products, it gives us nothing in return. But we have a right to get some of our money back. That's why I support Project Grab, the local organization that seeks moral covenants between Quick Paw and our community."

"Sounds serious," averred Adam. "What are 'moral covenants'?"

"Agreements to do ethical things with some of the money they take from us," snapped Karl. "That means putting some of the money back into our neighborhood. Perhaps they could spend it on local advertising or put it in local banks."

"But it's not true that Quick Paw gives us nothing in return," said Adam. "Market exchange benefits *both* buyer and seller. My new running shoes are a good example. I paid $60 for them because I wanted the shoes more than the money. And the company benefited because it wanted the $60 more than the shoes. *Each* of us *gave* something, and *each* of us *got* something in return. What we have paid no longer belongs to us, and what we have bought no longer belongs to the seller."

"Wouldn't Quick Paw be quixotic," continued Adam, "if it complained that it gets nothing in return when selling shoes? Imagine the company arguing for a 'moral covenant' to require us to return some of the shoes we bought!"

"But I'm talking about money," argued Karl, "and the company takes money from our community."

"Yes," agreed Adam, "and members of our community take shoes from the company. But the company doesn't *seize* our money, and we don't *steal* its shoes. Instead, individual mice willingly trade with Quick Paw. We end up with shoes we value more than the money we spend, so the company makes us better off. Are you saying that these instances of *voluntary, mutual beneficial* trade — in which each party both gives and gets — are unethical?"

"Perhaps not," answered Karl. "But I still support Project Grab's efforts to force the company to spend more money here."

"That would certainly benefit members of Project Grab," said Adam. "They could help dole out the money while taking credit for extorting tribute. But their personal political success would result from deceiving mice about the mutual gains of trade and from restricting a company's freedom to use its earnings as it thinks best."

"I must admit," admitted Karl, "that doesn't seem very ethical. It is just sociological silliness."

Economic Efficiency and the Spirit of Society

øøøø

In economics, few activities are more elemental than trade. And the elementary theory of exchange appears straightforward. After all, if in swapping assets *each* of the traders considers himself better off — if *each* values more highly what he gets than what he gives — it would seem that voluntary exchange is good. Economists do tend to be free-traders. But few are literally free-traders, opposing *all* restraints on *all* potential exchange under *all* circumstances.

How about the buying and selling of human organs? The community permits a market in blood, but some — including some congressmen — want to outlaw a market in kidneys. Why? I am willing to supply a kidney to you for some minimum amount of money; you are willing to give me the money for my kidney; if no third party is adversely affected, on what basis can the exchange be reasonably prohibited?

Well, even people of erudition and analytic competence do have major reservations. The formal analysis is not wrong, they concede, but it is psychologically and sociologically incomplete. It ignores implications for the community spirit: trafficking in human organs — perhaps with the relatively poor selling portions of their bodies to the relatively wealthy — dilutes our "integrity," inhibits the development of "altruism," and weakens the "principle of voluntarism." So, they suggest, third parties *are* adversely affected.

Economics cannot prove such wonderments wrong or ridiculous. But we do well not to reject identifiable, assured good in favor of avoiding nebulous, potential harm.

It is an unattractive world, to be sure, when the desperately poor feel reduced to selling organs to the rich. But the unattractiveness lies in the poverty, not in the poor trying to make the best of their limited lot. In forbidding the poor from selling organs, are we protecting them (by preventing them from doing what they believe would benefit them)? Are we protecting the patients (who also are God's creatures, even if rich)? When a patient has not been successful in obtaining a kidney, it seems not highly moralistic for a healthy senator to tell him that it would be gauche to offer to buy one. Perhaps the only ones being protected are those who find it somehow comforting to camouflage the unhappy essence of the situation — that is, the need of some for medical help and the need of others for income.

Society may try to persuade people to be more altruistic. Charity is to be commended. But, surely, the social objective of organ transplants is to improve health, not to provide an outlet for philanthropy.

At any rate, do not count on gifts. Can we realistically hope to achieve such angelic status that each will get what he requires simply from the goodness of his neighbors? And if we shall continue to have to rely generally on buying and selling, is it shrewd to exempt human organs? While expecting to pay the farmer for calves' kidneys, can we suppose that peoples' kidneys will be provided gratis when required?

We can encourage appeals to altruism, but a more reliable way to obtain what we want is to persuade through trade.

Property Rights

Games and Their Ground Rules

ØØØØ

Every game must have its ground rules.

The ground rules of the economy are summed up essentially in *property rights*. Property rights are the rights of people to use, in limited ways, the things they are deemed to own. Where are you allowed to live? What kind of work are you permitted to do? Who or what determines your wage? What may you buy and sell, under what circumstances, on what terms?

People everywhere are much the same in ultimate attitudes and aspirations. But the ground rules, the property rights, within which they act vary greatly from place to place and over time. Community differences are to be found not so much in genes and hormones as in heritage of the past and property rights of the present.

Some rules of the game give wide discretion to individuals. Then rules put the major emphasis on *private, personal* rights to use of assets. This means, of course, that the great bulk of resources are privately, personally owned: People cannot exchange things which do not belong to them.

In a zoo or a prison, Higher Authority makes decisions for the inmates, who are subservient and dependent. We can hope that Big Brother will be benign and kind — but the realism of the hope is thoroughly diluted by consideration of the tyranny which has pervaded history. Naiveté is poor protection against the strength of the unbridled state. And the only effective bridle to keep the state under community control is private rights to use of property.

The benefits of private property go beyond personal liberty and dignity and the morality of individualism The issue is not only how we live but *how well*. How well we live depends on how *productive* we are. How productive we are depends on the *incentives* people have in coping with a world of limited resources. And incentives to work hard, save much, invest wisely, and manage effectively are greatest when useful effort is proportionately *rewarded*. We reward each other for being useful to each other.

"*...useful to each other.*" It is not enough to produce much. *What* do we produce? *For whom* do we produce? We may be a veritable ant colony or bee hive, but whose wants are being catered to? For some of us, the very notion of "efficiency" requires an open, individualistic society of free men in free markets. For efficiency has to do with using scarce resources in accordance with revealed preferences of the whole community, not the whims of dominating Big Brother.

Over much of the world, yesterday's peasants and peons are now bestirring themselves. They are being roused from the coma of communism and the silliness of socialism by the fresh winds of individualism and its efficiency. Doubtless, there is strain and reason for concern in a process of personal responsibility and accountability. Not all will prosper greatly. But many are eager to play the more fulfilling game. And, in doing so, they may rejuvenate the blasé among us who were born free.

Property Rights, Conflict, and Harmony

◢◢◢◢

It is doubtful that Adam and Eve could have had a full measure of comprehension of the implications of their indiscretion. The consequences have been more dire than they should have been, for succeeding generations have not always adjusted shrewdly to the condition of scarcity which was seductively introduced into the Garden.

How is a society to deal with the competitions and conflicts inevitably associated with scarcity? We are forever cursed with sweaty brows in obtaining our daily bread, and it behooves us to minimize the costs and discomforts.

In our best adaptation to a lousy world, we want people to know of alternatives, to be able to communicate bids and offers, and to obtain goods and to bear costs in accordance with relative preferences. There is information to be acquired, and there are assessments and comparisons to be made and negotiations to be conducted.

In all this, we obviously are competing with each other. But there are ways and ways to compete. The competition can take place through mechanisms of the market, which yield civilized coordination, with people pursuing individual gain in a manner which yields mutual benefits. Or the competition can take place through machinations determined by decrees of Big Brother which spawn belligerent confrontation in which one person's gain is his enemy's loss.

These different approaches to living together in a stingy world are illustrated by administration of large blocs of valuable land. As recounted by economists John Baden, Richard Stroup, and Dwight Lee, the Audubon Society owns the Rainey Wildlife Sanctuary in Louisiana. The Sanctuary not only is home for much wildlife, it also contains natural gas deposits.

If the territory were owned by *government* — as is two-fifths of this nation — the Audubon Society and the energy companies would be natural enemies. Each party, in single-minded self-interest, would seek the jugular of the other through wielding political influence. But with *private* ownership of the land, there is room and incentive for mutually useful negotiation. The Audubon Society has found it advantageous to sell limited rights of gas drilling: in its own interest, the Society takes into account the preferences of the companies. By the same token, the companies are induced to acknowledge and adapt to the concerns of the Society.

This negotiated harmony is *not* a matter of metamorphosing greedy natures into brotherly love. Rather, it is mutually beneficial accommodation through voluntary market exchange. It is, thus, a matter of rights to use of property. When those rights rest with a governmental third-party dispenser of privileges, the Society and the firms inevitably fight, and resources are badly used as alternatives are restricted and costs are ignored. But when those property rights are privately owned, market negotiations replace grabs for politically exercised power, and persuasion is used through appeals to the interests of the other party.

The choice between such alternative arrangements is not difficult.

First Bison, Then Whales, Now Elephants

✐✐✐✐

The preservation of elephants is an economic problem. Economic problems are best resolved through markets.

We obviously can set up legal barriers to trade which will affect the *ease* of transactions and thus the *amount* exchanged; and they will affect the *terms* of trade and thus the *profitability* of trade. Even if the trading is made more inconvenient and the quantity exchanged is reduced, driving up the price may increase profits of those suppliers who are sufficiently bold in breaking the law and contemptuous of society's imposed proprieties.

In Africa, there is much wealth to be generated over an indefinitely prolonged future by appropriate husbandry in elephants. Such care and cultivation of the mighty beasts will not stem from pure goodness of men: there must be *incentive*, a *rewarding* of investment. Unless there is payoff from using scarce resources productively, elephants will be left to short-term plunder by poachers.

It has been demonstrated in parts of Africa that it *is* possible to earn adequate return from investment in private and state wild game reservations and parks. There are people who will pay well to participate in safaris of observation and restricted hunting. In regulated circumstances, elephants have flourished. Indeed, the elephant population can readily press against available subsistence, and the imposing creatures are to be appropriately culled. The slain animals can well supply a legitimate world trade in ivory and hides — and meat from the ecologically-based thinning of herds can be supplied to human residents of the area, maintaining local support for the property arrangement.

As long as there are elephants, they will be killed, and their tusks and hides will be sold. Banning legal markets in ivory will not stop the killing. Indeed, those African nations in which trade in ivory has been banned have suffered the greatest slaughter, and their elephant populations have fallen dismayingly. Effective private and communal rights to use of property also will not mean that no elephants will be killed. But in countries permitting orderly, commercialized treatment of elephants, the number of elephants has grown, and the herds have to be thinned.

Cattle are privately owned — and cattle are killed, and their products are sold. Cattle are cared for and their numbers increase precisely because of ownership rights. Ownership provides much incentive to nurture and protect the valuable assets owned.

Whales and bison, too, were valuable assets, but they had no owners to raise and finally harvest them. Instead of incentives of ownership to make long-term investments in whales and bison, there was the incentive of anarchy to take any whale or bison at hand, for your failure to take now what is available means only that a less restrained predator will make the kill tomorrow.

The question is: will we treat elephants as we treat cattle — or as we treated whales and bison?

Mouse Wisdom: Billboards and Property Rights

ᘓᘓᘓᘓ

Mouse Karl has a penchant for the heroic pose. "I insist," he insisted quite heroically, "that when *human* rights conflict with *property* rights, then human rights must prevail."

Mouse Adam, something of a missionary, felt obliged to respond. "There can be no conflict between human and property rights," he responded. "Property rights cannot exist by themselves. So-called property rights are rights of *people* to *use* of property."

"You are argumentative," snapped Karl belligerently. "Consider highway billboards. For us sensitive sorts, billboards are an abomination. And a Republican senator, supported by the Bush administration, has introduced a bill to protect humans on highways from the 'visual pollution' of billboards. It would ban new billboards along federally funded highways and permit state and local governments to abolish existing ones. If the bill passes, it *will* be a triumph of human rights over property rights."

Adam felt agitated. "I am not surprised," he said, "when certain sorts of politicians and environmentalists recite silly slogans, but a bright mouse should know better. The billboards are not living creatures with thoughts, feelings, and rights. They are assets owned, not by the Wicked Witch of the North, but by people."

"So," smirked Karl, "in demolishing unsightly and useless billboards, we make highways prettier for all, even if that may inconvenience a few."

Adam was aghast. "Inconvenience a few in getting rid of useless unsightliness?" he murmured unbelievingly. "This ham-handed action by Big and Little Brother would wipe out most of the billboard industry, two-thirds of which consists of small operators. It would reduce income of those who own land along highways. It would deny merchants — commonly small, local business people — relatively inexpensive advertising. And it would hamper tourists looking for motels, eateries, and service stations. This is not a battle of good people against bad property: It is an effort of some self-styled elitist types with government connections to expropriate property of other people."

A startled Karl tried to mollify his agitated friend. "Don't let your cheese melt, old boy," he said. "This cannot be expropriation. After all, the Constitution clearly says that 'private property [shall not] be taken for public use without just compensation.' *Just* compensation must mean *full* compensation; and *full* compensation must mean the *present value* of the future income which could be expected from the asset."

"You would suppose so," agreed Adam. "But, in actuality, as we are told by James Bovard and L. Gordon Crovitz in *The Wall Street Journal*, the bill provides no monetary compensation, at all! It lets government commander billboards if the owners are simply warned a few years before that their property will be taken."

Beneath his fur, Karl blanched. "How free can be the Land of the Free," he wondered, "if government can freely seize the property of citizens?"

Capitalism, Communism, and Pollution

ﬄﬄﬄﬄ

Supposedly — in some circles — a private-property, open-market economy fosters pollution. Business types are sensitive to costs, of course, because they strive for profits. But they take into account only those *private* costs which fall on their firm, and there are *social* costs which their firm can evade. The firm has to meet expenses of hiring labor, buying machinery and materials, and borrowing money; but it can spew noxious gas into the sky and put toxic wastes into streams and landfills for free. Businesses do not include in their production calculations unassigned social costs.

Well, now, if all this is an apt and adequate characterization of the pollution perils of capitalism — if private property and market pricing produce pollution — presumably a social/economic arrangement of state-owned property and economic activity directed by central decree would yield a pristine environment. Presume again.

Economist Thomas DiLorenzo has surveyed the distressing story of pollution in the Soviet Union and its satellites. It is a catastrophic catalogue of irresponsible waste and degradation by unaccountable people — a review of major rivers and massive lakes utterly despoiled by untreated waste and raw sewage, made unfit even for industrial uses; of denuded forests, erosion, and dust storms; of soil left useless for agriculture; of air so filthy that children are commonly sick most of the time, with appalling increases in mental retardation, rampant cancer and respiratory disease, and shortened life expectancy.

Every society will have some amounts of some kinds of environmental costs. To live is to pollute. But *capitalism* does *not*, in its nature, contribute to excessive pollution, and *communism does*.

At the core of capitalism is private rights to use of property. These rights are limited. You cannot use property designated to be yours to destroy property designated to be mine. We can compete for the favor of employers or consumers, but you are not permitted to burn my buildings, pour smoke and noise over my land, or dump garbage in my yard. Designated private property rights make people *responsible* and *accountable*. But when property rights are vested in "the state" and in bureaucrats and managers who have no occasion to be sensitive to the good will of members of the community, then it is a game of very different rules, and one is permitted and even induced to be cavalier toward the environment.

Our own environmental problems do not stem from too much of privately owned property and too little government. The communists have make it definitively clear that government-dominated societies become environmental disaster areas. Our problems stem, instead, from too *little* of privately owned property and too *much* ineptitude in government regulatory decrees to cover gaps in defining and enforcing those property rights which will guide owners to be good stewards of their assets.

The Pricing System in Action

Scarcity, Shortage, and Policy

ๆๆๆๆ

Ever since the serpent seduced Eve and Eve seduced Adam, we have been cursed with scarcity. No matter how much, how hard, and how well we work, we cannot produce all of everything we want. It is not likely that grubby people will soon stop wanting so much; it is no more likely that the supply of manna from heaven will appreciably increase. So it behooves us to be efficient, squeezing as much as possible of those things we want most out of the limited resources we have available.

When the objective is efficiency in using resources, the mind of man has not conceived, and the machinations of man have not evolved, a better arrangement than a private property, price-directed economy. Much of the world is belatedly learning this lesson. But many of our politicians and journalists, and even some business people, do not really accept the market economy. For them, free men in free markets is only a romantic notion, too fragile and too inequitable to rely upon when major difficulties arise.

Curtailment of oil can be a major difficulty. With current and prospective oil supplies reduced, it is not surprising that the valuation of oil would rise. There is nothing nefarious or subversive in gasoline prices going up when supply goes down — especially when, following the historical pattern, crude oil prices change proportionately more than gasoline prices.

But an increase in the price of a commodity as conspicuous as gasoline brings out the demagogic craziness of Senator Snort and his little friends, who love to snarl darkly about "gouging" by Daddy Warbucks. Even when the boys try to be terribly analytic, they make hash of good sense. A single story in the *Los Angeles Times* refers ten — count them, ten — times to oil and fuel *shortages* when what was meant was simply *reduced supply*.

If supply of oil is reduced, of course price rises. And the rise of price serves a purpose: the higher price leads people to *want* to cut consumption to the amount available — the higher price *rations* the reduced supply. But if people are *not* induced to curtail the amount demanded when supply falls, then we have a *shortage*. At a price too low, people demand too much. *Scarcity* is inflicted on us by a stingy world; *shortage* is inflicted on us by our adoption of price control.

Confusing shortage with scarcity is far more than a mere matter of formal terminology. Failure to understand the nature of the problem can lead us into bad policy which perpetuates and aggravates the difficulty. Faced with incipient shortage as supply falls, we bitch about evils of rising prices; we combat "gouging" by suppressing prices, and we then try to ration and allocate in costly patchwork ways. But holding down prices when the market can be cleared only by their going up intensifies the shortage.

Clumsy language leads to clumsy thought, which leads to clumsy policy, which leads to clumsy use of resources.

Water, Energy, and Prices

✍✍✍✍

"All Californians must seek every possible means to conserve water," assert editors of a newspaper. "One method," they indicate, "is by charging prices that more accurately reflect the value of water."

We do commonly waste water, for we use it for purposes worth less than the cost of supplying it. Such behavior seems sensible at the moment when we pay low, subsidized water prices. If a gallon of water costs 5 cents to supply but its price is only 1 cent, we use it in ways worth as little as 1 cent. But it is wasteful to put 5-cent water to 1-cent uses.

If the subsidy is ended and the price of water is allowed to reflect the higher cost, consumers will cut out uses of water they value less than the 5-cent cost. No government authority will have to specify the uses to deny or satisfy; each person decides for himself. And if the scarcity increases and price rises correspondingly, consumers will eliminate still more uses until the quantity demanded fits the smaller supply available.

Such conservation depends on the price of water accurately reflecting scarcity and cost of supply. But as the editors point out, some cities do not even have water meters. Indeed, one city charter declares that "Water meters shall never be attached to residential water service pipes." Instead, local governments charge residents a flat, subsidized fee. To end the consequent waste, the editors wisely call for increased use of meters and for prices that "more accurately reflect the value of water."

Yet, in writing about *energy*, the editors ignore the importance of prices. Instead, they emote about "the ultimate crisis" of running out of oil in the next century. If — a big *if* — we begin running out of oil in the foreseeable future, its scarcity and cost of production will rise. If government does not then control petroleum prices — that, too, is a big *if* — those prices will rise to reflect oil's growing scarcity and rising production cost. In response, consumers would conserve oil, and producers would supply more substitutes.

The goal is *not* to "conserve all the energy possible now," as the editors aver. We could conserve *all* petroleum by not using *any* of it! But that would be too costly. Instead, the objective is to eliminate only those uses of oil (and water) that individuals value less than the cost of producing and using it. And that means allowing prices to reflect scarcity and production costs — including the costs of environmental damage from using oil.

With the guidance of these prices, we will know how much to conserve and how much of substitutes to supply. The editors underscore this point in water use, but they ignore it in energy use. Instead, they call for government "social engineers" to tell us how to behave as consumers and producers of energy. But we know how to behave. All we need is guidance from accurate prices that reflect scarcity and costs.

Waste Disposal and Adam Smith

✍✍✍✍

Nearly three-quarters of the nation's landfills have closed since the 1970s. And the Environmental Protection Agency estimates that a third of those remaining will shut down in the next three years. What will Americans do with their mountains of trash?

Not only are there more people to create garbage today, but each also makes more now than in the past. Thirty years ago, Americans each discarded a daily average of 2.7 pounds of trash. Now they throw away close to 4 pounds of paper, paperboard, yard debris, metals, glass, food, and plastics.

Garbage has become a very big and growing problem, but it will not be well solved unless waste disposal is widely perceived as an *economic* problem. That is, landfills are *scarce*: they cannot satisfy all of everyone's wants for waste disposal, and we have to economize on their use.

Other goods, too, are scarce. Yet, Americans do not have a problem with tomatoes or shirts for one simple reason: These products have *market prices* that reflect their scarcity. If bad weather reduces the supply of tomatoes, their price rises. Tomatoes are scarcer, a fact communicated to consumers by the higher price. And since consumers pay according to the number of tomatoes bought, they reduce the amount purchased to fit the smaller available quantity. So there are no shortages of tomatoes when people pay market prices.

In contrast, there are persistent, growing shortages of landfills. These shortages occur because individuals can use landfills without having to pay prices that reflect their scarcity. People often do pay a flat, periodic fee for garbage collection. But that fee does not *vary* with the amount of trash discarded, so one can throw out more without paying more.

But market pricing can be included in trash collection, as Perkasie, Pennsylvania, demonstrates. *The Wall Street Journal* recounts that residents of this small town must pay $1.50 for each 40-pound bag of garbage collected. The fee compels individuals to pay *more* when discarding *more*. So people have incentive to economize on their use of the local landfill. They compost food and yard waste and buy fewer paper towels, plastic containers, and other products that generate much trash.

They also accumulate separated newspapers, cardboard, bottles, and cans for pickup without charge. Indeed, the community *requires* — and subsidizes, with the free collection — recycling of papers, bottles, and cans. Because of the town's charging by the bag for garbage collection and subsidizing of recycling, citizens have effective incentive to minimize waste and to help reuse the reusable.

It is powerful inducement to have to pay for what one gets — or gets rid of — and to receive reward for good citizenship. And it has worked: Costs of waste collection and disposal have fallen by a third. Says a city official: "We've let Adam Smith lead the way."

Resource Scarcity, Changing Scarcity, and Rationality in the Marketplace

✍✍✍✍

In 1980 a notorious, self-styled environmentalist bet $1000 that the real prices of five minerals chosen by him would rise over the next ten years. He lost the bet: corrected for inflation, the price of each of the minerals was *lower* in 1990 than in 1980.

A commentator has chortled that "the predicted scarcity of material resources as a result of increasing population and increasing industrial activity did not occur." The choice of chortled words was not entirely appropriate. Those minerals were already scarce in 1980, they remained scarce in 1990, and in all probability they will still be scarce in generations to come. But it is to be noted that they became somewhat *less* scarce during the '80s. Through a combination of changes in consumer preferences, technological refinements, and production requirements, along with greater physical availabilities of the minerals, the *supplies* of the resources increased more than the *demand* for them.

But suppose the real prices of the minerals had increased? Would salvation then require draconian constraints imposed on the community — policies of no-growth or even negative-growth, with Big Brother necessarily imposing a primitive lifestyle in order for us to live at all? What governmental policies and decrees are required when resource prices start to rise?

The most basic answer is simply to let the market fill its role. For rising prices of either inputs or outputs are reflections of changing circumstances, and they give us signals and incentives to act efficiently. Higher prices lead us to consume and use less or to produce more or to seek lower-cost substitutes.

A rising trend of resource prices would not by itself imply that greater conservation is rational. Some years ago, three sound economists — Gerhard Anders, S. Charles Maurice, and now-Senator

W. Philip Gramm — asked if further resource conservation would have paid during the twentieth century.

Consider a resource — coal, copper, iron ore, petroleum. The owner can either extract it from the ground now, sell it, and invest the net proceeds; or he can now leave it in the ground and hope that its price will rise over time. Which strategy will yield the greater future value?

If the rate of *return on investment* of the receipts of the current sale is greater than the rate of *price appreciation* of the unmined resource, then dig it up and let the community use it. And that, in fact, is the resource story of this century: "...enforced long-term conservation ... would have been a poor economic decision."

This is, indeed, a world of scarcity. But hysteria hardly helps. We do best to use our resources with analytic sense, comparing costs and returns of alternatives, rather than indulging in sophomoric silliness.

Poets, Comedians, and Replacement Costs

✍✍✍✍

If you would understand how the world works economically, put not your faith in journalists or politicians.

When the dictator of Iraq decided to take civilization to the oligarchies of Kuwait, the rate of increase in oil prices rose abruptly in fears of curtailed supplies. But why should a motorist have to pay a higher price on Tuesday for gas which was sold to the filling station on Monday at a low, pre-invasion price? Shouldn't yesterday's low cost to the retailer mean a low price to today's customer?

The august *New York Times* provided — in the words of one of its own columnists — "one of those fuller-explanation stories that make *The Times* indispensable to people who would ... know what's going on ...." The story accounted for the quick jump in gas prices essentially on grounds that "psychology ... is in charge," abetted by instantaneous electronic communications. Although "physical fundamentals" of the oil industry had not yet changed, "people expect the price to rise," a petroleum researcher was quoted, "so the price rises."

And, of course, psychology conjures visions of corruption, and Senator Snort quickly made noises about "greed," "collusion," and "war-profiteering."

Well, prices are generated through activities and anticipations of people in markets. And where there is people activity and anticipations, there is necessarily involved some "psychology." But more than simple-minded psychology is entailed. When a firm — whether Colossal Oil Company or a neighborhood outlet — searches for the best price to charge, there are certain objective conditions to satisfy. Most basically, if a firm's receipts do not cover its expenditures, the firm will not be long for this world.

A firm sells an asset this morning; it uses proceeds of the sale to replenish inventory this afternoon in order to make another sale tomorrow. If the firm is to survive, it must sell assets at prices high enough to replace those assets. The relevant expenditure of the firm is the *replacement* cost of the asset *today*, not the *historical* cost in acquiring the asset *yesterday*.

You sell a house to buy another house. The price you charge now had better reflect today's market valuation if you hope to replace it. The fact that you bought the house for less — or perhaps acquired it at zero price through inheritance — has nothing to do with its present value.

A savings institution acquired loanable funds last year when interest rates were low. Now, rates are higher, and the institution charges high interest on today's loans, for it will have to pay depositors high rates in order to replenish its loanable funds inventory.

Similarly, a seller of gas and oil and must charge today's high prices in order to cover replacement costs, even if the product sold today was bought yesterday at a lower price.

Poets of the press and comedians of Congress should try real hard to comprehend that past prices are not pertinent for present operations: today's values are provided by today's perceptions.

Problems of Peculiar Pricing

How Politicians Abuse the Law

৶৶৶৶

Good economics and good politics rarely mix well: politicians thrive by promising something for nothing, but economics shows that little can be had without someone bearing cost. By exposing the ruse that individuals do not have to pay their way, economics becomes the killjoy of the party. No wonder it is not invited to the political orgy.

That good economics is excluded from political festivities is illustrated by the pricing of water, airports, and health care. In each instance, politicians cultivate the belief that consumers can be excused from paying much of the cost of production. But by keeping these prices arbitrarily low, government abuses a fundamental principle of good economics: the law of demand, which points out that individuals consume more of something at lower prices than at higher prices.

Water prices are generally kept much below costs of supply. Individuals consume more than they would at higher prices. Farmers use more water by ignoring water-saving changes in irrigation methods; producers use more water by ignoring processes or products that use less water; and households use more water by ignoring plumbing and landscaping alterations that would conserve water. Although individuals would willingly use less water at higher prices, politicians keep prices low. So water shortages are commonplace.

A similar outcome occurs at airports. Airports are commonly owned by government. Here, too, politicians abuse the law of demand. Individuals demand more runway space at lower prices than at higher prices, but politicians commonly forbid airports from charging prices that vary with traffic. Unlike telephone companies which contain demand by charging more during peak hours, airports cannot price runways to restrain use. The result is a common mismatch between airport capacity and the number of people who want to fly — and congestion results.

Medical care is another example of foolish political pricing. Government does not tax employer-provided health insurance premiums, but it does tax income that would be used if one preferred to buy his own insurance. Not surprisingly, employer-provided health insurance has ballooned. As a consequence, an employer-labor-government consortium — not the consumer — is now in charge of the purse strings. One does *not* have to take a hard look at the cost of the health care he consumes. Instead, he can consume additional care while paying little or no additional cost. The low price to each consumer then increases the quantity of medical care demanded. And as everyone tries to obtain more care, its cost ratchets up for everyone.

Rising health-care costs can be contained and shortages of water and airport capacity can be eliminated—if government policies are in accord with the law of demand. But this is one law politicians did not pass and love to abuse.

Mouse Wisdom: Lanes, Planes, and Dr. Gridlock

✍✍✍✍

Mouse Adam and Mouse Karl had called a noted economouse to resolve a dispute.

"I say that new road construction is the only solution to highway congestion," exclaimed Karl confidently.

"Clogged highways are common," said Dr. Gridlock agreeably, "but new road construction by itself cannot be a solution."

"I agree," agreed Adam. "Congestion expands as fast as new highways are built. New roads will not solve road congestion any more than new airports will solve airport congestion."

"That's dumb," Karl demurely disagreed. "An airline executive says that our airport system lacks enough capacity to handle current or expected volume. And a member of the National Transportation Safety Board thinks a lack of airport capacity is today's biggest concern in aviation. I don't see how congestion can be eliminated unless we build enough new highways and airports to accommodate our needs."

"But so-called needs are not fixed," admonished Dr. Gridlock. "They depend on the price paid to satisfy them. Indeed, we economists prefer to speak of *demands*, not needs. And the amount of roads or airports demanded depends on their *prices*. The higher the price, the smaller the amount demanded. Prices are market-clearing when they balance the amount demanded and the amount available. But if prices are absent or are less than market-clearing, demand becomes excessive. So congestion results."

Karl persevered. "But we already pay prices for roadways when we pay gasoline taxes, and we pay prices for airports when we buy airline tickets."

"True," answered Dr. Gridlock, "but the gasoline tax is *not* a price that drivers pay to use a *particular* road at a *particular* time. Nor do airlines usually pay prices to use *particular* airports at *particular* times. So roadways and airports lack prices that influence decisions about where, when, and how to travel."

"Congestion occurs," Adam emphasized, "because roads and airports do not have market-clearing prices to keep demand in line with capacity."

"Correct," confirmed Dr. Gridlock. "Like other goods and services, roadways and airports are scarce. And being scarce, they cannot satisfy all travel wants of every mouse. Indeed, scarcity implies continually coping with insufficient capacity to satisfy all wants. But in the absence of market-clearing prices, we do not cope well with that limited capacity. Instead, we frustrate ourselves by trying foolishly to use more than is available, and in doing so we cause congestion and waste resources."

"You don't mean that new highways or new airports should not be built, do you?" asked Karl.

"Of course not," answered Dr. Gridlock. "Capacity should be expanded if the added cost is justified. But remember that additional capacity will not prevent congestion: no matter how much we build, only proper pricing of roads and airports can do that. Good engineering must be combined with good economics."

Auto Insurance and Consumer Protection

✍✍✍✍

Motorists are hotter than steaming radiators because of higher prices for auto insurance.

Insurance rates have risen faster than the inflation rate in recent years. But the increase is due mainly to higher costs of bodily-injury claims. Not only have these costs pushed up rates for consumers, they have also reduced earnings for insurers. *Fortune* magazine reports that auto insurance, on average, is not profitable.

So it takes a long leap of faith to believe that government rate controls — by further reducing those earnings — will attract more insurers into the industry and yield more insurance at lower costs. Yet, drivers are urged to take that leap by self-appointed consumer protectors, who moan about big, greedy companies preying on helpless insurance consumers. The only way to protect consumers, they say, is through government regulation.

Or is it? Eminent economist Milton Friedman observes that the consumer's most effective protection is a marketplace that is open to all potential competitors. "The consumer is protected from being exploited by one seller by the existence of another seller from whom he can buy and who is eager to sell to him. Alternative sources of supply," concludes Dr. Friedman, "protect the consumer far more effectively than all the Ralph Naders of the world."

When purchasing auto insurance, consumers can shop among many alternative suppliers. That shopping can take a little effort and cost a little time, of course, but many insurance companies compete fiercely with one another for the consumer's dollar.

Clearly, still greater sources of supply are *not* what government regulation promises for the auto industry. Government cannot effectively decree lower-price, lower-cost insurance any more than it can command the tide to stay out. Someone has to pay the high cost of claims which now saddles suppliers of auto insurance. If government price controls prevent consumers from paying the real cost of their insurance, companies will supply less. Some will refuse to cover young drivers or residents of densely populated, high-risk areas. Others will withdraw all services from a given state.

So consumers of insurance will end up with fewer competing suppliers. Many will find none at all. Perhaps this is what so-called consumer protectors really want. For by devastating the private auto insurance industry with government regulation, they can howl for socialized insurance. First, they shoot the horse in the foot; then, they cry about its inability to run.

But government-provided auto insurance presumably would compel lower-risk drivers to subsidize higher-risk drivers. And with oppressive regulation that drives out efficiency and reduces buyers' options, the real cost of auto insurance would rise. Drivers would then pay more money for less insurance. Thanks to an army of self-appointed consumer protectors, drivers would have the worst of all worlds. Who or what would then protect them from their protectors?

"I'm a Capitalist — But ...."

✍✍✍✍

"Exceptions prove the rule," we are told. I have never understood that. Exceptions weaken and dilute the rule, and make it less reliable.

The exceptions promoted by people in the marketplace are rarely reflections of dispassionate, disinterested analysis. Rather, they often are indelicate attempts to gain special advantage, discriminatory favor unearned by productive performance. Thus, we hear, "I am all for prices determined by activity in open markets — *but* don't touch the rent control which subsidizes my housing expense."

And there are the exceptions which reflect lack of analytic sophistication. One distinguishing feature of the solid, sober economist is that he really believes in his analytics and consistently relies on it. His opinions and proposals are logically *deduced* through coherent thought.

Alas, solid, sober economists are not numerous. But that does not mean that others decline to pronounce opinions on matters calling for analysis. Consider a pronouncement of fluff and foolishness on a serious question by a columnist in a major newspaper.

The serious question in question is ticket-scalping — reselling tickets at a high price which had been earlier bought at the lower face value. The occasion was an athletic tournament. Tickets were sold by the arena for $60. But some buyers then resold them for prices ranging up to $2,300.

Now, buying something low and selling it high sounds pretty shrewd to most of us most of the time. But not to the journalist when the low price is printed on the ticket. That initially stipulated price is, we are informed, the "honest" price, and only a "greedy" "creep" or "jerk" would resell it to a "sucker" in the "open market" for "profit."

Is the newspaper columnist some kind of commie? Is there something inherently wrong with people buying and selling at an agreed price? Well, the columnist stoutly insists, "I'm a capitalist — *but* scalping of tickets hits me as a rotten deal."

This is pretty strange talk — and it is wholly unsupported by any analysis by the journalist. The seller and the buyer of a ticket obviously did *not* consider the exchange to be a "a rotten deal." On the contrary, the exchange is productive, making both people better off.

In *any* uncoerced exchange, *each* party believes that he helps himself: *each* values more highly what he gets than what he gives up, *each* is using his *own* assets to enhance his *own* well-being in accordance with his *own* criteria and assessments. And *that* is at the crux of what capitalism — and the individualistic society generally — is all about.

It is sobering to find professed capitalists denigrating private rights to use of property, including the right to sell what one owns in order to buy things owned by others. Thus is capitalism subverted by professed but confused capitalists.

Mouse Wisdom: The Hurricane After Hugo

✍✍✍✍

"It's disgraceful how some mice take advantage of others' misfortune," complained Mouse Karl. "After hurricane Hugo smashed the east coast, sellers increased prices of ice, plywood, chain saws, and other goods. Fortunately, government blocked the gouging by making it unlawful to raise prices after the hurricane."

"But the hurricane *did* temporarily increase the scarcity of many products," answered Mouse Adam. "Supplies of many items fell at the same time demands for them rose. There were not enough products to satisfy all of every mouse's increased wants, so somehow these items had to be rationed. How could mice most efficiently adapt to the disaster, making the best of a tragic situation? Unfortunately, government controls — which are costly to enforce — prevented higher prices from rationing the products to those willing and able to pay, so *shortages* resulted. The goods were then rationed by *waiting in line*."

"A good thing, too," responded Karl, "for it is cruel to imply that a poor, unemployed mouse cannot receive immediate relief for her family because she does not have as much as a rich family."

"But price controls are not an effective means for helping the poor," admonished Adam. "Remember, price controls create shortages and cause rationing by waiting in line. Is it not cruel to imply that a poor, elderly mouse in ill health cannot receive immediate relief because she does not have as much endurance as others to wait in line?"

"Rationing by waiting in line does not guarantee poor mice a greater share of the pie," continued Adam. "Indeed, many mice will pay others to wait for them. If public officials were sensibly concerned about assuring the poor minimal access to goods in the marketplace, they would give the poor cash to supplement their buying power. Then, the entire community — not just suppliers of the purchased goods — would bear the cost of the subsidy."

"Well, government price controls do keep goods cheaper during the emergency," remarked Karl.

"They don't even do that," answered Adam. "The real price of obtaining a good is its money price *plus* the value of time spent waiting in line. The price control keeps the money price lower. But by increasing the waiting time, it often raises the time cost by a greater amount. So when money *and* time are considered, the good is more costly than it would be if its money price could rise to its market level."

"Moreover," Adam continued, "price controls make goods more expensive by reducing their availability. Without price controls, mice would have more incentive to transport greatly desired products into the devastated area."

"Self-interest isn't the only permissible reaction to the adversity," snapped Karl. "What about all those caring mice over the country who donate food and other valuable commodities?"

"That is noble behavior which ought to be praised and encouraged," answered Adam. "But it doesn't make sense to undo this charity by enacting price controls which further reduce already scarce supplies, make goods even more costly, and divert time from cleaning up to waiting in line."

Prices and Production

✍✍✍✍

Prices are important. Prices are critical in determining how much of different goods is demanded and how much is produced. Market-determined prices reflect preferences, anticipations, and costs. People, both consumers and producers, make decisions in light of prices of some goods relative to prices of other goods and prices of goods today relative to prices expected tomorrow and prices of outputs relative to prices of inputs.

The world is a changing place. Jungle instinct alone is enough to suggest that some sorts of changes best lead to price changes if we are to keep demands and resource allocations in proper alignment.

Some of the underlying changes are cyclical, following a well-defined path over the hours of a day or the seasons of a year. And so prices of goods can appropriately rise and fall over a cycle even when production costs per unit vary little.

Thus, ski-resort, cruise-ship, airline, telephone, restaurant, and theater prices often vary greatly, depending on the month or the hour. Demands for evening plays are greater than for matinees, while more telephone calls are made during the day than in the night. The optimal price to charge for the product varies with changing demand. To put the matter differently, the product itself is defined not only by its physical characteristics but also by the time of its supply and consumption: an evening performance at the theater is not the same commodity as an afternoon performance of the same play with the same actors.

Some electric power companies, reports *The New York Times*, are belatedly learning what theater and telephone company managers have long understood: The demand for their product is cyclical, and the price can best reflect the rising and falling demand.

A flat "average equilibrium" price per unit of electricity over the daily and seasonal cycles will be too low for peak periods (it will encourage still more demand when usage already is naturally great) and too high for slack times (it will further curtail demand when usage is naturally small). If production capacity is made great enough to handle peak demand, there will be much idle plant the rest of the time; if there is lesser capacity, there will be peak-period shortages.

Problems are compounded if production expenses are higher in peak periods because of utilization of equipment with higher operating costs, requiring, say, use of an oil-fired plant to supplement a hydroelectric dam.

Raising peak-load prices and lowering slack-period prices may leave total electricity consumption unchanged. But it would go some way to even-out consumption over the cycle. And that, in turn, would reduce both immediate operating expenses and the costs of producing more plant to satisfy peak demands. Smoothing the consumption cycle means making fuller and better use of smaller plant investment. Prices are, indeed, important.

Corporate Costs, Operations, and Profits

The Hard World of the Market

ＳＳＳＳ

It is a very hard world. Many have borne great pains and costs for us to reach our standard of living. And continuing the increase in that standard will require continuing effort, ingenuity, and initiative.

Even if we succeed in adding to our wealth, we still will be confronting a world of scarcity. One of the more foolish things said by a notorious social philosopher was reference to our "affluent" society. We are less unaffluent today than we were 100 or 200 years ago, but the necessity to *produce* will always be the central economic imperative. The ultimate purpose of production is consumption, but we cannot consume what we do not produce. If we do not produce well, we will not consume well.

Our production efforts are carried on largely through business firms. And firms must struggle to survive, much less prosper. Big firms may have become big by being relatively efficient in satisfying customers. But many a large outfit has run into difficulties and dangers because high efficiency was not maintained in the worldly context of change and choice and chance.

A story in *The New York Times* illustrates some of the agonies of business decision-making in a high stakes game. The story pertains to a large corporation in the automobile industry. The old firm has been severely weakened, and is being forced into do-or-die innovation. Survival and expansion require commitment of great resources. A fiscal fiasco now would be fatal.

"Designing a car from scratch is an immense financial bet," observes an industry analyst, "and one an auto maker must be strong enough to lose." The firm in question is not strong enough to lose its bet — but neither is it strong enough to last for long without betting and winning. And it has to win in a "viciously competitive market."

Winning requires more than sound engineering and attractive styling. Funds must be adequate to finance the massive, drawn-out project; suppliers must be dependable, and workers must be committed and well directed; customers must be receptive; and the national economy must be vigorous.

The company cannot control the overall economy, it is vulnerable to vagaries of suppliers, and advertising campaigns are notoriously uncertain. But the firm is experimenting with new production methods as well as with new product designs. All these aspects and activities must come together well, for failure begets failure; if this product line and its production are not effective, new loans to and investments in the firm are not likely to be enough to enable the firm to go on.

It is a hard world in the market. Many conditions and people must be satisfied for success. It requires much work, competence, steady nerves, and luck to produce appropriate products, produce them economically, and market them shrewdly. Assuredly, we do *not* live in a society of easy affluence.

Costs, Competition, and Prices

ss ss ss ss

A reader has written bitterly to the consumer editor of a newspaper. "What kind of rip-off are the airlines pulling," he asks, "when the fare from Los Angeles to Indianapolis is more than twice that from Los Angeles to New York?"

The editor agrees that such pricing is a "gouge" of Indianapolis customers. After all, the airline costs of flying to Indianapolis are smaller than the costs of a New York flight. So the Indianapolis fare should be smaller. Everyone knows that.

Well, many *believe* that costs determine — or, in a nice world, "should" determine — prices. But is it somehow wasteful, unfair, or otherwise wrong that matinee tickets are cheaper than those for evening performances?

Obviously, prices of goods are *not* always in the same relation as their costs of production. Then, how *do* we account for prices? How can a relatively short airline trip be priced higher than a longer trip?

The editor turned to an airlines analyst of a brokerage house for guidance. The analyst polluted the air by proclaiming that "the Indianapolis passenger is subsidizing the New York passenger." But the fare to Indianapolis is not high because the fare to New York is low; nor is the New York fare low because the Indianapolis fare is high. In a market free of government decree, airlines will not long continue routes which do not pay: they will not use net revenue from good routes to underwrite persistently bad routes. The carriers will try to set profit-making prices on each route independently.

The brokerage analyst finally — and grudgingly — lets the cat largely out of the bag. "Unfortunately," he observes, "price is a product of competition, and the competition between Los Angeles to New York is fierce, while the competition for traffic between Los Angeles and Indianapolis is nil."

So the direct basis of the fares is not respective costs; nor is it mysteriously a matter of discriminatory subsidization. Rather, it is a matter of *competition in supply* and the *amount of demand*. How many suppliers seek the favor of how many demanders?

Curiously, many more people want to travel to New York than to Indianapolis. If there were only one airline to New York and no imposed price control, the profit-maximizing fare and the amount of profit would be very considerable. But these profit possibilities have attracted many carriers. And that competition has driven down the price — and the profits.

The *motivation* of lowering the New York price is not some peculiar fondness of airline officials for people going to New York; and the lower New York price on *all* airlines is not made *feasible* through subsidization by the relatively few people going to Indianapolis on *some* airlines or by willingness of *any* airline to lose money on the route to New York.

The New York fare is low because of *competition* of many airlines which seek to survive in that market. And the New York fare would be no higher if every airline decided not to fly to Indianapolis.

Entrepreneurship, the Dynamic Economy, and Teaching

✍✍✍✍

The English have called them "undertakers." In the United States, "undertaker" has a different connotation. So we use the French word, "entrepreneur." And the entrepreneur does, indeed, undertake market ventures.

For most of us, entrepreneurship — like electricity — fortunately exists, but is hard to define.

Entrepreneurship may be found in a manager. But the entrepreneur surely is more than an administrator of a going concern. A robust, expanding economy cannot confine itself to producing and delivering the same old goods in the same old ways. We commonly associate entrepreneurship with *new* things and activities and procedures. The entrepreneur faces uncertainties in seeking *new* products, *new* markets, *new* production and distribution techniques, *new* sources of supply, *new* types of organization. Such newness is sought as an aid in *rivalry* with market competitors.

The entrepreneur collects information and coordinates activity in trying to exploit perceived opportunities for uncommon returns. He both instigates change through innovation and responds to change perceived with new and better interpreted information. Those firms prosper most who best accommodate preferences of consumers for goods which are different or better or less expensive or more attractively provided.

Much of modern economic theory has been quite static. It is commonly centered on market *equilibrium* in a given setting. Comprehending equilibrium and its conditions is not trivial accomplishment. And yet, analysis confined to identifying and comparing equilibria in a construct of full information in perfect markets leaves out much of what the real world is about. Indeed, it leaves out entrepreneurship. Theory which largely ignores the entrepreneurial *dynamics* of actual market competition is inadequate as analytic description and thus as policy guide.

We can try to characterize the entrepreneurial function. We can speak of the productive consequences of imagination, creativity, innovation, initiative, insightfulness, boldness, persistence, and luck.

We can try to identify conditions and circumstances most conducive to flourishing entrepreneurship, including public institutions and policies which can greatly affect the options and ground rules and circumstances of market activity. But can we *teach* people to be entrepreneurs?

We can go some way in training *managers*. At least, we can provide certain tools and techniques — accounting, statistics, business law, portfolio and personnel management. But can we teach people to be imaginative and creative and innovative, to be insightful and bold and persistent — and to be lucky?

Surely, effective entrepreneurs are born more than made. The contribution we can best make is not to try to teach the unteachable, but to get out of the way and let creative people create.

Employment and Profits

ℒℒℒℒ

Most people don't want welfare or charity. They want jobs in which they can be productive members of the community. But in the last year and a half, employment has gone down. Between September 1990 and September 1991, the number of employees on private, nonfarm payrolls fell by 1.2 million, or about 1.3 percent.

Employment usually falls during an economic slump. Yet, compared to employment reductions of past recessions, the current decline has been mild. In the same one-year time span in 1982, employment fell nearly 2 percent. And in the downturn of 1975, it dropped nearly 3 percent.

Still, any increase in employment is better than even a modest decline. And during the eight years of economic expansion preceding the current slump, employment rose steadily. Increases in private payroll employment in that period averaged nearly 2.8 percent per year, a higher average than in the 1950s, '60s, or '70s.

The current downturn in employment has many worried. They wonder how employment can again rise when noted companies, such as General Motors and IBM, have scheduled massive layoffs. But these and other big companies were not mainly responsible for the rapid employment growth during the 1980s. New and growing small businesses (those with fewer than 100 employees) created most new employment opportunities then.

But whether the source is big or small companies, the creation of new employment depends on an economic climate that favors entrepreneurs. These are the people who risk their wealth in trying to satisfy community preferences. If they correctly anticipate and efficiently satisfy those preferences, the community rewards them with profits. So the prospect of earning profits encourages and directs entrepreneurs to produce much and well. When they do so, businesses create new jobs as well as provide more output.

No wonder growth of employment depends on profitability of starting and expanding businesses. When owners and managers are

Percentage Change in Private Employment and Prior Year's Real Corporate Profits, 1960–1991

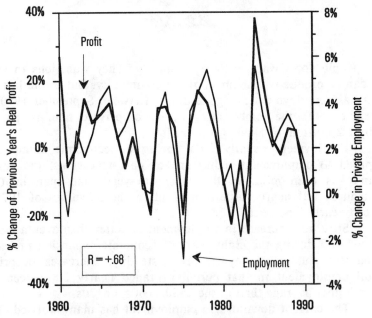

Sources: *Employment and Earnings*, October 1991, U.S. Dept. of Labor; *Economic Indicators*, November 1991; *Economic Report of the President*, 1991. 1991 data are for first half of year.

confident that their risk-taking has a better chance of earning a profit, they are more willing to hire workers and produce for the community. From 1960 to 1991, yearly growth of private employment closely followed growth of inflation-adjusted corporate profits the year before. When real profits went up (or down) in one year, employment grew faster (or slower) in the next year.

The strong relationship suggests that employment could again grow swiftly if we nurtured entrepreneurship. We do this by encouraging businesses and their owners to take risks, innovate, and efficiently create wealth for us all.

But this is not the environment we seem bent on creating. Instead, we burden businesses with higher taxes, more regulation, and greater uncertainty. What better way to dispirit entrepreneurs and discourage growth of jobs in America!

The Stock Market's Anchor

ॐॐॐॐ

"Beware the stock market!" advises a chorus of critics. The market has lost its anchor, they say, because stock prices no longer reflect the real economy. Instead, those prices mirror mainly crowd hysteria and whims of large institutional investors interested only in short-term gain.

Why else, they continue, would the Dow Jones Industrial Average have plunged by more than 500 points in October 1987 and 190 points in October 1989? And why else would variability of stock prices have increased in recent years? Surely, earnings prospects of corporations do not change so greatly and abruptly to explain these wide variations in prices.

Many factors determine a stock's price. But that price is essentially the market's *present* valuation of a corporation's *expected* earnings in the future. By buying a share of common stock, one becomes part owner of the company, and so receives a share of its earnings as dividends. If earnings grow, dividends, too, are likely to grow. So investors bid up the price of the stock today.

But even the most knowledgeable investor cannot know the future. The best one can do is *anticipate* it, and anticipations change like the weather — warming up stock prices one day and cooling them down the next.

Even if anticipated earnings remain constant, investors can change what they are willing to *pay* now for those future earnings. Having the right to a dollar next year is worth less than having that dollar now. So the future dividends expected from a stock are *discounted* to determine what one will pay for them today. And the *rate* of that discount is affected by the perceived riskiness of the investment. Greater risk means a heftier discount, and a heftier discount means a lower price for a stock — even if its stream of expected dividends remains unchanged.

Monetary policy, tax rates, trade policy, elections, rumors of war — such economic and political events alter the riskiness of stock investment. And earnings prospects, themselves, can quickly change. So stock prices can soar or plunge even though they follow expectations of the future economy.

That connection is illustrated by recent history. Consider the relationship between stock prices and corporate earnings. We can measure stock prices by the Dow Jones Industrial Average, and let corporate earnings be measured by after-tax profits as a percentage of stockholder's equity for all manufacturing corporations. Between 1948 and 1988, a substantial positive correlation exists — especially in the 1980s — between changes in one year's stock prices and changes in *next* year's corporate earnings.

So today's stock prices embody risk-adjusted anticipations of tomorrow's earnings. As anticipations of profits and perceptions of risk change, they can produce wide variations in stock prices. Those variations occur even though stock prices remain anchored to the expected economy of tomorrow.

On Doing One's Duty in the Business World

✍✍✍✍

Is a person to be deemed heroic and deserve extraordinary reward for doing his conventional duty?

The Pacific Coast Baseball League once paid bonuses to players who "hustled" — running, rather than walking, onto and off of the field, that sort of thing. These days, grade-school kids are paid money rewards for reading. But players are *supposed* to hustle, and students are *supposed* to read.

And business managers are supposed to administer shrewdly with a sharp pencil.

A highly able, successful businessman rejoices in the current "massive restructuring" of American enterprises. "Restructuring," he explains, "is a polite word for firing a lot of people ...." Something of a who's who of corporations has been laying off, not only thousands of troops, but also many officers, some of high rank.

We are told that such restructuring "could have a salutary effect on the economy." It means, indeed, that "the competitive spirit that is a hallmark of the American businessman is coming out, as our industry responds to the need to be globally competitive." "American business," we are assured, "is doing the tough things it needs to do and will become leaner, meaner and be more competitive," which "bodes well for the future of our economy."

But this would seem to be less than the complete picture. In their theorizing, economists generally assume that the business firm is producing at any time in the most efficient way, at lowest possible costs for a given rate of output. Evidently, this assumption has been too generous. The current massive and abrupt restructuring is intended to be a *correction* of past foolishness of managers. And some of those erring managers are now lauded as our likely saviors.

Particularly in the seven consecutive years of expansion in the 1980s, these supposedly hard-nosed and certainly well-paid managers grew sloppy and dull; they naively adopted silly administrative rules of thumb taught by business schools; they were analytically inept, intellectually soft, and showed lack of initiative; they hid behind government protection; they became preoccupied with interests other than productive efficiency — size of firm, diversification of product, cutesy advertising, glorification of the chairman of the board, community stature.

Doing less badly after restructuring will not necessarily mean doing well. Cutting excess personnel, rationalizing the table of organization, and dumping weak subsidiaries are fine — although it should not require a prolonged recession to inspire the boys in the board room to bestir themselves to do their duty. But will we then design products technologically better and in closer response to demand? Will we invest enough and well enough in research-and-development? Will we market shrewdly and energetically?

Any thick-skinned corporate officer can fire people (belatedly). But if the skull is as thick as the skin, we will dissipate our productive heritage and continue our retreat to defeat.

Motivation With a Bass Drum

♨♨♨♨

I am something of a lone wolf. That does not mean that most of my time is spent as a solitary predator stalking coeds. Rather, I do best in observing, reading, thinking, and writing when not in a crowd, whether or not the crowd is organized by cheerleaders.

Creativity, I have supposed, springs from individuality. The *individual* is the ultimate unit of analysis in the social sciences, for he is the ultimate unit of thought, motivation, and decisionmaking. Presumably, in a free and efficient society, we wish to exploit and clarify *personal* incentive and accountability.

None of this denies the significance of teams and societal coordination. But coordination is to be founded on mutual benefit. Each individual fulfills personal ends by using personal resources according to personal criteria, all in a context of procedures and ground rules which channel such strivings so as to make people useful to each other.

Obviously, there must be coordination within teams as well as within the community at large. Without coordination of the efforts of members of a team, there *is* no organization. Corporations are teams. Still, like other teams, they are composed of individuals doing their individual things. Workers work, managers manage, analysts analyze, decisionmakers decide, salesmen sell, accountants account. All these people require some intelligence, training, and tools — and their rewards are to be commensurate with their productivity, which strongly tends to inspire high productivity.

But reports in *The Wall Street Journal* and *Fortune* magazine indicate that many glamorous corporations find rationality and reward insufficient. Each now strives to build a common, coagulating corporate culture. Family fealty and paternal partnership are required, it is said, to convert apathy into allegiance and productivity. And so innate pride of workmanship and pay for production are to be supplemented with pop psychology from "motivational speakers" at fees of up to $20,000 per pop.

Well, if corporate managers and salesmen have the cultural attainment and intellectual professionalism of high school football players, then pep talks of halftime nature could be appropriate. We may hope that such "anecdotes, aphorisms, homilies, and platitudes" can help — until we realize that, if such junk food for the psyche actually is helpful, we have a very large problem of corporate sophistication.

Still, since there is a swelling market for "merchants of inspiration," perhaps I should offer my oratorical services. My high school had a great motivational cheer for football games, and we in the band boasted that — with the aid of the bass drum — we could make more noise than all the rest of the student body. For $20,000, I am willing to yell at business people. Of course, if I am to bring a band, complete with bass drum, the fee will be greater.

Economic Regulation and Intervention

Regulation and Production

Prices and costs come with the territory. The stingy nature of the world stipulates that we have to pay and bear them in producing our meager supplies. Producing well is neither easy nor simple. At our best, we shall never live as well as we would like. It makes no sense to make our poor lot even poorer by handicapping ourselves with dumb economic policy.

But dumb economic policy is what we are given by government — and the practitioners of politics do their dumb things in trying to please and placate the voting public. As a community — including both political masters and proletarian masses — we persist in fretting more about the frosting on the cake and the slicing of the cake than about the size of the cake. And when we perceive the cake to be smaller than it could be, we respond, not by cooking more and better, but by harassing and hamstringing the cooks with more regulation. The confused but cocky legislators and bureaucrats commonly cannot distinguish between a kitchen and a commode, but they incoherently mandate the only acceptable recipes, ingredients, procedures, and personnel, with cavalier disregard of cost.

We are now in a massive resurgence of regulation, imposed by people more animated by aggrandizement than guided by analysis. The Environmental Protection Agency itself refers to "massive" new regulatory programs of great "complexity" that present "a huge administrative challenge," if not "administrative nightmare," that is likely to "overwhelm" regulatory officials. If officials can be overwhelmed, businesses can be devastated.

Paul Craig Roberts, an economist conspicuous in both academic and government circles, notes that "government hostility toward business is stronger than at any other time in the postwar period." That hostility is commonly camouflaged: it can be kept out of the budget and off the 6:00 news by simply telling businesses how to do their business.

Firms are prohibited from doing some things in some ways and are required to do other things in only certain ways. Of course, they must file a mountain of papers to get permission to do what they are permitted to do, and they must submit an unending river of reports on what they have been doing. They must be prepared, financially and psychologically, to change their plans, investments, processes, and personnel instantaneously on Big Brother's flighty whims. And they must expect crushing court sanctions if they err in comprehension of or compliance with incomprehensible commands.

All this is decidedly non-trivial. It is enormously expensive to the entire community. Bureaucracy is bloated. Business costs are driven up, disproportionately for smaller firms. Prices are made higher for us all. Innovation and investment are made lower. We produce less well, and we produce less. We do not work as much, and we do not live as well.

There is more to life than economics, and there is more to economics than production. Still, production is critical. A community can use its output badly, but there can be little done well without much output. There will be little of comfort, of hope, of security, of equity, of gentility in a society which does not produce well. Dumb economic regulation gets seriously in the way of producing well.

Mouse Wisdom: The Sense of Auntie Trust

ØØØØ

Mouse Karl wiggled his tail with joy. "It's wonderful to have Auntie visit us," he squeaked to his mouse friend Adam.

"Yes, indeed," affirmed Adam. "Tell us, Auntie Trust, about your work as the government's top guardian against monopoly."

"You must have your whiskers full," suggested Karl, "trying to wiggle a little competition into the marketplace."

"Not exactly," Auntie Trust answered. "I have more difficulty opposing sellers who want to use my authority to *restrict* competition."

"I don't understand," puzzled Karl. "Don't you prevent businesses from monopolizing the marketplace? I thought the Sherman Act, the Clayton Act, and other important laws empowered your office to stop monopolists from picking the pockets of mouse consumers."

"That's what most mice suppose," replied Auntie Trust. "But often it's the other way around. Many mice oppose a particular merger of firms because they believe its success will encourage more mergers in the industry. The result would then be fewer competitors in the market."

"Correct!" chortled Karl crudely. "That would mean less competition. Don't you outlaw monopolistic mergers?"

"Hold on," said Auntie Trust calmly. "Neither the number nor the size of businesses in a given market is a good indicator of the degree of 'monopoly power.' A smaller number of larger firms can be more efficient, and that means lower prices for consumers. If a merger would create a more efficient enterprise, other firms in the industry would have to become more competitive to survive. Rather than confronting increased competition with greater efficiency of their own, the firms often try to use my authority to block the merger in the first place — and they do so in the name of protecting competition."

"But what about 'predator' pricing?" asked Karl. "History seems full of examples, such as John D. Rockefeller's Standard Oil Company, when big, wealthy businesses cut prices below costs and drove out competitors. Don't you have to use government power to prevent monopolistic price wars?"

"Predatory pricing is more myth than reality," responded Auntie Trust. "Rockefeller did *not* use costly price wars to drive rivals out of business. No matter how big or wealthy, no business would long find it worthwhile to sell appreciably below its cost in an uncertain attempt to put a competitor out of business. One company may *purchase* another, as Standard Oil bought other oil companies, but that strategy takes us back to evaluating the effects of mergers."

"Then why do many who complain about predatory pricing ask you to restrain price cutting in the name of competition?" asked Karl.

"Mostly because they want to prevent a more efficient company from underselling them," replied Auntie Trust. "It may seem as though these complainants are trying to *preserve* competition, but actually they are trying to *restrict* it. What they want is *not competition*, but *protection* from *competitors*. In the world of your dear old Auntie Trust, what seemingly is, often actually isn't."

Gainers, Losers, and Lousy Policy

Now, we have the Americans With Disabilities Act. It is wide-ranging legislation, intended to protect the physically and mentally impaired from discrimination and inconvenience in "major life activities."

While such intent is highly attractive, convoluted and arbitrary implementation will be daunting, and costs will be varied in kind and massive. But Senator Snort has made it explicit that cost is irrelevant in matters of civil rights. And when costs are deemed irrelevant, why fret about the equity of their distribution or their minimization in a given strategy or the possibility of more cost-efficient strategies?

So, is the Disabilities Act a good thing? Some will gain from it, while others will lose. But assessments will differ on *how much* will be gained or lost in what *forms* by *whom*.

Even if all agreed on all probable repercussions — long-term as well as short, and indirect as well as direct — there is a major *analytical* problem in comparing the value of the gains of some with that of the losses of others. If we cannot weigh gains against losses, we can hardly say with assurance that there is net benefit to the community.

And there is a major *procedural* problem in having policies made by people who can take credit for gains and largely avoid costs. Senator Snort not only is not spending his personal money to implement policies, no expenditure shows up in the government budget when he simply mandates business firms to pay the tab.

At least, there *are* some *winners* with the Disabilities Act. But consider another instance of trying to do good.

My office building is obliged by federal, state, and local laws to make certain facilities, if available at all, accessible to everyone. The building has always had a drinking fountain on each floor. But now the government people have decreed minimal spatial dimensions of accessibility, permitting convenient use of wheel chairs. The structure of the building does not permit opening more space around the fountains in their present locations. And architects have failed to find space in other locations — perhaps in corridors or near elevators — which will satisfy requirements of the fire marshal.

It is, in short, physically impossible to meet the mandated space requirements for fountains. What to do? Well, the political decisionmakers have said that facilities not available to all will not be provided to any. So the building is now removing all the fountains!

Economists suggest that a policy contributes to social welfare if everyone gains, or if some gain and no one loses. Social welfare may be said to increase even with some losers, if those who gain fully compensate the losers and still are better off than before. But clearly it is a lousy policy which hurts everyone, or hurts some while not helping anyone. Removing the fountains does not make the disabled better off, and it hurts everyone else.

Compassion with no sense, doing good badly, results in lousy policy.

Wetlands Policy: Sense and Subversion

⍦⍦⍦⍦

John Pozsgai is a poor, self-employed truck mechanic in Pennsylvania. He bought a bit of virtually barren land which had long been illegally used as a dump. The land bordered a small stream which was partially dammed by debris, creating several standing pools. Mr. Pozsgai cleaned away the junk and filled and leveled the land to build a garage.

All this seeming improvement of the land, it turned out, was a succession of criminal acts. Agents of Big Brother managed to convict Mr. Pozsgai of 41 violations of the Clean Water Act of 1972. He was sentenced to three years in federal prison (where he now resides), five years probation, a fine of over $200,000, and a court order to restore the land to its condition before others made it a junkyard.

This vicious governmental idiocy — this irrationality and absurdity — is part of the recent history of national "wetlands" policy.

A section of the Clean Water Act of 1972 was intended to safeguard waterways, water supplies, and fishing and recreational areas from contamination, with no reference to so-called wetlands. A 1975 court decision extended the province of the law to include wetlands which drain into rivers. Still later decisions included isolated lands which are sometimes wet but with no connection to waterways. Recent emphasis has been on any touching of wetlands — any land filling or even repairs of dikes — even though no pollutant is involved. Meanwhile, the very concept and definition of "wetland" has been ever-changing, capricious, and quixotic.

Richard Miniter, of the Competitive Enterprise Institute, and Rick Henderson, of the Reason Foundation, acknowledge that genuine and substantial wetlands — "marshes, bogs, swamps, mud flats, prairie potholes, and other forms of land flooded or saturated by water" — can be "of the greatest ecological importance." But historical wetland losses have been far from catastrophic; some of the losses have been beneficial in helping with mosquito control, providing significant building sites, and expanding food production; further, perhaps half of current annual losses consist of erosion caused by federal government projects of flood control, navigation, agricultural subsidization, and highway construction, while much of the most effective wetland protection is by private persons, conservation foundations, and corporations.

One can envision a policy which would properly preserve wetlands of value. We have not been provided such policy by the ineptitude, confusion, cowardice, and aggrandizement of the Congress, the courts, the White House, and the ambitious and officious bureaucrats of the Environmental Protection Agency and the Army Corps of Engineers.

And John Pozsgai — who has had taken from him property, money, and liberty — must regret his emigrating from Hungary to this Land of the Free.

Safety Policies and Indirect Costs

☙☙☙☙

Sometimes things are not what they seem. And sometimes the illusion is more satisfying than the reality. That is why cosmetics and foundation garments sell so well. But in the world of economics, being led astray can be costly. And we often mislead ourselves. We can easily mislead ourselves by stopping the thought process too quickly, noting only immediate characteristics of problems and effects of policies, overlooking indirect implications and consequences.

Safety is good. Granted, some extraordinarily silly things have been said in support of *zero* tolerance of risk in a world of substantial inherent risk. But it can be prudent to promote reduction of risk at reasonable cost.

So there is effort to impose a requirement that every airline passenger — including very young passengers — have his own seat. Currently, children up to two years can be held by an adult. But in heavy turbulence or a crash, surely the child would be safer buckled into his own seat rather than held. True, purchasing the separate seat, even at reduced fare, would increase costs of family travel. Indeed, with increased total demand for seats, prices of all seats might be higher — and airlines could be very brave about a substantial increase in revenue. But who would contend that the safety of children does not warrant greater expenses of travel?

Now, is that the appropriate end of the analysis? We like safety; infant safety seats can be protective; so we should make such seats mandatory. Economists Richard B. McKenzie and Dwight R. Lee suggest that we go further.

First, note the very modest gain in safety which would be achieved. Research in the Department of Transportation indicates that mandatory safety seats could have prevented just *one* infant death in the 12 years 1978-90. There were additional child fatalities in that period, to be sure, but they occurred in sections of planes where *no one* survived.

Second, demanders respond to changes in prices. If the expenses of airline travel rise, there will be less airline travel. Some of these who are then priced out of flying will stay home. But many will travel by automobile, instead. And automobile travel is much more dangerous than airline travel.

What orders of magnitude are involved? Using very conservative estimates of key variables, professors McKenzie and Lee calculate that the increase in expenses in airline travel could result in a shift to automobile travel which would yield five additional deaths per year — along with injuries and destruction of property. Five deaths a year for twelve years is *60* car fatalities, offset by only *one* life saved in an airliner crash.

The analysts reasonably conclude that government "should not be in the business of creating a travel safety problem (on the highways) that is bigger than the one they are trying to alleviate (in the skies)."

Mouse Wisdom: Markets and Mileage

ØØØØ

"Again we are victims of Middle-Eastern politics!" fumed Mouse Karl to his friend, Mouse Adam. "We should have taken precautions long ago."

"Calm down," reassured Adam. "A sudden drop in the world supply of oil would not be good news, but we can make the best of a bad situation."

"We're not doing that," responded Karl. "When oil prices declined during the 1980s, we squandered the chance to take measures which would have protected us now."

"What measures?" asked Adam.

"We should have tightened the government's mileage standard, which is now frozen at an average of 27.5 miles per gallon," replied Karl.

"Government fuel standards are doubtfully desirable," said Adam.

"Nonsense!" snapped Karl. "Government standards cut the use of oil by increasing the average mileage of new cars. Foreign oil producers then receive fewer dollars from us, and drivers here create less air pollution. The Transportation Department reportedly estimates that if government now raised the standard by 40 percent, we would save nearly 50 billion gallons of gas in just the first year. How can you be against saving gas, cleaning the environment, and protecting us against future oil shocks abroad?" wondered Karl.

"But a higher mileage standard would *not* accomplish these objectives," answered Adam. "First, that enormous saving of gas could be accomplished only after virtually all present lower-mileage cars have been replaced, perhaps in a dozen years. Second, consider the cost of producing cars that get 40 percent more miles per gallon. New cars already get much higher mileage than did those 20 years ago; these improvements were relatively easy, but further increases in mileage would be very expensive. As a result, new car prices would jump and thereby encourage mice to keep their older cars. And older cars use more gas and pollute more."

"Third," continued Adam, "the stricter standard would allow motorists to use less gas to drive an additional mile. They would then drive more miles, car-pool less, and use less mass transit. The result would be more highway congestion — which means more gas used, more air polluted, and more time wasted in traffic."

"Fourth," added Adam, "the higher mileage standard would result in production of lighter and smaller cars. More mice would then be injured or killed."

"I didn't realize," realized Karl realistically, "that a higher government standard could increase highway injuries and fatalities, make roads more congested, increase the proportion of older cars that guzzle gas and foul the air, and raise the price of new cars."

"If we want to make the best of an uncertain and ever-changing world," said Adam, "we ought to get the most mileage possible out of *markets*. For each good, markets continually inform us of its scarcity, cost of production and use, and value to the community. When any of these variables changes, markets quickly communicate that information so we can respond effectively."

"Maybe I should stop looking to government every time an ill wind blows and rely more on the efficient market," concluded Karl.

Living Standards, Income Distribution, and Productivity

Measuring Income Inequality

$\mathscr{SSSS}$

Even Karl Marx acknowledged that capitalism had been enormously productive. In a system of capitalism, personal income is determined basically by productivity: those prosper most who produce much of the what the community values most highly.

Since productivity varies much over the population, income shares vary much. Indeed, income varies widely in all societies — probably as greatly in the supposedly egalitarian Soviet Union as in the supposedly capitalistic United States.

Still, some of us are irked by and worry about the extreme ends of income distribution. If the rest of you shared my preferences, then gladiators and clowns — including baseball players, TV network anchor types, and other comedians — would not command annual salaries of $3 million. And none of God's children would have to survive with only $3,000.

Whatever the "appropriate" or "legitimate" amount of income inequality, just how unequal *is* the distribution? The average income in the best paid one-fifth of working families ($76,600) is six times larger than the average in the lowest fifth ($12,800). Whether or not a ratio of 6 to 1 be deemed scandalous, that measure greatly distorts reality as detailed by Robert Rector and Kate Walsh O'Beirne, of the Heritage Foundation.

First, there are *taxes*. Even a flat-rate income tax substantially reduces the dollar amount of after-tax differential: a 30 percent tax paid by everyone cuts the pretax income difference by 30 percent.

Second, gross data of family incomes ignore differences in *sizes* of families and in number of *workers* per family. Contrary to mythology, the average household in the top one-fifth of incomes is larger than that in the lowest bracket, so per capita incomes are closer than family incomes. Better-paid families also have more wage-earners than have poorer families — and the market *productivity* of those workers is greater.

Finally, the Census Bureau traditionally counts only *cash* income — before taxes, at that — and it undercounts cash and especially noncash *government assistance.* Oddly, it manages also to count some government assistance to relatively well-to-do families more fully than the same kind of aid to poorer families. Altogether, government spending on low-income families is undercounted by 50 percent.

After appropriate adjustments in the data, income of the top one-fifth of households is not six times that of the poorest families; instead, the ratio is about 2.8 to 1. Indeed, comparing families with at least one full-time worker, we find the after-tax per capita ratio is less than 2 to 1.

"... the remarkable thing about U.S. society," observe analysts Rector and O'Beirne, "is not the alleged gap between the rich and the poor but the astonishing overall level of equality."

The Plight of the Paycheck

ﻪﻪﻪﻪ

Are wages falling? The answer depends on how they are measured.

If the rate of pay fails to include noncash benefits like medical insurance, then one measure of the average real wage has fallen for more than two decades. But fringe benefits are part of wages. And for years Americans have been substituting more benefits for cash. Total hourly compensation, including benefits and adjusted for inflation, was a record high in 1988. Even after falling in the next two years, it was greater in 1990 than in 1980.

Still, this broader measure began growing more slowly after the late 1960s. Why? Might paychecks be leaner in the future?

The answer begins with productivity of labor. Higher real pay comes from baking a bigger economic pie, not from somehow grabbing a bigger slice of an existing one, perhaps by stealing from profits.

Indeed, labor compensation already represents about 75 percent of the nation's total income. In contrast, corporations' before-tax profits are only some six percent. So workers must produce more per hour if their average hourly wage is to rise.

Profit as a Rate of Return and Average Yearly Changes in Labor Productivity and Labor Compensation, 1950–90

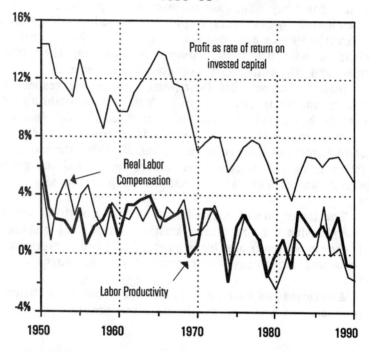

Sources: *Survey of Current Business*, U.S. Department of Commerce, April 1991; *Economic Report of the President, 1991; Economic Indicators*, June 1991.

Rising labor productivity generally has lifted real wages through our history. Yet, about twenty-five years ago, productivity growth began to slip. Predictably, decline in growth in real wages soon followed.

Why, then, did productivity grow more slowly? We have no simple answer. But we know that labor productivity rises because people have more tools and better technology to use. And we know that new tools and technology come from businesses making risky investments.

Investments are risky because businesses will lose wealth if consumers don't buy what the new investments produce. The risks are not taken mainly by customers, employees, or creditors. They are borne most directly by business owners — the proprietors, partners, and stockholders who bet their personal wealth that they can well anticipate and efficiently satisfy consumers' preferences.

Business owners bet their wealth on new investments only when they anticipate personal gain. Yet, the profitability of new investments has fallen, reports the Survey of Current Business. In 1965, before-tax profits for nonfinancial corporations represented almost 14 percent of their invested capital. By 1990, the rate of return had fallen to only 5 percent. The rate of return and the growth of productivity and of real wages all show a sharp decline since the mid-1960s.

The lower rate of return has depressed growth of real wages. For when business owners earn smaller rewards for risking their wealth, they make fewer new investments. And when workers use fewer new tools and technology, their productivity and wages rise more slowly.

Americans can have fatter paychecks — but not by listening to false prophets who would further diminish real profits.

Mouse Wisdom: Why Women Work

ﻼﻼﻼﻼ

Mouse Adam and Mouse Karl were debating why so many married women had joined the labor force in recent years.

"I don't dispute," fumed Karl in quite a disputatious manner, "that from 1967-83, the median annual income of families with husbands as sole earner averaged 96 percent of the median income of all families. But this fact doesn't support your conclusion that most married women have not been 'forced' to work."

"But it does," answered Adam. "It indicates that families with single-earner husbands have *not* been relatively destitute. So the married women joining the labor force during this period have not typically done so in order to maintain income parity with other families."

"It is just the opposite," rebuked an angered Karl. "The data show that all families receive nearly the same average income as those in which only husbands are earners. Consequently, many families are able to reach the median income only because of married women's earnings. So these women have been forced into the labor market."

"Some families surely do depend on women's earnings merely to reach average income," affirmed Adam. "And when an absence of their earnings means great hardship, they are compelled — as they always have been — to seek employment. But we are debating the reasons why so many *additional* women have joined the labor force in the last few decades. Why this modern surge of women seeking jobs? Families with sole-earner husbands have *not* generally experienced relatively low or declining earnings. So the threat of destitution has *not* clearly been a significant force propelling most married women into the labor market."

"In addition, and even more persuasively," continued Adam, "there is no systematic relationship between unemployment rates of married men and changes in the labor force participation rate of married women. If married women commonly were being forced into the labor force, they would do so in proportionately greater numbers when unemployment rates of married men were higher."

"But you forget," cautioned Karl, "that when jobs are tough to find for men, they are also hard to find for women. You should not expect the employment of married women to increase when it decreases for married men."

"I did not cite the *employment* rate of married women," corrected Adam. "I cited their *labor force participation* rate. The participation rate reflects the number of married women in the labor force. And the labor force consists of both employed and unemployed workers. The proportion of married women employed *and* unemployed does *not* rise and fall with unemployment rates of married men. This fact further suggests that married women have not been entering the labor force mostly because of severe economic hardship."

"When a rising proportion of married women has sought employment typically for some reason other than grim economic necessity," agreed a calmer Karl, "they must have done so by felicitous choice."

Sweatshops: Outrage and Analysis

ॐॐॐॐ

A major newspaper has run a series of stories and commentaries on southern California sweatshops. We are told much of morality and legality; but we are provided no analysis of economic efficiency or policy efficacy or appropriateness in personal adaptation to cruel circumstances.

In the garment industry, retailers — dress shops and department stores — buy merchandise from manufacturers; the manufacturers may contract with others to supply them; the contractors may sub-contract with sewing shops, which do the actual producing. The retailers, the manufacturers, and even the contractors may do well; the hard-pressed, viciously competitive sewing — or sweat — shops and their women workers do *not* flourish.

Journalists and political sorts deem sweatshops to be evil, and evil is to be directly eradicated. We are to pass strict laws, strictly enforced, to abolish low pay, long hours, unpleasant working conditions (including work at home), and use of children.

But is that really the end of the story, the end of analysis of the problem, the end of policy prescription? We simply outlaw the scourge of sweatshops and walk away in prim satisfaction?

What is to happen to the erstwhile workers — commonly uneducated, poorly trained, illegally in a land foreign to them, with little experience and marketplace sophistication — who have had their livelihoods abolished? They had been surviving — even if meanly by civilized standards — in market competition by selling their limited services of low value at meager wages. Taking away those miserable jobs, pricing them out of what had been their best option, does not magically provide them with better alternative employment. Reducing their already poor power to compete, leaving them more handicapped than before, is a strange way to help them.

The sweatshop situation does have tragic elements. But to alleviate the tragedy, we must get straight the base of the tragedy. It does little good to damn greed, for all of us — not just garment producers and sellers — are afflicted by abundant greed. The real source of the terrible circumstances of sweatshop workers is their few and unappealing alternatives. With better options, they would leave the sweatshops.

They do not voluntarily leave, for they have no better options, either here or in their native lands. Why not? Because they have little of value to sell in the labor market. And they have little to sell because they have little education and training, little geographical mobility and knowledge of employment possibilities, and their condition is made still harder by having no resident husband and too many children.

A policy which helps to generate a solution will have to deal with enhancing the productivity and market effectiveness of these workers. Abolishing their jobs can hardly help. Moral outrage has its place. But it is not an adequate substitute for systematic thought.

Marx and the Growth of Wages

✍✍✍✍

Karl Marx was not a good prophet. More than a century ago, he predicted that labor income would steadily fall in industrialized nations. Both average *pay rates* and *employment* would decline. Fewer people working and paid continually less per hour would result in the suffering that Marx believed would inevitably bring the overthrow of economies based on private property and markets.

The actual history of capitalism tells a different story: wages and working conditions have improved, not worsened, in these economies. In the United States, individual and total wages have risen substantially over the decades because both real wage rates and employment have increased. Since 1929, for example, employment has risen proportionately more than population; per capita work force compensation, adjusted for inflation, has expanded more than 2.5 times; and total wages as a fraction of national income have increased from 60 percent in 1929 to 74 percent today.

Why hasn't the gloomy prediction of Marx come true? A ready response cites the increased role of government. "Marx was ... 'wrong' in his economic vision," argues a popular Marxist apologist. "The economic laws of motion which his model of capitalism revealed may still be visible in American capitalism," he continues, "but they are faced with a set of remedies which spring from political and social attitudes quite beyond his imagination."

The political remedies often praised for stemming the Marxian tide of trauma include minimum wage legislation, unemployment compensation, and laws encouraging labor unions. If government had not made these changes, it is argued, American workers would long have known Marxian misery.

However desirable these government-instituted changes may be judged on other grounds, Professor Jack Hirshleifer, of UCLA, concludes that they have *not* increased wages of American workers. True, the minimum wage, unemployment insurance, and unions can raise pay rates of *some* workers. But it is true, also, that these higher rates of pay reduce total *employment* without increasing the real determinant of wage rates, the *productivity* of labor. With productivity unchanged and less employment, total wages would be smaller, not larger.

Wages have grown rapidly during our nation's history because the productivity of labor has increased. As technology advanced and businesses added to their stock of equipment and facilities, an hour of work became more productive. By *competing* against one another to obtain greater *quantities* of labor made more valuable by more capital, businesses bid up the *wages* they pay.

With more employment at higher wages, the standard of living of American workers has increased enormously. The rising employment and wages have been due mostly to the very economic institutions Marx condemned: private rights to property and voluntary exchange in the marketplace.

Poverty and Homelessness

The Persistent Problem of Poverty

ᗡᗡᗡᗡ

Poverty is, and likely will remain, a problem for us all.

We are properly to resolve the poverty problem by *getting rid* of poverty. The curse of the poor is low income, so their incomes must be raised. But this resolution can be satisfying and efficient only through raising incomes of the poor by increasing *output* of the poor. We will reduce total wealth of the community if we simply *redistribute* earned income from the more productive to the less productive. The nature of the game is not redistribution: both efficiency and equity require that producers receive their own product.

If we are to prosper, we shall have to maintain a basic linkage between a person's *performance* and that person's *pay*. One is to get what he earns, and earn what he gets. But *how* are we to increase the productivity and the industriousness of the poor so that they, too, will rise above poverty?

Tens of billions of dollars have been spent and decades of experience accumulated in devising and administering many sorts of welfare programs. Policies to help the poor face not only daunting detailed difficulties of formulation and application, they are plagued by seemingly inherent inconsistencies and tradeoffs. The dilemmas exist both at the conceptual level and the operational level.

Conceptually, in dealing with broad theory and philosophy, we run into the messy issue of how to induce people to give up a situation which we reward them for retaining. More bluntly, how can we encourage people to start earning income which they now receive for not working? For people moving from welfare into low-paying jobs, there is a huge tax in giving up the aid: there is little net income gain in taking the job. And how can we encourage them to have children only in wedlock and keep families intact when that would reduce their welfare assistance? In establishing requirements for dependent children and broken homes to qualify for aid, we encourage the conditions we deplore.

We cannot hope to induce responsible behavior by subsidizing irresponsibility. We do not induce eager productiveness by subsidizing slothful idleness. We do not induce independence by requiring dependency.

Operationally, we can try to break out of such dilemmas by significantly increasing the productivity of the poor, putting them in a position to earn enough to make work worthwhile. And this would be a genuine solution of the poverty problem, not just a stop-gap: instead of giving a fish to a starving person, teach the individual how to do his own fishing.

But it is difficult, expensive, time-consuming — and frustrating — to try to teach people tricks and techniques of high-level fishing, and to inspire them to bear the burdens, traumas, and risks of trying — belatedly — to learn and then to compete and earn. Realistically, many of them will not learn enough fast enough to leave poverty behind.

Poverty and Growth

ﻭﻭﻭﻭ

Can economic growth reduce poverty? At one time, there was little doubt that it could.

As our economy grew during the '50s and '60s, the percentage of families below the poverty line tumbled by more than half. But after 1969, the poverty rate stopped falling. The Census Bureau measure of those below the poverty line has hovered near 10 percent since the 1960s.

Does the rate's failure to fall further mean that poverty has become immune to economic growth? Surely not. Something else has been pulling hard to keep poverty up. This other factor is the rising proportion of families with children under 18 that are headed by women without a spouse. Between 1969 and 1989, this proportion doubled. Female-headed families with children have poverty rates that average at least five times those of married couples with children. So the rising percentage of families headed by women has pulled progressively harder to keep up poverty rates for all families.

Meanwhile, economic growth has tried to push poverty rates down. True, some remain mired in poverty even during periods of relatively strong growth. In particular, the culture of the underclass keeps an element isolated from economic opportunity — and from personal responsibility.

But the faces of the poor are not all the same year after year. Instead, poverty is often a temporary affliction, brought on by career change, divorce, retirement, or other major event. If the economy becomes more prosperous, more people escape from poverty, fewer slip

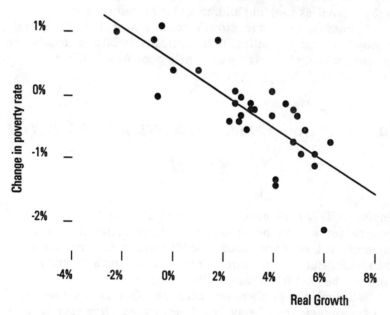

Growth of Real Gross Domestic Product and Change in Family Poverty Rate, 1959-90

Note: The correlation between real growth and changes in the poverty rate was −.790 for the period. But the relationship was stronger (−.879) from 1975-90 and weaker (−.771) from 1959-74.

Sources: *Poverty In The United States: 1990,* Bureau of the Census, U.S. Department of Commerce; *Economic Report of the President, 1992.*

into it, and many who are poor remain so for shorter periods. No wonder changes in poverty relate to economic growth.

Consider changes in poverty rates of all families (with and without children) and yearly growth of real (inflation-adjusted) gross domestic product. From 1959 to 1990, higher or lower growth accounts for most of the variation in these poverty rates. Higher economic growth usually meant bigger reductions in poverty rates, while lower growth brought smaller reductions (or even increases) in poverty rates. Indeed, the relationship between economic growth and changes in poverty was even stronger between 1975 and 1990 than when poverty rates fell between 1959 and 1974.

Do we find a similar relationship for families of different races? Census data for such categories go back only as far as 1968. Still, we find economic growth explaining much of the variation of poverty rates for white, black, and Hispanic origin families — even when these families contain children under 18 and headed by women.

Promoting economic growth doesn't have the sex appeal of other programs that put dollars into politically-influential hands. But a prosperous economy is a basic way to help poor Americans.

Nature of the Game: Production and Charity

✍✍✍✍

We individually get along either by producing or by mooching. We either earn our way by being useful to others or we rely on charity. When motivated by compassion and directed sense, charity can be commendable. But it is a costly error — costly both to giver and to receiver — when aid is confused with production.

We live in a *performance* economy. One is rewarded on the basis of *productivity*, being paid for productive services, for contributions to the social product. If one supplies substantial quantities of services which the community values relatively highly, the rewards are relatively great.

The performance, or productivity, economy is quite impersonal. For the great majority of people, *all* economies are quite impersonal. But the impersonality of the free-market economy is very different from that of the political-command economy. *All* economies are economies of scarcity; therefore, *all* economies are economies of competition. But there is a persuasive case for conducting the competition in the expansive market arena of work and trade rather than in the inhibiting governmental arena of centralized control and decree.

Better to earn personal favor through contributing to the well-being of the community than to gain group advantages from a favor-granting bureaucracy. Better to gain personally by economically helping to create more aggregate wealth than to rely on skewing the distribution of a smaller total of wealth by politically subsidizing low productivity. Better to prosper by effectiveness in market-coordinated wealth production than by effectiveness in government-imposed wealth redistribution.

Indeed, can large numbers of people persistently prosper through any strategy other than being economically productive? Some for some while can gain by pleading that all their difficulties stem from unfair discrimination. They have long been taught that ignoble and debilitating tactic. They have been led astray and crippled by both the knowing cynical and the confused compassionate.

Most of the political tactics promoted for redress of biased treatment not only stultify future, long-term competitiveness, but do more harm than good even immediately. In a performance economy, powers of competition and independence are *not* fostered by such paternalistic foolishness as minimum wage laws, rent controls, interest rate ceilings, and quotas in hiring and in college admissions.

To the extent that one wishes to prosper — not simply survive — economic performance is the nature of the competitive game in a stingy world. Neither expanding government gifts to the downtrodden nor opening market opportunities will help much if the beneficiaries do not respond with effort and, instead, remain detached from the world of work.

It is a monstrous misfortune for us all to cripple some of our neighbors and seductively divert them from the kinds of investments and strategies which would enable them to play the game to the utmost. Of course, we insist that we cripple them in the name of compassion — but that simply makes the crippling poignant and perverse rather than deliberately dastardly.

Doing Good Badly Through Welfare

ᴅᴅᴅᴅ

Wealth is not manna from heaven. For both the community and its individual members, much wealth requires high productivity.

Some produce little. We have not done a good job of making them, or permitting them to become, highly productive. Even the better welfare programs of basic education, job training, and job-search assistance have not accomplished much. A *New York Times* columnist has observed that, " at best, ... [such] programs gear up people to find ... unskilled jobs — minimum-wage jobs that do not come close to raising out of poverty a mother with a child or two."

We will not readily endow those who are desperately poor because desperately inept with the skills and orientation required for production of middle-class incomes. That will require much time and resources. But we can quickly begin to do better than we have done. A basic aspect of that effort is to revamp the ground rules and procedures of welfare so as to develop individual responsibility, incentive, and initiative of aid recipients. By such cultivation of personal accountability, we can relieve the poor of much of the present stultifying constraint and domination of the intrusive and expensive welfare establishment.

One promising tactic — associated mainly with Milton Friedman — is the "negative income tax." In determining taxable income, individuals and families are entitled to exemptions and deductions from gross income. For the very poor, exemptions and deductions are *more* than gross income, so taxable income is negative. But while taxes are *paid to* government by those with positive taxable income, those with negative taxable income do not correspondingly *receive* payment *from* government. Dr. Friedman would replace the current convoluted welter of various welfare programs by money assistance calculated on the basis of negative taxable income.

Obviously, giving solely *money* aid *directly* to the poor, determined by the *sizes* of their family and their income, would not in itself magically increase productivity of the poor. But it would greatly deflate the bulbous welfare bureaucracy, increase the responsibility to be borne by the poor in handling their affairs, and still leave much incentive to the poor to earn more income.

But increasing the independence and accountability of the poor would run counter to the interests of the huge, long-entrenched welfare machinery. One veteran welfare administrator acknowledges that "we have created such a rat maze that no one but a pro can get through it." And the rules perversely punish self-discipline, resourcefulness, and family preservation. "We who provide social services," she adds, "know that we need a continuing flow of people who need us," so we "continue to suppress America's underclass, to foster their dependency, to render them powerless over their own lives ...."

There is much craziness in our purported efforts to do good.

Government Housing Construction versus Housing Vouchers

ææææ

Contrary to cultivated misconception, the public housing program did not collapse during the 1980s. Measured by federal housing assistance outlays, number of families served, and quantity of housing units constructed, the '80s were a boom period for public housing.

True, authorizations for future construction fell dramatically, and the rate of construction in the second half of the decade declined greatly. But a public housing *program* need not consist of public housing *construction*.

"Urban renewal" housing acts of the 1930s and '40s created at least as many social problems as they alleviated. They concentrated low-income, largely minority people in "high-rise slums" and "instant ghettos."

In 1968, the federal government began an elaborate public-private partnership in housing construction. Within five years, reports William Tucker, these ill-designed and maladministered efforts were evident fiascoes. They had attracted as investors some thoroughly disreputable con artists, who bilked unsophisticated customers, dealt primarily with people who were not poor, and paid-off government officials who approved the shoddy deals. Housing construction and renovation through government subsidization obviously had not worked well.

The Housing and Community Development Act of 1974 did little to improve the program. While introducing a limited housing certificate to help tenants pay rent, it largely continued the discredited construction subsidies. Further, by the 1970's, a boom in suburban housing meant that the community's overall problem was then maintenance and utilization of existing facilities more than construction of still more units.

A presidential commission in 1982 came to a conclusion reached by scholars a decade earlier: instead of building more public housing, it would be better for government to subsidize the poor in use of facilities already existing or being provided through normal market activity.

Finally, in 1984, the strategy of federal housing subsidies through vouchers to individual beneficiaries was introduced. Aid was then targeted directly to the poor, rather than to construction investors and to middle-class residents. Further, since the recipients can use the aid to buy housing anywhere, the poor are not shunted together in cesspool slums. Such flexibility in use of the aid avoids the great problems of opposition to building large housing projects in particular neighborhoods. And the beneficiaries of the aid evidently prefer the options of its use over being placed in government projects.

If we are to help the poor with their housing, then it is shrewd to subsidize the users rather than the providers of the housing. But this good sense has been resisted by many in the Congress and by many who write editorials. Perhaps opposition from such quarters is the clinching argument in favor of housing vouchers.

Minimum Wages, Comparable Wages, Retirement Wages, and Unions

Minimum Wages, Market Wages, Employment, and Income

◢◢◢◢

"I'm so ticked off, I'd like to flee," cried Mouse Karl.

"Sorry to hear of your tick and flee problem," responded Mouse Adam. "What is the cruel cause of your current crisis?"

"Poverty!" shouted Karl. "There is too much of it, and it could be so easily eliminated! But the callous fat-cat members of the community don't care!"

"There *is* poverty," said Adam soberly, "even in this land of relative milk and honey. But I had not supposed that it could be easily and quickly corrected simply by civilized concern."

"Sometimes you seem innately inane," snarled Karl with patient gentility. "People are poor because of low income; most income is received as wages; higher wages thus mean greater income; so we can get rid of poverty by sufficiently raising the legal minimum wage."

"You do make it all seem pretty simple-minded," replied Adam wryly. "Just what is a 'sufficient' increase in wages? Would a wage of around $4.50 an hour be 'sufficient'? For a person working forty hours a week for the entire year, that would mean an annual income of just over $9,000."

"So be bolder," boldly suggested Karl. "Make the minimum hourly wage $6 or $7, which many beginning and menial workers are already getting."

"You call that bold?" chided Adam. "Make it $45 or $450 an hour!"

Karl twitched his tail nervously. "We have to be realistic," he grudgingly suggested. "Not many would be hired at wages that high."

"Precisely," confirmed Adam. "What is income to the worker is cost to the employer. It is not good for one's economic health — whether he be a consumer or a supplier — to pay more for something than it is worth. The market value of labor services is determined by what the worker does, how well and attractively he does it, and how many other workers are available to do the same thing. Unhappily, some people are not in a position to offer labor services which the community values very highly. If government then makes it illegal for those people to sell their services at low market prices, the services will not be bought. Pegging wages above market levels reduces the already limited competitive powers of people who are young, untrained, inexperienced, or otherwise disadvantaged. Pricing workers out of the labor market — denying them both income and work experience — is a pretty peculiar anti-poverty program."

Karl was crestfallen but no longer so confused. "Well," he sighed, "if there is to be employment only at market-determined wages, and if market wages reflect economic productivity, then evidently the only way to raise wages is to increase productivity. We will live better only if we produce more. And we *can* become more productive. But that will require much sense and commitment and investment — and time. No politician's quickie gimmick of market subversion will make us wealthy."

Black Teenagers and the Minimum Wage

✍✍✍✍

"An economic adviser should have only one hand," remarked Harry Truman. The president didn't want to hear inconclusive counseling, "On the one hand this, and on the other hand that."

Trouble is, few problems have simple solutions. Consider the relatively low employment ratios of Black teenagers. This ratio is the percentage of all 16-to-19-year-old Blacks who are working. In 1991, fewer than 23 percent of Black teenagers were employed. This was less than half the 47 percent ratio for White teenagers.

The lower percentages means fewer paychecks for young Blacks — and less investment in valuable skills and attitudes gained on the job. The lower labor market participation now is likely to lead to inferior and lower-paying jobs when they are adults.

How, then, to boost employment of young Blacks? There are no simple answers. But, surely, government policies ought to heed the medical profession's dictum: First, do no harm.

That guidance is ignored when it comes to the minimum wage. With fewer skills, Black teenagers have lower productivity. Since pay depends on ability to produce what the community values, their wages also are typically low.

Real Minimum Wage
and Difference Between Employment Ratios of White
and Black Teenagers 1972–1992

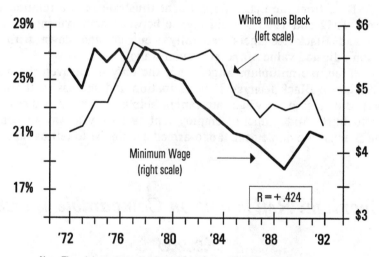

Note: The minimum wage is adjusted for inflation. The difference between employment ratios is the percentage of all white teenagers employed minus the percentage of all Black teenagers employed. Data for 1992 are for first 3 months.

Source: U.S. Department of Labor; *Statistical Abstract of the United States*, 1991.

The obvious remedy is higher productivity. But pushing aside this sensible long-term solution are minimum-wage proposals with short-term political payoff. By commanding employers to pay more than many Black teenagers can produce, these policies threaten to price the disadvantaged out of the labor market. Instead of receiving higher pay, many end up earning nothing at all.

Have higher minimum wages produced this effect in the past? We can check the changing *difference* between the greater employment ratio of White teenagers and the smaller ratio of Black teenagers. Higher White pay can be expected to be more immune to changes in the real minimum wages than are lower Black wages. If a higher minimum wage diminishes employment of Black teenagers relative to more steady White employment, then this difference in employment ratios should have *increased* when the imposed minimum went *up*. And the difference should have *dropped* when inflation *reduced* the stipulated rate's real value and increased Black employment more than White.

Data from the Labor Department illustrate such a relationship. Between 1972 and 1992, the difference between employment ratios of White and Black teenagers generally went up and down with the inflation-adjusted value of the minimum wage.

True, the minimum wage is not the only — or even the major — obstacle to Black teenagers' participation and success in the labor market. But raising the wage rate cannot help employment and strongly tends to hurt. And reducing employment is hardly a way to benefit young Blacks. We don't need a one-armed economist to tell us that.

Moonlight Reflections on Comparable Worth

◌◌◌◌

Ancient people incorrectly believed that the moon gives rise to its own light. We know today that light is not *innate* to the moon: moonlight is *reflected* light. But some commit similar error by arguing that economic value is *inherent* in a good or service.

It is asserted that a job has an *intrinsic* worth determined by the particular characteristics of the work and the worker. Two jobs believed — or decreed — to require the same degrees of skill, responsibility, and effort are alleged to be comparable in economic worth. Advocates of the comparable worth dogma decree — and maybe believe — that these jobs should pay the same wage. And if the wage of one of the jobs, held mostly by women, is lower than the wage of the other, held mostly by men, then sex discrimination is blamed for the difference.

Michael Levin, Professor of Philosophy at CCNY, has written of the charge that sex discrimination must be the cause of wage differences not ostensibly explained by selected characteristics of the job. "In the jargon of the moment," he says of the advocates of comparable worth, "they conceive discrimination as a 'residual. This means that certain variables are selected *a priori* as relevant to wages, and discrimination is then defined as what these variables cannot explain." Cavalierly dismissed is the likelihood that other factors, not identified and measured in this search for innate value, may be responsible for the unexplained wage gap.

But there is no innate value in a job or its product. The value of a good is instead conferred by individuals who offer to buy it. What a thing is "worth" in the market is simply what people are willing to pay to get it. "A thing's price," Professor Levin notes, "summarizes the ebb and flow of its performance in exchange, and has no independent meaning. And here is the intellectual black hole of comparable worth: there is no such thing as intrinsic economic value."

Two jobs may have comparable *characteristics*, but they are not necessarily of comparable *value*. Two artists with identical training may work with equal diligence for equal periods of time in the same studio, but their paintings may sell for different prices because the public does not value them equally.

By enabling individuals to record their preferences for various goods, voluntary exchange generates the relative economic values required to direct resources to the uses that people most value. Proponents of comparable worth seek to seize from the community the freedom to confer values through exchange. To disguise this coercion, they pretend that the job values they wish to force upon the community are somehow inherent in those jobs.

But economic value is not innate. As the sun gives luminosity to the moon, so, too, do individuals bestow values on goods. This is the axiom of economics eclipsed by faulty arguments in favor of comparable worth.

Producing and the Rules of Retiring

✐✐✐✐

Most of what we consume in this poor world has to be produced. So long as the bod is warm, each of us is a consumer. But not each of us is a producer, and many at any given time produce less than they consume.

One of the non-producing and little-producing segments of the community is the "elderly." How old is elderly? If we take retirement to be an indicator of elderliness, the beginning elderly are getting younger. In many circles, conventional retirement age long was 67 or 68; then 65 became customary — some 90 percent of people older than 65 are not working. Indeed, it is not uncommon to find people ceasing to be producers at 62 or being even more callow. As sociologist Kingsley Davis points out, a person who retires at 62 will continue to live for a period equal to over 40 percent of his working years.

As retirement has been coming at earlier ages, the average life span has been lengthening. On both counts — retiring earlier and living longer — the proportion of the senior population has been rising. And the elderly will be an increasing portion of the total population over the coming half century. By 2040, those over age 65 may be a fourth of the total.

So the producing part of the population has been, and will continue to be, a falling proportion: the ratio of workers to consumers is getting smaller. Within another half dozen years, there will be only three workers for every retiree.

Is there something illegitimate or naughty about more and more retirees currently consuming what is currently produced by relatively fewer and fewer workers? Certainly, there is nothing dastardly or decadent in a given individual, through assiduously producing and prudently saving, accumulating enough wealth to retire while the vital juices still freely flow. Given the rules of the game, one should not be castigated for playing it well according to one's own criteria and objectives.

But what of the rules? We can reasonably ask if government has been wise in making early retirement increasingly attractive — or, to alter the emphasis, in making continuation of production increasingly unattractive.

Under present rules, people below age 70 earning more than a very modest yearly income lose one dollar of Social Security benefits for every three dollars of additional income earned — a 33 percent marginal tax. And after including federal and state income taxes and the Social Security tax, the aggregate marginal tax on income can be around 80 percent!

The world is poor; it is poor because we cannot produce all we want; and we will be less poor, the more we produce. There is much sense in government getting out of the way of people — even if they are in their late sixties — who want to continue to produce.

Workers and Employers, Wages and Profits

ØØØØ

The labor market is, indeed, a market, where something is bought and sold at a price. How much is exchanged on what terms?

As a supplier of labor services, what do you have to offer? What talents, skills, and mannerisms do you have; what can you physically, mentally, and socially do? How unique is your product? In light of what you can do and of how many others can do it, how attractive are you to potential buyers? And what are your alternatives either in competing for a variety of jobs or in getting by without working at all?

There are considerations from the demanders' side, as well. A buyer will buy, as a seller will sell, only if he anticipates gaining from the transaction. And a buyer will pay a price no higher, as a seller will accept a price no lower, than seems to him sensible, given his objectives and alternatives.

As in other markets, activity is guided and results are generated by forces of supply and demand in a context of competition. But who is competing with whom? Well, in our cell meetings, as we sit in a basement making little round bombs, we are instructed by Marxists that labor market competition is a class phenomenon. Even non-Marxists are much inclined to speak in terms of "labor versus management."

But the real competition is not all workers against all employers. When I seek a job, I compete with those *other workers* who are trying to get that job. If you get the job I wanted, you were more attractive to the employer than I was, either because you were judged to be physically more productive or because you were willing to accept a wage low enough to offset my superior productivity.

I do *not* like fellow workers competing with me. The competition I *do* like is among employers. The wage one employer is obliged to pay for labor is affected mightily by how much other employers are offering, and it is a happy situation for me when rival employers bid against each other for my services.

So competing workers offering labor lower my wage, and competing employers bidding for labor raise my wage.

Organizing workers into unions does not change the fundamentals. A union may raise particular wages — and thereby reduce the number employed in that line of work. Those displaced workers then increase labor supply elsewhere, reducing wage rates there. Unions redistribute wages *among* workers rather than raise *all* wages.

Even in principle, wages cannot be increased perceptibly by further reduction of profits. Wages already account for some 75 percent of domestic income and after-tax profits about 5 percent. Aggregate wages can rise only if national output is increased. Output will be raised, not simply by working harder, but by saving and investing more, managing better, and innovating with greater boldness. But resources will not be used more effectively by destroying the profits which provide much of the motivating engine and the guiding rudder of the economy.

Timber, Water, Oil, and Power

Waste and Efficiency: Historians and Economic History

ᛞᛞᛞᛞ

Historians — like politicians and journalists — often feel obliged to talk about economics. Unfortunately, they seem not to feel obliged to talk economic sense.

One topic on which many historians have been analytically adrift pertains to United States timber activity. In the late 19th century, massive forests around the Great Lakes were heavily cut. "Timber barons" are pictured as frenzied exploiters, ravaging prime timberlands and then quickly moving on to devastate new areas. As told, it is a story of irresponsible, irrational waste and aesthetic insensitivity.

But not all use of resources is wasteful. Efficiency has to do with producing those things which the community values most highly and doing so with minimum cost for a given output. There was a nation to be developed and an economy to expand. There were farms to foster and buildings to build. This activity required labor, cleared land, and materials. A century ago, labor was relatively expensive and land relatively cheap. So the tactics of producers — farmers and manufacturers as well as timber-cutters — reasonably made expansive use of land and its attributes while economizing on labor.

This story is summarized by economists T.J. Iijima and Jane S. Shaw, of the Political Economy Research Center. They point out that per capita real income a century ago was just one-tenth of today's income. People were concerned with food, clothing, and construction — not with nature-study backpacking. For them, unused forests were a wasteland, resources to be used. Self-designated "conservationists" of the time were not concerned basically with how the land looked, but with possible timber famine from excessive exploitation.

But no timber famine occurred. Indeed, resources are not physically exhausted. Instead, as they become more scarce from dwindling supply and increasing demand, their prices gradually rise. As a resource becomes more expensive, the amount demanded falls, and alternative sources are found or alternative inputs are used or alternative production methods are adopted. People are not dimwitted: in the face of rising resource prices, they require no pretentious tree-huggers to tell them to conserve, and they require no officious bureaucrats to direct patterns and modes of production.

Not only did the widely-feared timber crisis not materialize, much of the cut forests have been restored, and the rest of the land has been otherwise productively used. Our priorities and predilections have changed as our wealth has accumulated.

But that does not mean that our great-grandparents were fools and slobs, and that we belatedly have corrected their primitive errors. Given their condition and options, they were efficient. And the happier condition and wider options of our wealthier society reflect largely the sense, work, boldness, and investment of our sensible forefathers.

Liquidity Crisis

◢◢◢◢

Water is a liquid asset. And it is scarce: we don't have all we want. For many, *scarcity* means *shortage*. So we are told that we must now act appropriately or gasoline shortages of yesteryear will pale in comparison with future shortages of water. Drought, population growth, industrial expansion, pollution, increasingly thirsty appliances — all supposedly are disastrously gulping our limited fresh water.

A common bureaucratic approach to scarcity is to wonder simply how to get more. In the case of water, rain dances are a possibility, but — with due respect to Native Americans — this does not strike many as highly promising. We might try to salvage more of the river water which now runs off into the sea, but those concerned with fisheries and environment fear the consequences of still heavier tampering with nature. We might invest more in desalination plants to produce fresh water from the ocean, but such water costs perhaps 10 times as much as current supplies. And importing water from places as distant as Canada would be even more expensive.

If we are not to go far in increasing water *supply*, perhaps we can cut water *consumption* and improve the efficiency of *use* of the water we have. Some want water police to implement controls and decrees, prohibiting ornamental and golf course use of water, unrequested serving of water in restaurants, use of hoses in cleaning driveways and automobiles, and dampening construction sites to keep down dust.

We need not surrender to officious officials the right to choose acceptable uses of water. Freedom of individual choice is compatible with — and, indeed, required for — socially efficient use of a scarce resource, with people paying and receiving market-clearing prices. If water becomes more scarce, its *market-clearing* price will rise; individuals would then use less water. But they would decide for themselves the extent to which water uses are not worth the higher price, and the quantity of water demanded would fall to equal the supply available.

A "shortage" of *anything* occurs *only* because people demand more than is available at the *existing price*. With market-clearing prices, water can be put to its best uses and rationed in accordance with community valuations. This will entail correcting the current massive subsidization of agriculture, which consumes over 90 percent of California's fresh water while producing less than five percent of the state's income. Urban residents pay some 200 times as high a price for water as do irrigation districts. We cannot afford to continue to make it economically feasible to grow monsoon crops in a virtual desert. We cannot afford federal and local laws which make it illegal for some areas to sell excess water to other areas which want to buy it. We cannot afford, in short, to perpetuate a staggering subsidization of waste.

"If California's farmers used just 10 percent less water, enough additional water would be available to everyone else," says *The New York Times*, "for decades of urban growth with some left over to restore the plundered salmon streams and wetlands."

The problem of sensible water use is more economic than technological, but economics is commonly omitted from both diagnosis and prescription. The major, most fundamental water problem in California is not inadequate water. We *can* prosper with what we have. The problem is that we do not distribute and use what we have as well as we could if we were to make our water decisions through the devices and procedures of a freely flowing water market.

Why Oil Imports Went Up

ⅅⅅⅅⅅ

In 1985 the United States imported 27 percent of the oil it consumed. By 1989 the proportion had risen to 42 percent. What caused the increase?

The popular diagnosis is an oil binge. After cutting back oil consumption in the '70s and early '80s, consumers have returned to wasteful ways. Americans, we are repeatedly told, are addicted to oil. So efforts to increase domestic oil production only feed the habit. Unless government requires strict oil conservation, the binge will persist, and imports will provide an ever-larger share of the nation's oil consumption.

But this diagnosis doesn't square with evidence. True, we consumed more oil in 1989 than we did in 1985. But the increase was due to *economic growth*, not profligate *oil consumption*.

To take into account economic growth, consider oil consumption *per dollar of national output*. This measure declined between 1985 and 1989. Indeed, by 1989 oil consumption per dollar of real output had fallen to two-thirds of its level when the first oil shock hit in 1973. So we use more oil today because we produce more output. But each unit of output takes less oil than in past years — clear evidence of efficient oil utilization, not wasteful consumption.

Why did oil imports per dollar of national output increase between 1985 and 1989? Domestic oil production provides the answer. While oil *consumption* relative to real GNP fell, oil production fell even more, so oil *imports* soared. More imported oil began replacing domestically produced oil.

One reason for the decline in domestic oil production was the steep reduction in the price of petroleum. Oil producers respond to price changes just like other producers: They supply less oil at lower prices and more at higher prices. So when an increased world oil supply reduced the price after 1985, producers cut back exploration and drilling, yielding less oil production, and consumers used more foreign oil in its place. This was sensible, and thus predictable: Americans benefited by increasing imports of cheaper oil and conserving more-costly domestic reserves for future use.

Still, price changes do not explain the whole story of domestic oil production. From 1973 to 1989, oil production per dollar of national output declined in 13 of 17 years. Yet the inflation-adjusted price of oil fell in only eight of those years. And while the real price of oil was higher in 1989 than in 1973, domestic oil output per dollar of national production was lower.

So it will be wise for energy policy to look at all incentives to produce oil instead of simply ham-handed government requirements to conserve it. Oil imports have gone up because of declining domestic production — not extravagant consumption.

Nuclear Power, Coal, and Wastes

ⱮⱮⱮⱮ

Some industrial processes yield hazardous wastes. But we can produce in different ways — it is a world of choice in production as well as consumption — and we can obtain a given output with more or less wastes.

As Petr Beckmann has noted, the alleged problem of waste disposal is the last refuge of the anti-nuclear, know-nothing element, who have largely failed to persuade the community to believe fictions of nuclear plants exploding or melting. But nuclear wastes supposedly will get us.

Dr. Beckmann, an engineer and mathematician specializing in energy matters, has been telling us laymen for a dozen years that the nuclear waste disposal problem is essentially solved, in contrast to the problem of disposing of wastes from burning coal. But somehow dirty coal lacks the fearsome, mysterious glamor of split atoms. And in the business of fear-mongering and hysteria-promoting, mesmerizing mystery is everything.

Certainly, in quantity, there is no contest between nuclear waste disposal and coal waste disposal. "If all the U.S. power capacity were nuclear," writes Dr. Beckmann, "the total amount of wastes per person per year would amount to one aspirin tablet, and that can easily be disposed of deep in the earth .... The amount of wastes generated per person per year by coal-fired plants amounts to 321 pounds of ash and other poisons, of which as much as 10 percent is spewed into the atmosphere...."

With production and use of *any* kind of energy, bad things *can* happen. But the probability of great misfortune with nuclear wastes is as inconsequential as the amount of generated wastes — again, in contrast to coal.

Nuclear physicist Bernard L. Cohen reports that air pollution from coal burning causes about 25 deaths per year per large plant, far more than 1,000 times the eventual deaths to be expected from disposed wastes of a nuclear plant generating the same amount of electricity. Some of the chemicals released in burning coal are carcinogens which will eventually cause 80 more deaths. Another material from coal-burning is uranium, a generator of radon gas, which will cause an additional 30 deaths. Twenty-five plus 80 plus 30 is 135, which is 7,500 times the corresponding nuclear deaths.

Further, notes Professor Cohen, nuclear power removes uranium from the ground, which reduces radon exposure, thereby *saving* 500 lives each year per plant operation. Five hundred lives *saved* is nearly 30,000 times the number *lost* due to nuclear wastes.

It should not be hard to choose between 500 lives saved through nuclear plant operations and 135 lives lost through coal plant operations. But the problems of nuclear use and waste are those of propaganda and politics, not science, and silliness often gets in the way of sense.

Environmentalism

Science, Sense, and Sensationalism

✍✍✍✍

Nearly everyone supposedly supports truth and beauty over the false and the ugly. But some, it appears, seek not so much *victories* of causes as *participation* in causes.

A hot cause of the moment is vaguely defined "environmentalism." Ecological doomsday flower children are enjoying a flurry of hysteria. If we do not lose our skin to cancer, we shall drown from melting glaciers or retrogress to a stone age because of exhaustion of resources.

Inevitably, there are questions to ask and difficulties to resolve in use of the resources and attributes of a limited earth. Wise administration of scarce means of production and their products is the essence of economics. But wisdom stems from passion to comprehend, sophisticated analysis, and accurate measurement.

There is little apparent wisdom in being told that we should not dig for iron ore or coal or drill for oil or split the atom or cut trees or inconvenience fish and birds or use arable land for houses, factories, schools, and roads. It is not shrewd to insist that production should be primitive and consumption should be minimal. It is not insightful in a world of ubiquitous risk to insist that no degree of risk can be tolerated. It is not helpful to hold that the human race is a mistake of the Deity and that human artifacts are an abomination against deified nature. It is not sophisticated to insist that, in humble contrition, we should don sackcloth and ashes — except that production even of sackcloth requires energy and creation of ashes involves pollution.

And now we have advertising types pontificating on meteorology, chemistry, and astrophysics as well as economics. A trendy clothing company has published an ad promoting "environmentally conscious style." "Thoughtful consumption," we are told, requires "simply asking yourself before you buy something ... whether this is something you really need."

Now, economists can say useful things about *preferences* and *demands*; but for the economist, "need" is a non-word, a notion of no analytic content. The ad writer, however, can actually subdivide non-existent needs. "We can buy for *vital* needs," he allows, but "not *frivolous ego-gratifying* needs." How extraordinarily perceptive!

Since the fiasco in the Garden of Eden, this world of resource scarcity has been plagued by an abundance of problems. Doodlers with models and computer simulations too restricted, using data too few and too questionable, purport to have found complications of holes in ozone layers and greenhouse effects and resource depletion. Such complications — in some form, to some extent, with some degree of probability — may be real. But writers of clothing ads and scientists who seek media celebrity status are not likely to go far in identifying problems, their magnitudes, causes, and corrections, and the likelihoods of corrections being worth the costs. For that, sense must prevail over sensationalism.

Green and Mean

♨♨♨♨

Many Americans are genuinely concerned about how their consumption affects the environment. And they often follow popular guidelines for the so-called green consumer.

But Lynn Scarlett, of the Reason Foundation, concludes that, "Consumers who try to follow simple rules when they shop may end up harming the environment more than if they were simply to ignore the environmental consequences of their behavior." The unintended harm occurs because many of the popular rules are based on myth, not fact.

Consider some of the myths identified by Ms. Scarlett.

Myth No. 1: we are running out of landfill space. The fact is, all the solid waste Americans will produce for the next 1,000 years could fit into an area 44 miles square and 120 feet deep. Modern landfills endanger neither the environment nor human health. But the politics of Not-In-My-Back-Yard keeps enough new landfills from opening to replace those that close at the end of their natural lives.

Myth No. 2: Americans are wasteful compared with consumers in other countries. Many nations exclude from their definitions of solid waste things we include in ours. When statistics are adjusted to reflect the different definitions, U.S. households end up producing about the same amount of garbage as households abroad.

Myth No. 3: all packaging is bad. Actually, packaging often reduces waste. Packaging and processing allow rinds, peels, and other parts that would otherwise end up as garbage to be turned into useful by-products. Packaging also eliminates much solid waste by reducing damage and spoilage.

Myth No. 4: plastics are necessarily bad. But plastic containers are much lighter than glass or aluminum, so they save energy in packaging, handling, transportation, and disposal. And plastic containers require much less energy to manufacture, so they can end up using fewer total resources than those made of glass or aluminum.

Myth No. 5: diapers and other disposable items are bad. Yet, in the total lifespan of these goods, disposable products often save resources. Production and use of cloth diapers require much more water and energy than disposable ones, and produce a great deal more air and water pollution. In addition, cloth diapers can be less sanitary, convenient, and comfortable.

Myth No. 6: recycling is always good. But recycling requires more collection trucks, production facilities, and use of water and energy. So recycling can easily consume more total resources than new production and subsequent disposal in landfills.

We want our behavior to reflect the value of environmental and all other resources, of course. But bowing to the irrationality of mythology does not help. That is not being green. It is, instead, being mean to the environment — and to ourselves.

Mouse Wisdom: Property Rights and Pollution

ØØØØ

"A sell-out to big business!" fumed Mouse Karl.

"What's raising your blood pressure now?" wondered Mouse Adam.

"A proposal to grant rights to pollute," gasped Karl. "In Southern California, the Air Quality Management District is considering a plan to trash its regulatory procedures for curbing smog.

Instead, the agency would set an overall level of allowable air pollution, divide the total allowance into shares, and then distribute the shares among local firms. The total allowance would decline each year, but businesses could trade the shares they receive."

"Sounds reasonable," said Adam reasonably.

"Ridiculous!" jeered Karl. "The plan would grant businesses the right to pollute. A company needing less than its allowance could sell its pollution rights to another needing more. Businesses could then profit by selling shares in poison!"

"But the reason air pollution is a problem," explained Adam, "is because property rights to air have not been established. Unlike private resources, air has no owners whose personal wealth is at stake in managing and monitoring its use. And without private owners to charge mice for its use, fresh air has no market price. No wonder we fill the air with excess pollution."

"As a remedy," countered Karl, "governments have regulatory standards."

"True, agreed Adam. "But even regulations give individuals and businesses rights to pollute. Eliminating *all* pollution would mean prohibitive sacrifices by the community. So government regulation, like the proposal you scorn, gives mice the right to put some dirt and toxins into the air."

"Maybe," conceded Karl. "But at least regulation doesn't let mice profit by selling their right to pollute. With old-fashioned regulation, government just orders businesses to limit pollution by telling them how to change their activities and technologies."

"That's the problem," answered Adam. "Compared to owners and managers of businesses, government officials have little knowledge of the complex processes they regulate. Their mandated methods of reducing pollution usually are inefficient and clumsy. So the community wastefully uses too many resources to reduce pollution to an allowable level. And regulation provides no incentive for firms to cut pollution beyond required levels or to develop new methods and technologies to clean the air."

"All these shortcomings are overcome," continued Adam, "if regulation is replaced by marketable rights to pollute. Then, companies with lower costs of reducing pollution have an incentive to exploit their competence in keeping the air clean. They can profitably sell their rights to other companies whose costs of curbing pollution are higher. Greater efficiency in limiting pollution benefits the community, which gives up less income, production, and employment to clean the air."

Convinced, Karl concluded: "And business will have incentives to develop better methods of restricting pollution."

Power Play: Politics, Technology, and Economics

ぷぷぷぷ

In even this Land of the Free, Big and Little Brother have often diddled, in various degrees in myriad ways, in how citizens may use resources. The California Air Resources Board recently refused to delay or otherwise modify a 1990 mandate requiring, in effect, that a progressively increasing proportion of automobiles be electric-powered. The state government is requiring that, beginning in 1998, 2 percent of "vehicles produced and offered for sale" in California generate "zero emissions."

Then, three years later, the quota rises to 5 percent, and in 2003 it will be 10 percent. Producers who do not comply are to be excluded from the California market. Several other states are happily intrigued by this procedure of problem-solving by pronouncement.

But some of us who live in the real world, rather than in Sacramento, fret about some questions and complications. We do not do so out of enormous affection for the gasoline-powered engine, which is noisy, dirty, and not very efficient. But casting aside what we have simply by premature, willy-nilly stipulation is not likely to improve the situation.

1. *Technology.* The technology to provide a satisfactory substitute for the internal combustion engine is not here, although basic design for the 1998 model year should be locked in by now. And, disconcertingly, some expectations have been deteriorating with research experience. General Motors announced in 1990 its forthcoming electric, two-seater automobile, the Impact.

Four years ago, the expected range of the Impact before battery recharging was some 130 miles; today, it is given as 70-90 miles — if the air conditioner, heater, headlights, or windshield wipers are not used. Four years ago, the top speed was to be 110 miles per hour; today, it is 80. Four years ago, the anticipated recharging time was about 1 hour; today it is seen as 2-3 hours (on 220 volts) or 10 hours (110 volts). Four years ago, battery replacement (after 20,000 miles) was to cost $1,500; today, replacement (after 3-5 years) may be as much as $15,000.

No one can know what tomorrow holds, and hope springs eternal. But we have had more than a century of experience with electric automobiles, and batteries have long been the subject of research. A professor of mechanical engineering, writing in *The New York Times*, has remarked that "the chances for a great advance" in battery technology "are remote for something as thoroughly familiar as electrochemistry."

2. *Price*. It is acknowledged that this "weak-kneed contraption of batteries on wheels," as it has been dubbed by one engineer/scientist, will carry a price premium — unless camouflaged by heavy governmental subsidies. Estimates of the premium range from $3,000-4,000 to over $20,000. (Toy cars can be cheaper. One spartan two-seater due for production this year may be priced at under $15,000 — with a range of just over 40 miles.) In 1990, the target price of the Impact was $20,000; now, educated guesses suggest at least $30,000.

3. *"Efficiency."* Technological efficiency is not everything. More subtle and encompassing is economic efficiency, the value of outputs relative to the value of inputs. Value stems from valuations, and, in our sort of society, the valuations are made in the market by the community. We define efficiency in terms of how well consumer preferences are satisfied. When government mandates or subsidizes or decrees prices or outputs, it muddies the market waters and dilutes the efficacy of consumer preferences, thereby reducing economic efficiency.

Proponents of minimum market quotas for electric autos have argued that production and sales decrees and guarantees are necessary to ensure adequate investment in such cars and in the associated battery-recharging infrastructure. But that is an admission of consumer demand which is apparently inadequate: the project has not met the engineering/market test.

Those producers prosper who adequately perceive or predict sufficient demand for prospective products. Genuinely promising products do not require paternalism. The hope of increasing personal wealth has led venturesome, acquisitive individuals to test and pursue supposed or potential demand for automatic transmissions, television, video recorders, instant coffee, credit cards, personal computers, supermarkets, miniskirts, and hula hoops.

And government-sponsored infrastructure was not universally required. Automobile production was not delayed until a network of filling stations appeared; movie makers did not wait until theatres were built; radios did not wait for radio stations; frozen foods and freezers for home use did not "bottleneck" each other; color television did not require a law compelling television sets manufacturers to make units with color capabilities.

Electric autos do not require government mandates if the product pleases the community; and they will be inefficiently supplied if they are not demanded and are offered merely by state decree.

4. *Mandate.* The Air Resources Board decree is in terms of "vehicles produced and offered for sale." What if the community will not buy a battery-driven 2 percent of the cars produced in 1998? Government can mandate production quotas; it cannot mandate consumer purchases.

Well, presumably, those cars *will* be bought at some price greater than zero! If customers will not pay a cost-covering price, they can be seduced by a sufficiently lower price. But if the price is less than the cost, the value of the car is less than the value of the resources which constructed the car. This is known in some circles as "resource misallocation," or "waste."

5. *Alternative pollution reduction.* The internal combustion engine is, indeed, a polluter. But (a) present fuels pollute less than those of a couple of decades ago; (b) the major part of the emissions problem is not dirty fuels, but untuned cars, with fewer than 10 percent of the cars creating over half the pollution and 15 percent generating 75 percent of the emissions; (c) even battery cars are not entirely pollution free, for there is pollution in generating the electricity which powers the cars.

While continuing to improve fuels and combustion engines, we can winnow out untuned cars (which are not invariably ancient), and require owners to fix them. It is now feasible quite readily and inexpensively to detect dirty cars on the road by remote sensor.

The ham-handed, clumsy belligerence of Little Brother in decreeing deadlines for battery cars can hardly be called a coherent strategy. It resembles a king standing on the beach commanding the tide to behave itself — and getting his feet wet. The electricity-powered automobile may be the vehicle of some tomorrow. Through effective market processes over time, we can anticipate evolving consumer demands, production costs, and technological refinements to meld into a new equilibrium alignment.

Health: Concerns, Care, and Costs

Health Care and Other Good Things

ØØØØ

The very *best* things in life are free, of course, but not much is free in this world of scarcity. Ordinary *good* things are more often found, but are not free.

Homes, for example, are costly ro produce, for the resources used could have made other things instead. That cost is reflected in the price of new housing. People buy less than they would consume *if* housing were costless, or free.

Health care is another good thing that is not free. Resources must be diverted from producing other good things — like housing — in order to produce health care. But unlike prices of new housing, the price paid by an individual when consuming health care is far below the cost of producing it.

Thanks to private and government health insurance, consumers in the medical marketplace are spending mostly someone else's money. So each decision about the kind and quantity of medical services to consume is made without much attention to the real cost of those services. Economist Henry Aaron and physician William B. Schwartz report that in 1987 patients paid, on average, about 10 cents of each dollar of hospital-care costs. So individuals choose more care than they would *if* others did not pick up most of the tab.

No wonder health-care expenditures have grown much faster than the rest of the economy. Victor R. Fuchs, professor of economics at Stanford University, analyzes the gap between faster-growing health-care expenditures and the slower-growing general economy. From 1947 to 1987, health-care spending grew at an average annual rate 2.5 percentage points greater than growth of the general economy. As a result, health care has mushroomed from under 5 percent of gross national product in 1947 to more than 11 percent today. And the proportion continues to grow.

Expenditures have two components: prices and quantities. So a gap between health-care growth and general economic growth can occur if health-care *prices* rise faster than the general price level or if the *quantity* of health services increases more rapidly than the economy's output. *Both* factors contributed to the growth gap during the period. But price increases usually contributed more, a fact Professor Fuchs attributes mostly to the difficulty of increasing labor productivity in health-care services, which depend greatly on individual personal contact.

Still, prices or quantities of health care would not continue to rise so fast without persistent, rapid increases in demand for those services. And that demand continues to grow faster than the general economy because consumers pay only a tiny portion of the cost of those services when consuming them.

But what seems nearly free to an individual consumer is costly to the community. For as more resources are diverted to production of health care, fewer remain for housing and other good things.

Medical Folks and Artichokes

ØØØØ

What shall we do about the persistently rising cost of medical care? Artichokes may suggest the answer.

The price of artichokes depends on many things. One is the number available. As with virtually all goods and services in the marketplace, a greater supply makes the price of artichokes lower than it would otherwise be. And a smaller supply makes it higher.

But doctors are not like artichokes, concludes a study about health-care costs. For medical folks, a larger supply is likely to raise, not lower, the price of medical services.

Why the difference? Because doctors are smarter than artichokes. Artichokes do not consult with consumers and advise them to buy more of their services to promote good health. Doctors do. As the number of doctors increases, the study suggests, on average they perform and bill for more services, and thereby maintain their incomes.

Doctors, not consumers, control demand for medical services, so more doctors means more demand for those services. And increasing demand means higher prices and greater expenditures for medical care. As proof, the study shows that during the 1980s the number of physicians and their average income both increased.

The suggested prescription for rising medical costs is to limit the number of doctors. But before we begin closing down medical schools, we ought to ask if physicians *really are* all that different from artichokes.

True, doctors can influence spending for their services. But that influence results largely from the way we finance most medical care. Consumers of medical services pay out of their own pockets for only a small fraction of the services they buy. Since 1981, out-of-pocket expenses have been less than 25 cents out of each dollar patients spent for health care.

Medical Care Prices and Percentage of All Health Expenditures Paid by Patients, 1970–1987

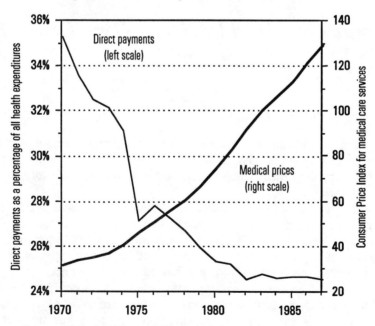

Sources: *U.S. Statistical Abstract,* 1990; *Economic Report of the President,* 1991.

If shoppers knew that private and public food insurance would pay for most of their artichoke purchases, they would stuff their carts with them. And as demand increased, artichoke prices would rise, farmers' incomes would go up, and growers would be motivated to produce more of them. A larger supply of artichokes would then occur along with a bigger income for farmers. But we would not conclude that artichokes are somehow influencing buyers and bloating demand. Nor would we advocate limiting the number of artichokes on the market. Doing so would only make their price still higher.

Similarly, demand for medical care is bloated because consumers usually are spending someone else's money when they buy doctor's services. Limiting the number of physicians in the face of that subsidized demand would raise doctors' fees and fatten their average income. Yet, such a recommendation of supply curtailment comes from the study, which was authored by (you guessed it) two doctors.

We can contain the cost of medical care. But we aren't likely to do so by pretending that, in the marketplace, medical folks are not at all like artichokes.

Families and Healthy Health Care: Choose It or Lose It

Politicians are falling over themselves to try to show support for the American family. It is easy to talk a caring, compassionate game; it requires seemingly uncommon comprehension and courage to promote helpful policies.

Medical care is an illustration. Most of us receive health care through employer-provided insurance. The reason is the tax system, not business benevolence. Government allows employers to pay some of our wages as tax-free health insurance. But it does not give us a tax break if we take cash wages and then buy our own insurance.

No wonder families prefer tax-free employer-provided medical benefits rather than taking an equivalent amount of cash, paying taxes, and then buying their own insurance. The tax code has transferred decision making about health care from the family to the employer.

But if the family is the thread of our social fabric, then why weaken it by having employers make these decisions for it? Do politicians suppose that American families are too dumb or too cavalier to make such decisions? At any rate, they have stacked the tax code against family responsibility in health care.

By doing so, the politicians have created other problems. One is so-called job-lock, in which an employee stays in a job only from fear of losing medical benefits. Indeed, the Kaiser Family Foundation reports that 25 percent of those surveyed said that job-lock affects them or someone in their family. "This ... has transformed the health care problem," says the Foundation's president, from a limited "'social issue' ... into a mainstream, pocketbook issue."

So why not return decisions about medical insurance to the family? Government could do so by ending the tax deduction for employer-provided medical insurance and creating a deduction for insurance that families buy. Families would than choose to have employers pay them more cash and less insurance. And with the added cash and new tax deduction, they could shop for their own insurance. This would not prevent government from helping to finance insurance for lower-income families.

The change would eliminate job-lock because a family's medical insurance would stay with it when changing jobs. In addition, it would do wonders to contain runaway medical costs. For families who directly spend their own money for health insurance are much more likely than their employers to make cost-conscious choices. Savings from health-insurance premiums go directly into their own pockets, so they are more willing to buy insurance tailored to their personal interests. They are more willing also to economize on use of health care which is paid for more directly with their own money.

Health care in America could be much healthier. Part of the prescription for improving policy is for government to allow the families who use it to choose it.

Education

Public Schools for the Public

øøøø

The odor of rotting economies is pungent in Eastern Europe and the Soviet Union. In other nations, too, people are holding their noses and acknowledging the inability of government to plan and command a successful economy. These people have learned through bitter experience that higher living standards do not come from government mandates and controls. They result, instead, from individuals who are free to produce and trade in open markets and have incentive to do so.

Yet, in our own public schools, we continue to follow the same failed system of government decrees and direction. Should we then get government out of education as many nations now are getting government out of their economies? The answer is yes — and no.

No, because government serves a legitimate function in education. When youngsters learn basic skills of communication and calculation and obtain basic knowledge of our history and institutions, they are gaining the general education required for good, productive citizenship. So students and their families are not the only beneficiaries of training and cultivation. The community benefits, too. By helping to finance such education, government assures the community of this commonly-shared and highly-valued benefit.

But providing the money for people to obtain general education does not mean that government, itself, must always produce it. *Financing* education is not the same as *producing* education.

Keeping government in the financing of education makes sense. But allowing government to continue as a monopoly producer of education prevents the changes that would make schools efficient providers of educational services. Like the failed government enterprises of other nations, public school monopolies serve largely their government workers and directors at the expense of the consumers they are supposed to benefit.

But how can government finance education without also being its monopoly producer? The answer is to change the way we fund public schools. Stop assigning each school a given amount of the available funds. And stop guaranteeing customers by assigning schools a given share of available students. Instead, divide available funds into per-pupil shares and allow parents to direct their shares to the schools of their choice.

Parents could choose from a menu of schools satisfying minimal requirements of graduation. The menu could include existing public, private, and parochial schools and any new schools that communities or enterprising individuals want to provide. In the new, competitive school market, public education would mean education largely financed, but not necessarily produced, by government. And the financing of each institution, no longer an entitlement, would stem only from parents choosing to send their children to that particular school.

Accountability through provision of choice in the marketplace would make schools innovative and efficient. At last, public education would serve the public.

Education and Society

øøøø

Everyone knows that you get only what you pay for, and the more you pay, the more you get.

Well, maybe we do *not* really know that. By any standard, we pay a lot for primary and secondary education, and the amount we pay has been steadily and significantly rising for many decades, but the educational product persists in deteriorating. If generous, and increasingly generous, school financing has yielded increasingly poorer results, one has reason to wonder about the wisdom of spending at a still greater rate.

The sorry and frustrating record of school financing has been surveyed by John Hood, associated with *Spectator* and *Reason* magazines and the John Locke Foundation. He reports that the United States now spends, in real terms, much more per pupil in public primary and secondary schools then ever before and that the United States spends more per student than do the majority of other nations.

And yet, by standards of both our own history and of international comparison, our students perform poorly.

How are we to account for such seeming perversity, with more educational spending yielding less education?

Well, how is the money spent? Much experience indicates that lowering student/teacher ratios, increasing teacher salaries, increasing school district consolidations and centralized administration, and adding noninstructional frosting on the cake have little correlation with — and sometimes even negative effects on — student performance. So what to do?

Mr. Hood responds enthusiastically in terms of more individual school autonomy and freedom to innovate, of parental choice in schools for their children to attend, and of more parental involvement in determining educational content and procedure.

Still, this can hardly be the entire story of reform. For one thing, the existence of massive waste by the educational establishment does not negate the necessity of very considerable resources. *Average* educational expenditures across the country *are* very considerable, but there remain huge pockets of poverty. Schools with few and outdated textbooks, dilapidated and crowded buildings, and semi-literate teachers are poor places in which to cultivate young minds.

Certainly, more than money *is* required — and also more than a voucher system of parental choice among competing schools. Those choices are not likely to be sophisticated when the choosers are not sophisticated. Poor, uneducated communities, inhabited by people from and in broken homes, with no tradition of or hope for success, with, indeed, little notion of or interest in the nature and requirements of professional accomplishment, plagued by teenage pregnancy, drug consumption, and other improprieties — such communities cannot be expected to generate or participate in effective educational programs.

Better communities will require better education. But better education will require better communities. Where and how are we to begin improvement?

Training, Education, and Business Competence

ぷぷぷぷ

What is business competence, how is it to be identified at an early stage of personal career, and what sorts of experience are most conducive to its development? We speak abstractly of "the business firm." But it is particular *people*, not an entity called "the firm," who define questions, conduct investigations, deduce answers, and, often at much risk, make decisions.

One might suppose that business schools and business leaders would have made great progress in dealing with the dilemmas of providing superior business guidance. Unhappily, the boys in the dean's office and in the board room seem commonly naive in the area of identifying and developing problem-solvers and decision makers.

A senior vice president of a major corporation has commented on his gaining of consciousness of certain elemental aspects of the personnel world. He recounts that his company had long been "seeking to hire only MBAs, accountants and engineers, whose skills could be used immediately .... But," he goes on, "then we looked around us, and noticed that our own senior officers came from a variety of educational backgrounds, heavy in the liberal arts. And we began to wonder if short-term performance pressures were forcing business units to look only at people trained for entry level positions, with little thought for the long-range needs of the company."

That is a remarkable confession: the corporation was hiring simply for first-jobs people who had been trained simply for first-jobs.

Surely, even an officer below senior vice president could be expected to comprehend that key recruitment of personnel is properly concerned, not primarily with the detailed chores of the day, but with acquiring people with the qualities and characteristics providing promise of development over decades. And he could at least suspect that the qualities and characteristics which distinguish those with potentialities of growing into top-level analysts, problem-solvers, and decision makers pertain to and reflect, not the particular classes taken in school days, but to reading and writing, intelligence and alertness, ambition and energy, poise and sense, courage and integrity.

Further, in so far as particular course work is of any interest, the emphasis obviously should be, not on training in nitty-gritty procedural mechanics — the firm can always hire mechanics for the mechanical problems of the moment — but on education conducive to growth in effectiveness in fundamental analysis and implementation of deduced policies.

It is notoriously the case that a substantial proportion of business leaders have limited comprehension of, or interest in, the economy in which they work, prerequisites of survival of their professional world, and identification of allies who can best help repel the barbarians who seek to subvert that world. It is apparent, in addition, that some business leaders are muddle-brained even on the matter of finding and developing the talent required eventually to succeed them.

Financing College Education: Gifts and Investments

✍✍✍✍

It may be inevitable that a world of scarcity will be also a world of snarling. For scarcity not only leads to competition and conflict, it can give rise to acrimonious confusion, as well. Confusion about corollaries of scarcity are rarely as conspicuous and corrosive as in the realm of financing higher education.

Most of the most renowned colleges and universities are private. Even at private schools, payments by the customers fall far short of covering all costs of the institution. Even so, tuition at Harvard is much higher than the fees charged at the University of California.

Although state schools are striking bargains for students compared to private schools, there are many — faculty members as well as students at ol' State U. — who insist that the public school fees are too high and certainly should not be pushed a penny higher. How can we reasonably approach the problem of how best to finance state universities? Consider a few considerations.

1. Non-market-clearing prices inevitably give rise to questions of allocation and rationing, economic problems to be resolved through

shortage and discrimination by arbitrary political and bureaucratic decree.

2. "He who gets should pay" is a solid rule, a first approximation which permits little legitimate tampering. Simply distributing educational services at low or *zero price* does not magically make them *free*. The low price makes the services appear free to the student, but the costs to society still exist.

3. When subsidization is begun, there are few good guidelines for determining *who* should subsidize *whom* in what *form* in what *amount* in what *way* on what *terms* for how *long*. The proportion of total state taxes paid by poor people is greater than the proportion of the University of California student body which consists of the poor. The poor are subsidizing the non-poor.

4. The case for subsidization of a selected few in the form of college tuition is not made persuasive simply by reference to educational "investment" being beneficial to us all. The world abounds with illustrations of possible subsidization which would yield some positive feedback to the subsidizer. I could bribe my neighbor to spend more on his lawn, and I would enjoy some return from his doing so, but most of us reasonably presume that each person should pay for his own lawn.

5. If it be insisted that subsidization of education is uniquely appropriate, *how* shall it be done? Must it be by *gift*? If the direct beneficiary of the subsidization has legitimate business in college — if he really is a resource worth cultivating on the campus — he is *not poor* in basic competence and commitment. He may now be financially pinched. If he is potentially productive, it is rational for him to *borrow* in order to make his *own* investment in his *own* career. And it is rational for the community to make such borrowing feasible. The student can later repay the loan out of his enhanced earnings.

If educational investment is shrewd, then he who most directly and fully benefits from the investment should finance it and bear its risks.

Mainly Macroeconomics:
Income and Monetary Analysis

☙☙☙☙☙

Introduction

The foundations of economic analysis are in price-and-allocation theory. But there are interesting questions and significant problems which must be considered on a large scale — matters of government spending, taxation, inflation, fiscal and monetary policies, exchange rates, the balance of payments. We can deal with some issues only with the aid of big aggregates and big averages of the economy — although we must keep well in mind that real, live individuals are behind those aggregates and averages. Great masses of data are likely to remain mere summary measures and mechanical indicators if we do not ask how the world looks — its options and constraints, its incentives and perils, its payoffs and penalties — to the particular people who make decisions.

A commonly used aggregate is "national output and income," measured generally as gross domestic product. GDP can be subdivided into its spending components and into its components of income dispersal. The *spending* on the output of the economy over an accounting period determines and measures the marketplace *value* of that output, and all of this received spending is disposed of in various forms of *income*. Thus:

GDP = C + I + G + X, from the standpoint of income-creation, and GDP = C + S + T + M, from the standpoint of income-disposal, where C is consumption spending, I is investment spending, G is government spending, and X is foreign spending (exports) on currently produced, domestic, final output; and S is saving, T is tax collections and M is imports.

The GDP figure is imperfect and inadequate, conceptually as well as operationally. In addition to physical difficulties in accurately gathering the mass of data, there are questions of what to *try* to include and what we *do* measure in this summation of economic activity. And in using the measurement of analysis over time, there are corrections to be made for changes in prices, varieties and qualities of goods, population, and income distribution. Still, there would be absurdity in throwing away usable information because it does not perfectly measure all we should like to measure.

Such national income accounting has sometimes been used — and misused — as a basis of discretionary fiscal policy. Simple models seem to demonstrate that government can diddle with its own spending (G) and collection of taxes (T) to attain targeted values of GDP. Doubtless, government spending and taxation (and regulating and mandating) can affect national income, but the models provide only limited guidance in real-world policy making. They do not well incorporate considerations of what the government will buy, through what taxes and borrowings it will finance the spending, what will be the side effects on money supply, interest rates, and community expectations, and how long will be the lags between policy conceptualization and implementation and repercussion.

Discussions of large budget deficits (G larger than T) also have exhibited some of the perils in moving from accounting tautology to analytic theory to policy prescription. Many have blamed the deficits, which began to balloon in 1975 and reached an impressive peak in 1992, on T being cut while G was being bloated by increased defense spending. In actuality, since World War II, both government receipts and outlays have increased proportionately faster than GDP, with outlays leading receipts — but not because of a massive explosion of defense spending. See Table 1. Most politicians and editorial writers — and even some economists — have yet to learn the source of the deficits, what are and are not the problems of deficits, and the relative significance of the size of *deficits* and *budgets*.

Table 1

Federal Outlays, Receipts, Deficits, and
Defense Spending as Percentages of GDP

		Outlays	*Receipts*	*Deficit*	*Defense*
Truman	1946-52	17.0%	16.9%	0.1%	8.7%
Eisenhower	1953-60	18.6%	18.0%	0.6%	11.2%
Kennedy/ Johnson	1961-68	19.1%	18.1%	1.0%	8.9%
Nixon/Ford	1969-76	20.3%	18.6%	1.7%	6.8%
Carter	1977-80	21.4%	18.9%	2.5%	5.0%
Reagan	1981-88	23.3%	18.9%	4.4%	6.1%
Bush	1989-92	22.9%	18.8%	4.1%	5.3%
Clinton	1993-95	22.0%	18.9%	3.1%	4.3%

Source: *Economic Report of the President,* February 1996.

Matters of national output, national income, and price level can be approached through monetary analysis, as well. Instead of breaking down aggregate expenditure into components of C, I, G, and X, we can state it as M times V, the amount of money multiplied by the average number of times a dollar is spent on output during the year. GDP = MV. And the expenditure on output determines the value of the output, which can be noted as price times quantity, or P times Q, an index of price per unit multiplied by a measure of the units of output.

So spending on output (MV) necessarily equals the value of output (PQ). And the *sum* of the proportionate (percentage) changes in the money supply and monetary velocity approximately equals the proportionate change of the price index *plus* the proportionate change in the real amount of output, both being equal to the proportionate change in the value of output, which is GDP in current dollars.

Consider some of these relationships since the 1950s, broken into three sub-periods: 1959-72, 1972-81, and 1981-1995.

Table 2

Money, Velocity, Price Level, Output, Spending,
Money/Output, and Productivity
Annual Rates of Change

	M	V	P	Q	PQ	M/Q	Productivity, business sector
1959-72	4.5	2.5	3.3	3.7	7.1	.8	2.8
1972-81	6.5	4.1	8.2	2.4	10.8	3.9	.8
1981-95	7.0	−0.7	3.6	2.7	6.2	4.3	1.3

Source: *Economic Report of the President,* February 1996.

The period 1959-72 had the lowest rate of inflation. It also had the smallest rate of money increase; and it had the greatest rate of increase in output. The large rate of output expansion was consistent with a large rate of increase in productivity, although productivity per worker is not the only determinant of output. Aggregate output is a function not only of worker productivity, but of the number of workers; and the number of workers depends on the population of the community, the proportion of the population in the labor force, and the proportion of the labor force which is employed.

From 1972-81, the money supply increased more rapidly, and the increase in velocity of money spending also was greater than in the preceding period. The rapidly rising expenditure combined with a considerably smaller rate of output increased to generate much greater inflation. Expenditure rose at nearly 11 percent per year while output went up at 2.4 percent, so prices rose more than 8 percent.

In 1981-95, the inflation rate fell well over half from the preceding period, *not* because of a massive surge in productivity or total output and *despite* an increased expansion of money, because monetary *velocity*, which had expanded rapidly in 1972-81, actually fell at close to 1 percent per year.

Obviously, in different periods of several years, inflation can be dominated by any of a number of variables. But over the long pull, look to money. In particular, see if money is rising faster than output. If the ratio of money to output is going up, then expect the price level, too, to go up.

All of the micro and macro analytics find a home in the realm of international economics. The bases of trade are the bases of trade, and the gains from trade are the gains from trade, whether the traders reside in the same country or in different countries. And in both domestic and foreign trade, we gain from what we get, not from what we give.

What a country has available for its own consumption and investment "absorption" (A) is mainly its own production: We live better when we produce much. But some of that domestic output is exported to foreigners, and some foreign output is imported. So $A = GDP - X + M$. If imports are greater than exports, then the nation absorbs more of the world's output than it produces: we live better also by being subsidized than by subsidizing.

FISCAL CONCERNS AND THE ECONOMY

Measurement and Data

GNP: The Baby and The Bath Water

✍✍✍✍

Gross National Product — fondly known as GNP — is a money measure of aggregate output, the dollar value of all goods and services produced in the economy over some period. It is an imperfect measure, and a few have suggested throwing out the notion.

There *are* problems and limitations in using GNP figures.

For one thing, the *dollar value* of a basket of goods is determined by both the *physical quantity* of goods and the *price tags* on those goods. From 1979 to 1980, GNP in this country went up almost 9 percent. That sounds great. But prices went up close to 10 percent, with real output actually falling over 1 percent. There is a big difference between 9 percent and –1 percent. In dealing with GNP, watch out for inflation.

Another problem pertains to *qualitative* changes. Automobiles and refrigerators today are hardly the same commodities as automobiles and refrigerators of thirty or fifty years ago. But these differences are not indicated by the number of units produced and their prices at different dates.

There is also the complication of *population* change. If real output goes up 15 percent over a period while the number of people increases by 20 percent, output per person falls. Some countries have such a large rate of population increase that most of their output is absorbed in simply maintaining per capita income: they run hard just to stay in the same place.

And what of income *distribution*? Several oil-producing countries experienced huge increases in GNP per person during the 1970s, but 95 percent of the residents did not gain.

So there are these and other technical issues in interpreting and using GNP data. There remains an even more basic matter of exactly *what* is being measured.

GNP is only a money measure of the economy's *output*. It is not a comprehensive measure of the community's *well-being*. The human condition is a function of many variables — psychological, sociological, philosophical, theological, as well as economic. How well established and how well respected are the standards of the community? How confident and committed are the people — and confident and committed with respect to what?

Now, GNP *is* pertinent to many of the more subtle aspects of life. People are more likely to be content and get along well when the economy is flourishing. But GNP figures themselves — the money value of production — do not include measures of propriety, gentility, courage, discipline, love ... which most fundamentally determine the quality of people and their lives.

But, then, GNP was not *intended* to try to measure such things. What GNP *does* measure is very important, however. Properly used, GNP data can tell us useful things about some vital aspects of the world.

Fiddling and Fudging with Figures: Heroines of the Household

✍✍✍✍

Perhaps the most important things in our lives cannot be measured to the fourth decimal place — a case being the beauty, grace, and charm of Winnie, my noble dog. But it can be useful to measure what we can. Certainly, it is good to have data on many variables in economics.

Gross national product has long been a conspicuous economics measure. GNP is the *money* measure of the community's productive activity, the *marketplace* value of our output.

Every one knowledgeable in such stuff is aware of problems and inadequacies in GNP data. In making comparisons over time, we should correct the numbers for changes in prices; for per capita comparisons, we take into account changes in population; we may want to note changes in the distribution, as well as the amount, of production; it would be nice, but hardly feasible, to measure also changes in quality of goods.

Criticisms of GNP measurement go beyond mechanics of adjusting raw numbers. There is concern about the *limited scope* of what we have been *trying* to measure.

Some profess to be intellectually outraged and emotionally offended by the GNP figures being a *marketplace* value, stemming from transactions and their prices. As such, it omits much actual economic activity, including house-work and home-making. And since such activity is done predominantly by women, the contributions of wives and mothers are understated.

We may conjecture that hell hath no fury like that of a woman whose contribution is understated. "No one," says one with dubious grammar, "should have their work remain invisible." "But," she goes on with dubious syntax, "we're told again and again it only counts if it's exchanged for money."

There is a good reason for counting only marketplace exchanges: that is where the data are. Without transactions and prices, how are we to tell the money value of housewifely activities? We cannot well count the amount of unrecorded labor or calculate its money value simply by comparisons of values of allegedly similar services. That clumsiness and arbitrariness would get us back into much of the absurdity of the recent "comparable worth" belligerence.

And what would such attempted measuring of the immeasurable accomplish? It would make GNP numerically bigger, to be sure, but it would add nothing to our actual productive activity or real income. We would continue to do what we are doing now, but would try to fool ourselves by giving it a larger dollar value — and, in the process, make current and future GNP figures non-comparable both with historical data and with data of other countries.

The dilution and distortion of wedging a figure for unpaid labor into a GNP measure of paid activity *would* accomplish one reasonable thing: acknowledgment of extensive labor outside the market. But instead of fiddling and fudging with figures, it would be better just to give medals to non-market workers. The medals could read: "Heroine of the Household."

The Unknown Future Lies Ahead

ॐॐॐॐ

We cannot know what our conditions and circumstances will be in six years or six months. And even if we felt confident of tomorrow's problems and possibilities, we could not certainly know what to do, or when to do it, or how far to go in doing it. Our future is risky in its uncertainty, and our powers of control and adaptation are limited.

To be sure, we can try to predict the economic future, partially through use of an index of "leading indicators." But there are inherent difficulties of conception and operational difficulties of calculation in such devices. The index of indicators sometimes waffles, not clearly pointing either up or down; it sometimes is found to have pointed in the wrong direction; it sometimes gives us warning much too late and sometimes much too soon.

Instead of trying to predict the future and adjust to it, we can try to force and mold the future through decrees of Big Brother. The essence of centralized economic planning is to impose results which a market mechanism based on private use of property would not generate. The open market yields productive incentives through market-clearing prices reflecting demander preferences and supplier costs, broad work and investment options, and reward linked to performance. But the economic czar decrees disequilibrium prices and puts the community — except for the governmental elite — into a harsh yoke of capricious discipline and deadening conformity.

Are we, then, helpless in shaping a fate of freedom? To forego the clumsy paraphernalia of planning and the mindless bumbling of bureaucracy is *not* to forego order in favor of anarchy. Lack of knowledge about, and capacity to do, *everything* does *not* mean we know and can do *nothing*. We can have efficient coordination without — indeed, *only* in the absence of — controls.

We have much evidence on the productivity of free men in free markets, and we know much about the optimality of simple and stable rules of the game which permit ambitious people to work, plan, save, and invest. Simple and stable rules which maximize options and incentives will not preclude all error and disappointment. It is, after all, a fluctuating world of costs and pains. But we do best not to exacerbate our problems and difficulties by misconceived and inept intrusions, directives, and restrictions.

We will continue to be frequently — and not always happily — surprised. But we will cope best with an uncertain, even erratic world when we have wide options, many opportunities to exercise discipline and skill, and incentives to use sense, exhibit courage, and nurture ambition.

We shall not get far in *predicting* the future, and we shall certainly lose our way in trying to *prescribe* the future, but we can appreciably *provide* for the future, largely by promotion of those institutions which enable us individually to be economically productive.

Nature, History, and Significance of the Deficit

The Federal Financial Fire

♌♌♌♌

All the sparks about federal budget deficits are turning heads away from the real financial fire: government expenditures. These *expenditures*, not taxes or budget deficits, show the amount of national income absorbed and redirected by the federal government.

Think of it this way, advises eminent economist Milton Friedman: "If the national income is four trillion dollars, and the federal government spends a trillion dollars, that leaves three trillion dollars for state and local governments, private individuals and institutions to spend or invest as they separately wish, whether the government finances its spending by explicit taxes or by borrowing."

Since the 1940s, we have shoveled progressively more of the nation's income into the government furnace. True, government requires income to provide valuable goods and services that would not otherwise be available. National defense, the administration of justice, and care of the destitute illustrate legitimate, even if costly, functions of federal government. But none of these legitimate functions has been the wind fanning the fire of federal spending. Indeed, the most conspicuous — national defense — has generally *declined* as a fraction of national output since the Korean War in the early 1950s.

The primary reason for greater government spending has been increased transfer payments and subsidies, most of which benefit those with at least middle incomes. These programs — Social Security, Medicare, farm subsidies, and the like — have grown from about 3 percent of GNP in 1948 to over 10 percent in 1988. The rapid growth of transfers and subsidies has pushed federal spending up faster than federal tax receipts, swelling the budget deficit.

Although the deficit has recently declined as a proportion of GNP, its considerable size still has kept Congress from spending all the money it would like. No wonder that many of the congressional

Federal Spending and Receipts
as Percentages of GNP, 1948–1987

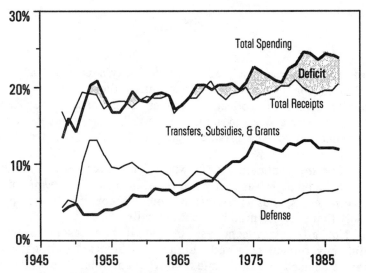

Sources: *The National Income and Product Accounts of the United States 1929–1992*, U.S. Department of Commerce, September 1986; *Economic Report of the President*, 1988.

statesmen cry for increased taxes. Though touted as deficit reducers, the additional revenue would more likely fuel greater spending. More taxes, advises John G, Makin of the American Enterprise Institute, would indulge "Congress' 'pent-up demand' for new programs for everything from the environment to affordable housing for yuppies."

Anyone doubting this conclusion need only check the record of Congress since 1948. As percentages of GNP, higher taxes have been associated with bigger, not smaller, deficits.

The track record confirms that members of Congress have prospered by spending other people's money. The spending strategy has succeeded: incumbent Congressmen almost always are reelected. Now, under the ruse of deficit reduction, they seek still more money for vote-getting transfers and subsidies that barely trickle down to the poor. If they continue to succeed, the budget deficit will not come down. Instead, more revenue will stoke the federal financial fire — and the burden of profligate and wasteful government will grow.

Real Budget Balance: Government Purchases and Transfers

ஐஐஐஐ

Government acquires much of the community's production. It pays with dollars for what it gets. It acquires those dollars from the community either by collecting conventional taxes or by deficit-borrowing through sales of bonds. In either case, there is a direct wealth reduction for the private sector, and that wealth reduction *is* taxation.

"For the community as a whole," observes Milton Friedman, "what is called a *deficit* is really a form of *taxation*. The *whole* of what the government spends is extracted from the community's resources, not solely that part financed by what are called taxes."

Not all government use of output and resources will be wasteful: government may build highways which not only have value but may be deemed more valuable than what could have been done with those resources by private people. But whether the sequestered stuff is used well or poorly, it *is* sequestered, so cost is borne as less is left in the hands of the private sector. Government financing thus involves real taxation equal to government purchases, whether or not the conventional budget records a deficit.

This is not to deny that the mode of financing can be of interest. Perhaps the most basic significance pertains to income redistribution: there will be one pattern of redistribution if conventional taxes are levied now; there will be a different pattern if conventional taxation is deferred through sale of bonds. But in either case, government sequestering of output and resources constitutes taxation, so the real budget seems to be balanced.

But suppose the government spending is *not* to obtain goods and services. Instead, it may be direct income redistribution through *transfer* payments. In this transfer case, government is not "absorbing" or channeling the productive use of real resources: there is left with the public no net reduction in wealth when Mr. A is forced to subsidize Mr. B.

If the public as a whole loses nothing by the redistributive transfer, there is no real taxation, no governmental extracting of real resources. But then there is also no real spending — and so no real deficit is created.

Transfer payments and their financing are only "financial" operations in shuffling existing assets within the community. In no real sense can a deficit be involved. In contrast, when government buys things, there is a real sequestering and cost — but the real budget remains balanced because the real sequestering from the public is also real taxation of the public, regardless of the immediate mode of financing the spending.

Many seem to be mesmerized by the conventionally measured "deficit." There *are* important problems — problems of efficiency and equity, both immediately and over time — associated with the size, structure, and financing of the government budget. But to hold simply that we ought to "balance the budget" provides more confusion than guidance. One step toward clarity in the area of government finance is to note that, in a real and significant sense, the budget always balances.

On Chewing Gum and Understanding Deficits

✍✍✍✍

The federal government deficit is a common cause for consternation. Politicians, editorial writers, and such find it convenient to pose as born-again budget-balancers. Big deficits, they proclaim, will stifle economic growth, mainly, it seems, because deficits must generate high interest rates. In so saying, they falsify history and bastardize analysis. To the extent that their problem is not one of integrity, their performance may stem from trying to think while chewing gum.

Consider some selected points.

First, on the one hand, there has been very *little* correlation between current or anticipated federal deficits and inflation or interest rates. On the other hand, the correlation is *large* between the money supply and inflation, and between inflation and interest rates. The major linkage is from money to prices to interest rates — *not* from deficits to interest rates.

Second, a deficit must be either *financed* or *eliminated* — but it matters much how either strategy is carried out. *Financing* the deficit requires government to borrow. But government may borrow already existing money from the public or borrow newly created money from the banking system. And what happens to inflation and interest rates, be it remembered, is determined most basically by what happens to the amount of money. *Eliminating* the deficit requires greater tax collections or reduced rate of increase of government expenditures. But saving and investment, productivity, and output will be affected by *which* taxes and expenditures are changed by how much. The grubby details of the particular taxes and expenditures will be more significant than what happens to the summary deficit.

Third, psychologically, one would not *expect* to find, and, historically, one *does* not find, that increases in tax receipts lead to reductions in deficits. Commonly, more taxes have meant more spending instead of a smaller deficit. As economist David Meiselman observes, over-eagerness to balance the budget has made fiscal conservatives mere tax collectors for Congressional spenders.

Fourth, even if — to the astonishment of all — increasing taxes closed the budget gap and then kept pace with spending, the major fiscal problem would not be resolved. For the real budgetary burden of government, the real issue of government "crowding-out" private users of our scarce resources, is reflected in the *size*, not the *imbalance*, of the budget. And the *size* of the budget is measured by government *spending*, which, even in proclaimed days of "bare-boned austerity," consistently continues to surge to ever more rarified heights. Government spending itself *is* a tax, for it shifts resources from private use to the government sector. And the government sector is not notorious for using resources well.

If they would stop their gum-chewing and think real hard, these are some of the things politicians would be tempted to admit in public.

The Indirect Harm Done By Deficits

ØØØØ

Jungle instinct suggests difficulties with big, continuing government deficits. But it is not easy to pin down precisely *what* those problems are. Some argue that, under circumstances and on the basis of assumptions they deem likely and plausible, it makes *no* direct, immediate difference whether government spending is financed by taxes or by borrowing. Even if that is the case, everyone would still agree that the running of big deficits would have *some* repercussions.

Things like consumption and interest rates may be little affected by deficits, but there would be unplanned redistribution of income. For people do not hold government bonds in the same pattern they pay taxes — almost everyone pays taxes, but some get no government interest while others hold disproportionately large amounts of bonds and receive much interest.

The difficulties with deficits go further than income redistribution, largely because many *believe* that, somehow, in some way, it *does* matter whether a given rate of government spending is financed by government collecting taxes or by government borrowing through selling bonds. At least, government types obviously believe that their constituents believe that it makes a difference, for congressmen keep spending more than they tax — and voters keep re-electing the congressmen. Financing government spending by government borrowing is widely perceived to be economically less costly to citizens than financing by taxing. And if the supposed political costs to politicians of spending is reduced by borrowing, we can expect increased spending and thus continued transfer of resources out of the relatively efficient private sector into the more wasteful government sector.

Bigger *deficits* certainly have been associated over the past thirty years with greater government *spending* relative to GNP. In 1960, we had a small surplus, and for 1960-62, the ratio of budgetary deficit to government spending was not much more than 3 percent. In 1991, the ratio of deficit to spending was over 20 percent. Meanwhile, government spending relative to GNP rose by one-third. And, in turn, it was this large, persistent growth of *spending* which created the monumental deficits beginning in 1975, for *tax revenue* as a proportion of GNP did not fall, but actually rose moderately.

So, concludes economist Dwight R. Lee, deficits themselves have "little direct economic effect," but a debilitating "economic environment ... is created when politicians face little resistance to relying on deficit financing. The move to such an environment increases the control politicians have over productive resources, reduces the responsibility imposed on them in exercising that control, and, as a consequence, diminishes the productivity of our economy."

Deficits themselves may not harm us much directly, but they do harm indirectly by making it easier for politicians to spend too much.

The Tax Pen Writes Red

✍✍✍✍

The red ink is still spilling in Washington. Even so, the annual budget deficit has dropped more than $65 billion since 1986. And as a fraction of GNP, it has fallen to about the same relative size of the late 1970s.

Still, on Capitol Hill the tax bugle blows the same flat note: taxes must be raised to reduce the deficit. Even corporate chiefs want President Bush to forget his pledge of no new taxes. In its poll of chief executive officers, *Fortune* magazine finds 68 percent of them agreeing that taxes or user fees should be increased to reduce the budget deficit.

But would higher taxes really accomplish this objective? Or would the additional receipts only fuel more spending? It is no secret that Congress is itching to throw more money at child care, health care, housing, education, highways, and other programs. With new revenues, Congress might indulge in a still bigger spending binge. In that case, federal outlays could rise more than the additional tax revenue, resulting in a bigger, not smaller, deficit.

So what will Congress do if it gets its hands on more tax receipts? An answer is suggested by reviewing its track record. Consider the period, 1960-88. During this time, red ink flowed in all but two years. And with the exceptions of 1971 and 1983, tax receipts went up every year. But when tax receipts increased in a given year, Congress has *not* used the additional funds to reduce the deficit in the next: More than two-thirds of the time, bigger tax revenues in one year are *not* tracked by deficit reductions the next year. Indeed, there is a strong association between relatively *large* tax increases in one year and increases in the deficit in the following year. Fifteen times in the last three decades government receipts have risen more than 10 percent in one year, and in thirteen of the fifteen instances the budget deficit *increased* in the following year.

More taxes have not produced lower deficits. Instead, more taxes commonly have been immediately followed by spending increases greater than the revenue increases, with the deficit rising.

Given this record, current pleas for higher taxes look more like a ruse for increasing federal spending. More taxes would then stake Congress so it can continue to fatten the special interests which lobby fiercely for government largess. The distribution of largess through redistribution of income has become the main business of Congress. It would be contrary to its character and history for Congress to restrain spending in the presence of tempting new taxes.

We ought to pay less attention to what members of Congress say and more to what they have done. And what they have done is tax and spend. If taxes are raised, Congress will very likely spend the additional revenue — and something more — rather than reduce the deficit. Just look at the record: the congressional tax pen usually writes red.

The Budget and Economic Performance

Medical and Fiscal Prescriptions

ΔΔΔΔ

An article in *The Journal of the American Medical Association* documents the slowness of even medical authorities to adopt improved modes of treatment. Many years can pass before patient care catches up with conclusive clinical evidence — and thousands of lives are lost in the lag.

Medicine is not the only area in which many are slow to reject what hurts and accept policy stances which could do better. Even economists have been known to continue stubbornly to ride hobby horses which were born lame.

So-called fiscal policy is a striking case. In recent months, we have heard the old rallying cry: "Lets's get fiscal!" But even among the criers there is confusion to the point of chaos over what is meant and intended by "getting fiscal."

The basic tools of fiscal policy are government spending, taxing, and borrowing. But why and how to use those tools? Is the focus to be short-term anti-recession policy or long-term revamping of the foundations of the economy? How much are we to spend and how quickly and on what? And how are the massive funds involved to be raised? Does government borrow or tax? Borrow from or tax whom?

Proponents of "active" fiscal policy commonly concede that this would involve *more* government spending, not merely a redirection of spending; and the budget deficit would be *bigger* even if some of the new spending is balanced by further reduction in national defense.

For two generations we have been told of the stimulative effects of injecting more government spending into the income stream. But government spending now absorbs and channels nearly one-fourth of our national income, and the deficit continues to set records as it approaches $400 billion. If huge spending and exploding deficits are highly effective in stimulating the economy, why aren't we prospering?

Consider the record since 1960, when the budget was balanced and the ratio of government spending to national income was much smaller than it is today.

More times than not over these 30-odd years, government spending and the economy's output moved in *opposite* directions. Production increased most in years of relatively *small* increase in spending, and production commonly suffered when spending was *large*. In 1975, spending ballooned by more than 23 percent, and output change was actually *negative*; in 1980, spending soared by over 17 percent, and again output *fell*.

To take longer periods, from 1962-66, government spending rose at a moderate annual average of 6.7 percent, and national output expanded at a robust rate of 5.3 percent. In contrast, from 1975-81, spending galloped ahead at a horrendous 14.2 percent per year, and output growth was a discouraging 2.5 percent.

If big and expanding government spending would make us rich, we would be rich. But we aren't.

Budgets, Deficits, and Economic Performance

✍✍✍✍

There is this Sunday television discussion program. As such things go, it is quite a good show. But the regular participants and most of the guests are specialists in *politics*. This is a problem, for national politics and policies are heavily connected with *economics*. And political sorts commonly are not very good economists.

A recent session on the federal budget and its deficit was sanctimoniously summed up with the crack, "We must start to pay for what we get." That sounds puritanically proper. But what does it mean?

Who are *we*, and have we been getting things without *paying?* *Government* pays for what it gets. And the funds with which payment is made come from nominal taxation of and borrowing from the *community*.

With a given pie, when government buys more resources or products, less is left for the rest of the community. This sequestration of private wealth — whether or not government does good things well with what it takes — *is* taxation, regardless of the financial procedures by which it obtains the dollars it spends. The government does pay for what it gets, and the community gives up what government gets. Government borrowing (instead of explicitly taxing) does not mean that we have managed to delay payment. When government spends now, it is, in reality, taxing now.

For Senator Snort and television philosophers, the sum of good public finance is: balance the budget — with the proviso that the balancing be by raising tax collections still more, not by curtailing the increase in spending.

This is sophomoric economics. First, the *size* of the budget is vastly more important than the *imbalance* of the budget — and the size

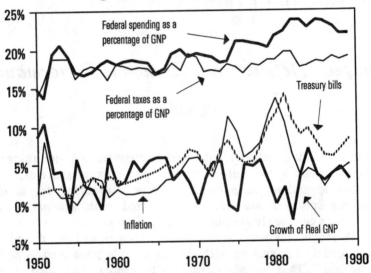

The Budget and the Economy, 1950-1989

Note: As federal spending rose from an average of 17.9% of GNP in the 1950s and '60s to 21.2% in the 1970s and '80s, the average yearly growth of real GNP fell from 3.83% to 2.75%. The average rate of consumer price inflation also increased from 2.22% to 6.32%, and the return on 3-month Treasury bills increased from 3% to 7.59%.

Source: *Economic Report of the President*, February 1990.

is measured by *spending*. Second, the simple prescription of balancing the budget tells us nothing of the *nature* of taxes or the *direction* of spending — or government-imposed *mandates* which do not show up in the budget. Third, the budget-balancing prescription ignores how well the economy has *performed* with budgets and deficits of different sizes.

In the decade of the 1950s, the budget was close to balanced, and the deficit was not large in the ˙60s. The deficit became conspicuous in the 1970s, and then, relative to GNP, it doubled in the ˙80s. The deficit did not rise because of tax starvation. As a proportion of GNP, government revenue in the 1980s was 10 percent larger than in the ˙50s; but spending was over 30 percent greater.

Our problem has been the growing *size* of the budget. And as government spending rose each decade, the rate of national output growth fell significantly, and the rate of inflation and interest rates in the 1970s and ˙80s were much greater than in the 1950s and ˙60s.

Big government budgets — that is, much spending — have hurt our economy. Spending relative to GNP hit a peak in 1985. Further containment of spending not only will help the economy, it will, as a bonus, correct the deficit.

O, Deficit, Where Is Thy Sting?

✍✍✍✍

There has been much concern and heartburn over "the government deficit." Few have a kind word for the historically huge deficits beginning in 1975. But while it is generally deemed unseemly to applaud the deficit, it is well to wonder why we should be so apprehensive about it.

Even the quantitative dimensions of the annual deficits and the accumulated debt are obscure, and analytic deductions are commonly confused.

For one thing, the feds are not the total government. There are states and cities. And there has been a combined state-and-local *surplus* every year since 1967. From 1983-88, that average annual surplus was equal to about one-third of the federal deficit. So the total government deficit has been only some 60-70 percent as large as the federal deficit.

There are many additional considerations, more subtle and harder to measure Government accounting does not distinguish between budgeted consumption and investment, between current and capital costs. And if appropriate account were taken also of inflation in valuing assets and obligations, the government debt — like the net international debt of the nation — might be eliminated.

Even if we were to get the numbers straight, there would remain much to figure out in assessing the impact of government spending and taxing — along with government regulating and mandating — on how the community uses its resources. And if, after all this, we were to conclude that there is a deficit to be reduced, there would be awesome questions of how best to do the reducing.

Politicians and journalists are not obsessed by such complications. What *are* their budgetary concerns? Well, it has been often claimed that large, persisting, and unanticipated deficits, as conventionally defined and measured, increase both interest rates and the price level — and higher interest and inflation rates hurt our domestic output and balance of payments.

Does the record show deficits associated with rising interest rates and prices? Over the past two decades, it shows quite the opposite! In every substantial change in the deficit — up or down — the rate of 3-month Treasury bills and the change in the Consumer Price Index moved in the *other* direction. Most notably, from 1980-81 to 1986, the annual deficit *rose* spectacularly from $74 billion to $221 billion; but during that period the interest rate *fell* from 14 percent to 6 percent, and the inflation rate *fell* from over 13 percent to 2 percent.

Year to year, the deficit and changes in the price level moved in the same direction only three times in the twenty instances; the deficit and the interest rate moved together just four times. By contrast, price level changes and the interest rate rose and fell together seventeen times.

Not only have deficits generally not led to inflation, but inflation generally has not accompanied prosperity. Periods of high national output — as around the turn of the century, the Roaring Twenties, the late 1950s and early '60s, the 1980s — have had very low or even slightly negative inflation; and when we have had roaring inflation — as in the 1970s — there has been puny production.

While changes in inflation have understandably had much effect on interest rates, changes in the deficit have *not* been accompanied by similar changes in interest rates and inflation. O, deficit, where is thy sting?

National Defense

Peace, Prosperity, and Politics

ঙঙঙঙ

Possibly promising changes in the Soviet Union and Eastern Europe are producing plans for scaled-down United States defense spending. The Secretary of Defense has suggested cuts of $180 billion over the three budget years beginning in 1992. What then would be in store for our economy?

The answer depends partly on how the diverted funds and resources are used. Defense reductions could shrink total federal spending and the budget deficit. The government would command fewer of the nation's resources, and private individuals would command more. But big public spenders are already drooling over prospects of a so-called peace dividend. They want more dollars for government-provided health insurance, child care, and housing. And there are regional constituencies to please by delivering federal money for construction and repair of roads, bridges, parks, and such.

Getting their hands on defense dollars would be a dream come true for those who perpetually prowl around the military budget like wolves around sheep. They have sometimes been successful. Real spending on the military actually declined during the 1970s. Expenditures for defense fell from 8.4 percent of GNP in the 1960s to 5.8 percent in the '70s. As a fraction of the federal budget, defense dropped from 44 percent in the '60s to less than 28 percent in the '70s.

This proportional reduction in defense spending from the 1960s to the '70s was much greater than what is now proposed. If the ratio of defense spending to GNP had been as large in the '70s as in the '60s, such spending would have been $47 billion more per year. That $47 billion cut is nearly 3 percent of the average annual GNP of the 1970s. In comparison, the $180 billion total cut in 1992-94 would be less than 1 percent of anticipated total GNP in those three years.

But the large defense cuts of the '70s did not mean more dollars to spend by American taxpayers. Despite scaled-down *defense* spending, *total* federal spending still *rose*, from an average of 19.2 percent of GNP in the 1960s to 21 percent in the '70s. And what did we get for the padded diversion of funds from the military to other government spending? Hardly a robust economy: during the '70s, productivity growth declined, inflation soared, unemployment rose, and output expansion was modest.

Evidently, if defense spending is reduced, the result will not necessarily be a healthier economy — even if we survive the security gamble. First, even a large proportional cut in the defense budget represents only a small part of national output. Second, that modest diversion of output to nondefense uses may or may not be used well. The experience of the 1970s is not highly encouraging.

The "Peace Dividend": Growth and Budget-Cutting

♨♨♨♨

Events in Eastern Europe and the Soviet Union suggest enhanced prospects of peace. So our defense budget is to be reduced. The cut in defense spending supposedly will provide a "peace dividend" of ever so many tens of billions of dollars for government to spend on ever so many splendid social projects.

Reducing the defense slice of the national output pie correspondingly increases the remainder of the pie available for other uses. There will inevitably be many competing uses for this dividend of greater nondefense output. What are the probable dimensions of the dividend?

We can acquire a dividend over time simply by holding real defense spending *constant* while the economy grows. Suppose output grows at a modest annual rate of 2.5 percent over the next five years. Defense purchases of goods and services amounted to 6.2 percent of GNP in 1989; those *same* real expenditures would be just 5.5 percent of the larger GNP in 1994.

This seemingly small fall in the defense proportion of output and associated increase in nondefense uses of output yield a "growth dividend" of $544 billion (measured in 1982 prices) in 1994 over 1989. This increase in real nondefense output — even while annual real defense output is unchanged — is a considerable 14 percent.

Indeed, this growth dividend is more than twice the defense spending of 1989 — and defense spending is not going to be reduced to zero. Suggested cuts in the real defense budget commonly have ranged between 10 and 25 percent over five years — that is, annual reductions of 2 to 6 percent.

A five-year real reduction in defense by 10 percent would mean an additional increase in nondefense output of only $26 billion: the "defense-cut dividend" would be less than 5 percent as large as the growth dividend. Even a defense reduction of a whopping 25 percent would add a defense-cut dividend of just $64 billion to the growth dividend of $544 billion.

Growth Dividend and Defense-Cut Dividend With Alternate Percentage Reductions in Defense Spending, 1989–1994

Billions of dollars

		1994		
	1989	0%	-10%	-25%
Real GNP	$4,140	$4,684	$4,684	$4,684
Defense	258	258	232	194
Nondefense	3,882	4,426	4,452	4,490
Growth dividend	--	**544**	**544**	**544**
Defense-cut dividend	--	**0**	**26**	**64**
Defense/GNP	6.2%	5.5%	5.0%	4.1%

Note: Assumed annual growth of real GNP is 2.5% for 1989-94. Real GNP is measured in 1982 prices.

Source: *Economic Indicators*, November 1989.

While the defense-cut dividend is relatively small potatoes, a 10 percent reduction in defense would reduce the ratio of defense to GNP to just under 5 percent; a 25 percent reduction would mean defense spending of barely over 4 percent of GNP. For comparison, note that the defense/GNP ratio in the late 1940s was a near-disastrously low 4.6 percent.

We can generate a considerable dividend by holding real defense spending constant as GNP grows. We can add marginally to the dividend by seriously cutting defense. But no attainable dividend — presumably only a fractional part of which would go to government — will make feasible a vast expansion of social programs. It will remain a world of scarcity.

Taxation: Costs and Consequences

A Tale of Tax Cuts

ₔₔₔₔ

Listen to politicians clamoring for federal tax cuts. What should we make of the commotion?

Shakespeare offered a clue. Life, he wrote, "struts and frets [its] hour upon the stage" — as some now parade upon the political stage and fret about tax cuts to spur the economy. Shakespeare also alluded to "a tale told by an idiot, full of sound and fury, signifying nothing."

The unfolding tale of tax cuts certainly is full of sound and fury. But does it signify nothing?

Politicians tell us that a tax cut would put life into our listless economy. But none of the plans can change taxes right *now*. Proposals must be concocted and submitted, and then wind their way through the labyrinth of Congress. If a bill survives the tortuous process of review, debate, and compromise, it would become law only far in the future.

Then, there is further delay. If the tax law is capable of stimulating the economy — and that is a big if — the full effect would not be felt until well after Congress passed the law. A tax cut may allow us to keep and spend more of our incomes, but we must first earn the income and then decide whether and how to spend it. Still more time must pass for an initial spending spurt to ripple through the economy.

When all these delays and lags are combined, many months will have passed since the tax cut was proposed. And by then inflation, not recession, could be the political preoccupation. If so, statesmen will be fretting about a tax hike.

Indeed, aren't we witnessing a tactical reversal now? After silencing lips that were mouthing "no new taxes," Congress and the President got a whopping increase in taxes in 1990. Now, the higher taxes are helping to dampen an already tired economy for which politicians want — you guessed it — lower taxes.

Lower taxes basically are a fine idea. Reducing the government proportion of absorption of national income reduces waste, on the one hand, and strengthens production incentives, on the other. Rates which are permanently reduced encourage and direct us to work, save, and take risks. Individuals, not governments, produce wealth. And we produce more when tax rates don't sap incentives, squander resources, and misdirect effort.

The lesson of lower taxes has been spreading throughout the world. But politicians here just don't get the distinction between improving the *long-term* context of productive activity and *short-term* fine-tuning. Minimal taxes are a splendid *strategy*; tinkering with taxes is a terrible *tactic*.

Why, then, the current sound and fury about lower taxes? Next year is an election year, so it is again time to woo voters with empty promises of more for less. Shakespeare was suggestive. This latest tale of tax cut talk signifies nothing positive for our economy.

Taxing Costs

✍✍✍✍

The federal government costs a lot. But the most expensive government program is not Medicare or even defense. And the bulk of the cost of that program does not show up explicitly in the federal budget. The most expensive program by far is the tax system — the way government collects taxes and the repercussions of the collection.

For 1990, the budget listed $6 billion for the Internal Revenue Service and related tax-collection units, but analyst James L. Payne makes clear that this is only a piddling part of the total costs of the federal tax system: The costs of government taking other people's money.

The largest component of such costs is economic disincentive effects. Whether or not by design, Mr. Payne reminds us, "every tax amounts to a penalty for engaging in the activity being taxed." Taxes on labor, corporations, and capital investment reduce work, innovation, and investment. Various studies suggest that the disincentives associated with raising one more dollar of revenue will reduce output worth about 33 cents. This reduction of production amounts to well over $300 billion a year.

Another huge category of cost, along with heartburn and trauma, is generated by individual and business compliance with tax laws. Conservative estimates indicate some 5.5 billion hours (the equivalent of close to 3 million people working full-time) are annually spent in taxation paperwork. This compliance cost comes to over $230 billion.

Disincentive and compliance costs, along with the budgeted expenses of the tax collectors, are not the whole of the burden on society. There are also costs of tax enforcement, including audits and identifying of under-reporters and non-filers — activities made even more onerous by IRS errors in a huge proportion of cases. There is the sprawling area of filing penalties, surveillance, and litigation, with convoluted law often enforced with confusion and carelessness. The greater the tax load, the greater the attempts to avoid, if not to evade, payments, and these efforts entail still more expense and lost production. All these additional burdens amount to perhaps $65 billion.

Total costs of the tax-collection system thus added up to around $620 billion in 1990. This is equal to over 60 percent of total government receipts. So when government takes from the community a dollar in taxes, the cost to the community is not $1 but more than $1.60.

All this is more than just getting the social accounting straight. It questions the very logic of government spending programs. A project may look good on benefit/cost grounds when the benefit is valued at least as much as $1 when the seeming tax cost is $1. But it is a lousy deal when the complete tax cost really is $1.60.

Government, it turns out, is very expensive; and many government deals are lousy.

Prices and Taxes

ᴂᴂᴂᴂ

"Taxes are what we pay for civilized society," observed Oliver Wendell Holmes in an era of very low taxation. But more taxes do not necessarily produce more civility. Nor do higher tax *rates* necessarily provide more government *revenue*.

For higher taxes are like higher prices: they affect the way people behave. Take the rental car industry. Hertz and other companies had announced the biggest rate increases in years. But consumers rented too few cars at the higher prices. When companies realized they were making less money at the new rates, prices tumbled back toward their original levels.

Similarly, government can receive fewer tax revenues by charging higher income tax rates for its services. Economist David R. Henderson reviews the growing body of evidence that higher tax rates can reduce total tax collections by affecting incentives to work and to avoid taxes. He reports that tax changes have the most impact on individuals paying the top rate.

That impact is not surprising, for a proportionate change in all tax rates *disproportionately* affects incentives of higher-income taxpayers. A 10 percent rate increase allows someone initially in a 50 percent bracket to keep 45, instead of 50 cents, of an additional dollar earned. The loss of 5 cents — which is 10 percent of the original 50 cents kept by the taxpayer — appreciably increases incentives for tax avoidance and leisure. For someone in the 20 percent bracket, however, the same 10 percent rate hike reduces the after-tax earnings of a dollar from 80 to 78 cents, a reduction of only 2.5 percent. In this later case, the incentive to avoid taxes or earn fewer dollars rises much less than for the taxpayer in the higher tax bracket.

If the top rate rises sufficiently, it can so magnify incentives for tax avoidance and leisure that tax revenues actually fall. Various studies confirm this result. In the United States, a top rate of about 35 percent appears to come close to maximizing government revenues.

Other countries might have different rates which maximize their tax collections. Still, many government leaders seem to be learning that the road to greater revenues can be paved with lower, not higher, tax rates. *The Wall Street Journal* reports that 55 of 86 nations with income taxes have cut their top tax rates from an average of nearly 56 percent in 1985 to 47 percent in 1989. And here at home, government officials sooner or later will have to admit that higher income tax rates for *wealthy* individuals are unable to provide the additional funds they seek for more government spending or for a balanced federal budget.

So beware, *middle*-income taxpayers! If the expansion of government spending is not constrained, and if there is great pressure to balance the budget, then taxes on your *moderate* incomes are likely to rise.

Taxes: The Corporation, the Chairman, and the Community

ØØØØ

The bigger are marginal income tax rates, the more they misdirect both consumption and production. With heavier taxation, we produce less and use less well what we produce.

Following an illustration of Lawrence B. Lindsey, of Harvard University, consider a compensation tactic of a corporation and its chairman. Initially, let the marginal income tax be 70 percent, as it was in 1981.

The corporation can provide the chairman a Big Car each year, which costs $60,000. Or it can increase the chairman's salary by $200,000; the chairman would pay $140,000 in income tax and have $60,000 in take-home pay, with which he could buy his own Big Car. But $60,000 is less than $200,000, so the company pays the chairman the car instead of money salary.

Alternatively, the company could give the chairman a $30,000 Little Car and also a $30,000 salary increase. The chairman then pays $21,000 of his additional $30,000 salary to the tax collector, leaving him with an increase of $9,000 in take-home pay.

Does the chairman prefer a Big Car worth $60,000 or a Small Car worth $30,000 plus $9,000 cash? Only he can say. But he will be more likely to take an alternative package of a Small Car plus cash the lower is the tax rate.

Let the rate be only 30 percent, roughly what it is today. Now, the corporation provides the chairman with a $30,000 Small Car plus $30,000 additional income, as before. But, with the lower rate, the chairman pays only $9,000 in extra tax, leaving $21,000 as increased take-home pay. And he may well prefer a Small Car and $21,000 to a Big Car.

The corporation has a business expense of $60,000 in each case. The chairman cannot lose from a lower tax rate, and may deem himself better off. (Note that any increase in the chairman's *well-being* is smaller than the increase in *income*. Income rises by $30,000, but take-home pay is up only $21,000, and the gains from use of that take-home pay are at least partially offset by having a lesser car.)

The general economy does not lose from lowering the tax rate — although the Big Car company may have less business and other firms more. Indeed, the economy can *gain* if the chairman chooses the second option as a result of the low rate. First, the government gets more revenue as the chairman is now paid taxable income, and that can finance either a cut in other taxes or more government services. Second, we could expect some of the increased take-home pay of the chairman to be saved and invested, thereby increasing the economy's productivity.

High taxes distort. They encourage conspicuous consumption while discouraging production of stuff to consume. Government's power to tax is power to make us poorer.

Saving, Investing, and Growth

On the Meaning and Measurement of Saving

ØØØØ

Saving and investment — how much they are, what affects them, and their relation to economic growth — would seem to be a serious subject. Unhappily, there are big problems in *measurement* of saving and investment, in the conception of *what* we should *try* to measure, and in both domestic and international *comparisons* of measurements.

Saving is generally taken to be a residual, the difference between "income currently received and income currently consumed." So the measured amount of saving is determined by the measurements of income and consumption. If income is 100 and consumption is 95, then saving is 5. But if income is measured 1 percentage point too low and consumption 1 point too high, the saving residual is only 3 — 40 percent smaller than the real amount. Or if income is overestimated 1 percentage point and consumption is underestimated 1 point, nominal saving is 7 — 40 percent too big.

Aside from the mechanical problem of compiling the official data, what do we *want* to measure? Wild and crazy sorts live only for the moment, but most of us most of the time have some anticipation of, and make some plans for, the future. So we build factories, machines, houses, automobiles, computers, and other durable things; we go to school for training with long-term payoff; and we organize pension funds to finance retirement living.

All these future-looking, deferred-consumption uses of currently available resources would appear to be activities in the saving-and-investment game. But, in gathering data to measure such activities, some of that durable production (factories, equipment, and houses) is classified as investment financed by saving, and some (personal automobiles, computers, and education) is considered consumption, and money put into some pension funds is listed as saving but other pension money is not. Social Security contributions are a pay-as-we-go tax rather than funded savings — and anticipated Social Security benefits tend to reduce other forms of saving.

The saving, consumption, and investment measurements can be made in different ways. Certainly, the measurements are made variously in different countries. It is customary to say that the Japanese saving rate is several times the savings rate in the United States. Because of different definitions of saving, that differential is surely much exaggerated, and a respectable — even if minority — interpretation is that the Japanese rate of saving is actually smaller than the U.S. rate.

Even within the U.S., the Department of Commerce measures "personal saving" one way, and the Federal Reserve has been known to measure it differently. The alternative ways give roughly similar *changes* in the savings rate, but the Fed *level* has been much greater than the Commerce measurement.

We can agree that saving and investment are important. But that does not mean that it is easy to define and measure them or to understand their determinants.

Saving and Investment: Private, Public, Domestic, Foreign

✍✍✍✍

By conventional hair-shirt wisdom, Americans have a small savings rate which is getting smaller. Various explanations have been offered — in accusation or in apology — for our alleged "alarming" propensity to consume too much and save too little.

Perhaps we do not save much of current income because our stock market and housing assets have grown greatly. Perhaps the safety nets of Social Security and Medicare have reduced the pressure to save. The yuppie baby-boomers have not been big savers. Much of the resources devoted to future uses have not been officially classified as saving and investment.

Most such thought and talk pertains to the *personal* savings rate, which held steady in the 1950s and '60s, rose in the 1970s, and then fell considerably in the '80s. But there is also *business* saving, which is some three times greater; and business saving has risen a bit over the past four decades, especially since the early 1970s. So the rate of gross private saving — personal plus business — has been strikingly steady over the post World War II era.

In the 1980s, annual "gross private saving" has averaged nearly 17 percent of GNP, and "gross private domestic investment" has averaged nearly 16 percent. As with the savings rate, the investment ratio is virtually equal to the average for the whole period since 1950. But we are told by the keepers of the national income records that *private* saving and investment is not all that matters.

To obtain *total* "gross saving," the boys in the back room subtract the government budget deficit from the amount of private saving. This subtraction of the deficit from private saving makes gross saving appreciably smaller, and many have said that a major way to increase saving would be to balance the budget. A favorite proposal is to do so by raising taxes. But do we really improve the situation by having the public finance a certain amount of government spending by giving more dollars to government in taxes and correspondingly fewer dollars in purchase of government bonds? The channeling of current income into savings would be little affected simply by the community acquiring more tax receipts and fewer bonds.

Statisticians also modify the investment data. They subtract the inflow of foreign capital from private domestic investment to obtain "gross investment." The net inflow of capital from abroad accompanies an import balance of goods. One might suppose that foreign investment in the U.S. is more a supplement to than wholly a subtraction from domestic investment, especially since over half of current U.S. imports of merchandise consist of industrial supplies and capital goods.

Our saving and investment rates have not been either gradually falling or abruptly collapsing. And perhaps we cannot definitively say even that they have been too low: by reasonable criteria, they may have been just about right.

Gunfight at Narrowing Gap

∅∅∅∅

The world economy is intensely competitive, but is it a battlefield? Many see American producers squaring off against foreign competitors like Wyatt Earp and Doc Holiday confronting the bad guys at O.K. Corral. But this time, the bad guys are winning, and we can see the wounds inflicted at Narrowing Gap.

Narrowing Gap refers to the shrinking excess of U.S. output over foreign production. Reuven Glick of the Federal Reserve Bank of San Francisco reports that Germany's per-capita domestic output was only one-half of ours in 1950, but by 1988, it had risen above 80 percent. Similarly, Japan's per-capita production jumped from under 20 percent of ours in 1950 to nearly 60 percent in 1988. And France, Italy, and the United Kingdom, too, have made substantial gains.

So the difference between higher U.S. per-capita production and that of other nations has narrowed considerably over the last 40 years. But that news is good, not bad, for the narrowing gap is due to rising world prosperity — a prosperity we have conspicuously shared.

Mr. Glick reports that other nations have not gained on us because our production has lagged behind our historical average. Indeed, during the '60s, '70s, and '80s, growth of the U.S. economy was a bit better than its average from 1919 to 1960.

Other nations have gained because their economies have grown somewhat faster than ours. But most of the foreign growth surge came in the 1950s and '60s. Nations devastated by World War II experienced extraordinary "catch-up" growth as they rebuilt their economies with modern technology. Between 1950 and 1973, yearly growth of Japan's real domestic production averaged about 9 percent. Germany's averaged more than 8 percent in the 1950s and more than 4 percent in the 1960s.

But the relatively high growth rates began to diminish in the 1970s. Then in the '80s, growth of our domestic production generally equaled or exceeded that of Japan, Germany, and other nations. True, a recession in the early 1980s caused real output to tumble in the United States. But from 1983 to 1989, the U.S. economy grew by 3.8 percent per year, while yearly growth averaged only 3.1 percent for Germany, Japan, France, and the United Kingdom.

"This does not imply that current or recent past rates of U.S. output growth are the highest that can be achieved," explains Mr. Glick. "However, it does suggest that U.S. performance through the 1980s has not displayed any evidence of long-term output growth slowdown." Economic competition among people of different nations is not a gunfight where winners gain by plugging losers. Instead, gains come from producing much for each other and making the world more prosperous.

Unemployment

Diddling With Data

❦❦❦❦

There is vastly more to economic analysis than counting things and comparing numbers. Measurement is at places vital in identifying the sizes and shapes of problems and in deducing what might best be done about them. But tools can be used badly and for inappropriate purposes. There are those anxious to diddle with data, not to comprehend the world, but to promote a political purpose.

The calculation of the employment rate provides illustration. The unemployment rate is simply the ratio of the number unemployed to the number in the work force. But the measurement of that ratio is inherently tricky and tenuous, involving not only estimates, but also preferences of the people involved.

Who is in the labor force? We include everyone within an age range who has a job or who supposedly wants a job and is seeking one. In measuring unemployment, we do not count those not looking for work. And some who are not working but would like a job have given up looking. But when they are so discouraged about finding employment that they give up, they are no longer participating in the labor force: The dropout reduces both the measured labor force and the number officially unemployed, making the calculated unemployment rate smaller than before.

There are journalists and politicians who make much of this reduction in the official unemployment rate by discouraged dropouts. A *New York Times* report acknowledges that the number of those who have given up seeking work is "unknown," but somehow guesses that it is "perhaps more than a million." If we correct our calculations by quite arbitrarily adding 1 million to both the labor force and to the number of unemployed, then the unemployment rate would be raised by about 0.7 percent.

So the true state of unemployment is somewhat camouflaged by our pretending that dropouts are not there. But the long newspaper account says nothing about another accounting quirk with opposite impact: the bloating of both the labor force and the number unemployed by those who pretend to want a job but actually will not accept work. No one denies that there are people who officially but falsely state that they are looking for work in order to be eligible for unemployment and other welfare benefits. And through padding the reported size of the labor force and thus of the number considered unemployed, the determined unemployment rate is made too big.

But some find it politically convenient to make things look as bad as possible. While failing to note the welfare-seekers who deviously make the unemployment rate larger than it is, the story puts some emphasis on those who are employed but allegedly are "on the edge of unemployment, ... facing the hardships and insecurity of the jobless." "Probably ... more than 3 million" temporary, part-time, free-lance, and underpaid workers, the paper suggests, really ought to be considered unemployed. Thus goes the dubious diddling with data in an election year.

Government and the Conditions of Employment

✍✍✍✍

What prerequisites and circumstances are required for would-be workers to find work?

To be hired, (a) people must *have* something to sell, (b) they must *want* to sell what they have to offer, (c) they must be *permitted* to sell what they have to offer, (d) they must be occupationally and geographically *mobile*, and (e) there must be *demand* for their services.

A worker sells productivity, labor of mind and body. If he can contribute much input which the community much desires, he will be valuable to employers and can sell his labor at a high price. With only modest talent, poor training, and limited experience, he can offer little of value.

In any game of performance and productivity, even with uncommon talent and coaching, much turns on energy and ambition, commitment and discipline, initiative and reliability of the players. Character, molded by and reflecting the customs of the community, is critical.

Some are priced out of the labor market by imposed minimum-wages, and some are kept out by union restrictions on them and by mandated preferences for others.

Few jobs come to the worker: the worker must go to the market. And, over time, he may have to adjust to changes in the market, moving to another employer in a different location or a different kind of business. Those who will not adapt to an ever-evolving economy will be displaced and not easily reabsorbed.

Finally, employment is a matter of demand as well as supply. And demand turns on myriad considerations affecting perceptions of the present and prospects of the future. Employers do not hire for the thrill of the activity. They must use resources carefully in producing items which may be attractive to buyers. And they can sensibly and systematically plan and produce only within a predictable context of a stable price level, rational regulation, and readily manageable taxation.

The contribution of government to all this is enormous. Unhappily, the governmental contribution is commonly of negative value. Government — eager to intervene and slow to learn — has discovered more ways to hamper than to promote productive employment.

At every link in the employment chain, government has subsidized ineptitude and inefficiency. Big Brother has educated miserably in the public schools, destroyed families and work incentives with crazy-quilt welfare, reduced options and curtailed trade between employer and worker, subsidized immobility by increasing the costs of adjustment by both workers and employers, and distorted demand which has been made smaller and more erratic than it could have been.

And yet, Senator Snort, instead of learning from predictable mistakes and belatedly admitting error, with no economic analysis and much sloganeering demagoguery, continues stubbornly to call for still more foolishness, financing still more waste with a still greater budget.

Impoverishment Through Plenty: Historians and the Depression

ssss

In his book, *Coolidge and the Historians*, Thomas Silver makes it depressingly clear that partisan history can be a weapon in a war of ideology. Perverted scholarship is the more reprehensible when directed against the innocent young.

A well-known high school history textbook explains the Great Depression of the 1930s. The world abruptly became poor, we are told, because the United States produced too much. Having "mastered the problems of production," American manufacturers could not "find the mass markets for the goods they had contrived to spew forth in such profusion." "The nation's ability to produce goods," the textbook tells us, "had clearly outrun its capacity to consume or pay for them."

The historians surely do not really mean that we had become so productive that we could not *consume* all our output. But why could we not *pay* for it? The answer: "Too much money was going into the hands of a few wealthy people, who in turn invested it in factories .... Not enough was going into salaries and wages ...."

The silly thesis that we suddenly produced ourselves into poverty did not originate with the textbook authors. They were repeating mythology perpetrated by luminaries of the historians' fraternity, sensitive scholars preoccupied with the wickedness of wealth.

Dr. Silver documents some of the errors of the story-tellers.

One, it is held that monetary policy of the 1920s accelerated inflation and fueled speculation. Actually, the amount of money rose very little in the '20s with the price level *declining* a bit.

Two, supposedly, tax cuts vastly aided the rich and hurt the poor, stimulating a speculative craze and leading to over-saving. Actually, the *individual* income tax cut came some four years before the major stock market surge; it was a minute reduction overall, with taxes paid by the very wealthy increasing enormously and those paid by the bulk of the population almost eliminated; and the *corporate* tax was *increased*.

Three, income was purportedly becoming more and more maldistributed in favor of the wealthy. Actually, over those few years, there was virtually no change in the proportion of national income received by the wealthiest segment of the community. Following three decades in which real wages increased very slowly, they expanded greatly — while profits rose only moderately — during the decade following World War I.

Finally, the alleged over-saving and over-investing by the wealthy was accompanied by deficient consumption by the poor and thus failure to absorb all of the increasing output. Actually, consumption expanded steadily and did *not* decline as a proportion of growing gross national product.

The scholars are guilty of simple-minded use of badly selected, and sometimes invented, scraps of evidence. Such a pattern of performance is consistent with — and thus inexorably suggests — a bias which is deliberately devious.

Health Care, Welfare, and Assistance

A Prescription for Healthy Health-Care

ØØØØ

Some politicians suppose — and hope — that we are stupid. They are counting on our buying the argument that socialism is the answer to the high cost of health care.

True, we worry about rapidly-rising medical costs. But we are not persuaded by political promises that the burden will be shifted from middle-income people. After all, most of us fall into that group. Together, we middle sorts earn most of the income, pay most of the taxes, buy most of the output, and use most of the medical services. So we know that no scheme of political redistribution can shift the costs of health care from middle-income Americans to others, who are not sufficiently numerous to earn sufficient income to pay the tab.

We could foolishly confiscate the income of all filthy rich types and recklessly tax away every dollar of grubby corporate profits. But even then we would not come close to paying the health bills of the middle class. We cannot afford through government what we cannot collectively afford on our own.

So nationalizing the medical industry cannot ease the burden on middle-income people by shifting the cost to other citizens. The only way to ease the burden is by reducing the cost of health care by making its production more efficient. And the only way to do that is by getting socialism out of the health-care industry and putting market incentives and calculations back into it.

Milton Friedman, a Nobel laureate in economics, suggests two significant steps to accomplish this objective of efficiency. First, replace the socialism of Medicare and Medicaid with a requirement that every family have a major medical insurance policy with a large deductible. Government would help low-income families buy the insurance, and would allow other families to deduct their premiums from income taxes. People could also buy tax-deductible supplementary insurance. These changes would cut health-care costs — and associated taxes — by eliminating the massive government bureaucracy that now supervises nearly every nook and cranny of the industry.

His second recommendation is to make employer-provided health insurance a fully-taxable fringe benefit. If we eliminate the current tax bias in favor of employer-provided insurance, employees would then bargain for less medical insurance and more take-home pay. With more take-home pay, they could finance their own medical insurance and health care. As a result, they would take a bigger, more responsible role in doing what they do better than employers: making sure that health-care providers efficiently serve their personal interests.

With these reforms, claims Dr. Friedman, "the demonstrated efficiency of private enterprise would have a chance to operate to improve the quality and lower the cost of medical care."

But don't hold your breath waiting for politicians to prescribe private enterprise for health care. They are more likely to cite clumsy, costly socialism as the remedy for, not the cause of, the disease.

Welfare and Wisdom

⌀⌀⌀⌀

There are major problems with welfare programs. The problems pertain to both conception of the program and its administration. How *much* aid should be given to *whom* for how *long* in what *form* for what basic *purpose*? How can the aid be given with minimum dilution of incentive to seek employment? And can the aid be given with little bureaucratic expense and with little fraud by either dispensers or recipients of the aid?

Ideally, all those physically and mentally capable of contributing to the social output will appropriately do so if they are to receive rewards. And we all are to be prudent and reliable, meeting family responsibilities, spending wisely today and saving for other expenditures tomorrow, while producing efficiently.

Alas, we commonly fall short of ideal attitude and activity. We sinners in search of heaven are to reach further than our grasp. But sometimes we do not reach even as far as we could grasp. And welfare officials are not always angelic.

The Wall Street Journal recounts a sobering story of welfare. The story is one of prudence and responsibility being penalized.

A single woman with a young daughter has been receiving $500 a month in aid, $440 of it in cash. With much effort, cleverness, attention to detail — and dreams of a better future, including college for her child — the woman managed to save a few dollars. Indeed, over several years, she accumulated more than $1,000 in a savings account.

Many might say that such thrift was both remarkable and commendable. Some did say that it should be punished.

Big Brother, in his wisdom and sensitivity, decreed in the program of Aid to Families with Dependent Children that welfare recipients are not to be allowed to hold savings above $1,000. The woman, in her shrewdness and commitment to a better future, had broken the law.

County officials charged her with fraud and demanded in court that she repay the more than $15,000 received in aid after her savings exceeded the limit of $1,000. The district attorney, wise beyond his years and full of the milk of human kindness, reduced the demand to $3,000. The judge, making it known that he considered this law to be absurd, reduced the fine to $1,000 — approximately the amount saved.

The law is, indeed, the law. But the welfare administrators defended not only the principle of abiding by laws in general, but also the spirit of this particular law. Evidently, only the relatively wealthy are to be forward-looking and encouraged to save, and the poor should be directed to live abjectly only for the moment; indeed, if anyone persists in saving more than minuscule amounts, evidently that person has no proper claim to aid.

We may presume, with generosity, that the welfare officials were pure in heart. But surely something went wrong. They did their formal duty, but, surely, this should not have been their duty.

Unemployment Compensation: The Short-Run and the Long-Run

ℐℐℐℐ

There are short-run problems and long-run problems. Short-run problems are the natural habitat of the politician, who loves to cry that the sky is falling and then try to appear heroic in saving us.

The distinction between short-run and long-run would not matter if the long-run were only a stringing together of short-runs. If easing the short-term problem invariably improved the long-run situation, we could afford to plan simply from day-to-day.

But life is not so simple. Some tactics to ease the pain of the moment can mess up long-run strategy. Indeed, some short-term tactics can worsen even our short-run situation. All this applies to the debate over how much and how long unemployment compensation should be provided in a recessionary economy.

Of course, a happy way to escape the difficulties of determining recession-policy is to avoid recession. But we have been reminded by analyst Herbert Stein that recurring recessions, like the relatively poor, will always be with us. It is not in the power of government either to avoid all recessions completely or to bring an incipient recession to an abrupt end.

But while there are imposing limits on what discretionary, interventionist policies can do to help, government has demonstrated ample aptitude for making a bad situation worse.

Unemployment compensation is an *unemployment* policy of sorts, but it is not an *employment*, or anti-recession, policy. Surely, no one would deny the humanitarian and compassionate aspects of providing some support for those who are temporarily unemployed and genuinely seek employment. But few seem to recognize — or to give perceptible weight to the recognition — that unemployment compensation is unemployment *subsidization*. And we generally get more of what we subsidize.

People like income, and they are not fools. To the extent that they are offered income without working, we provide inducement to delay seeking or accepting employment. Economist Alan Reynolds notes that "those who have supposedly been 'unable to find a job' in 26 weeks miraculously find one within a few weeks after their benefits run out." And economist Morgan O. Reynolds reminds us that "unemployment boils down to a question of pricing. ... Unemployment is a labor service offered at too high a price ...." And, in fact, the asking price for labor services offered drops dramatically when unemployment benefits are exhausted.

In all this, we have dilemmas of policy. Government can do little to eliminate wiggles in the level of economic activity, and it cannot quickly correct downturns, but it can intensify problems of recession and of inflation. It can soften the trouble and trauma of temporary unemployment, but those very efforts tend to widen and prolong unemployment. And excessive diddling and preoccupation with comforting constituents in the short-run can get in the way of sensible, market-oriented strategies which would promote wealth-creation over the long-run.

Social Security and Social Investing

Social Security "Trust Funds" and Deception

✍✍✍✍

The Social Security program for more than half a century has been a governmental con game. The shenanigans have been knowingly and sometimes admittedly shrouded in mystery and mythology.

The deception continues. In his State of the Union address, the President asserted that the Social Security "promise" would be kept. "We rescued the system in 1983 — and it's sound again," he proclaimed. Not only does "our budget fully fund today's benefits," but "it assures that future benefits will be funded as well." The assembled members of Congress roared approval. But the future is *not* funded.

In contrast to nurtured common misconception, Social Security is *not* a program of personally funded pensions. It is *not* a process of individuals accumulating their own retirement accounts.

Rather than a saving process of building retirement funds, the operation is inevitably consume-as-you-produce for the community as a whole and pay-as-you-go in financing retirement benefits. Indeed, since Social Security tax payments now are much greater than benefits dispersed, it is a pay-*more*-then-you-go scheme. Today's workers are *not* accumulating money which will be returned to them years later; instead, today's workers are paying taxes to finance benefits for today's retirees — and to finance other government spending, as well. Today's workers can only hope that when *they* are retired, the people *then* working will pay benefits to them.

The ballyhooed 1983 legislation provided for still higher tax rates and still higher levels to be taxed in order to build up a "reserve," a "trust fund," from which future benefits would be paid. But the intended secret is that there *is* no reserve being accumulated. There *will be* no reserve, no matter how great tax collections.

The surplus Social Security tax receipts are not spent in government purchases of stocks and bonds of productive businesses.

And economist Paul Craig Roberts notes that such purchases would entail massive socialization of the economy. Instead, as specified by law, the money is loaned to the Treasury in buying special government bonds, and the Treasury spends the proceeds to pay current bills.

So when Social Security benefits are to be paid to people entering retirement, what to do? Big Brother could renege on at least some of the previously promised payments. Or he could finance them by cutting back other government programs. Or he could borrow by selling more bonds. Or he could raise taxes. But these *same* options would exist even if earlier Social Security tax collections had *not* been in surplus. No bookkeeping "trust fund" accumulated *today* will take care of *tomorrow's* retirees. The community and its government will have to provide and pay for *tomorrow's* benefits out of *tomorrow's* production and income.

It is appalling if the President and Congress do not understand the ridiculous situation; it is repelling if they understand but deliberately misrepresent.

Social Security, Government, and Productivity

ＤＤＤＤ

We are told of both good news and bad news about Social Security. Supposedly, it is good news that economic growth and higher tax rates have pushed Social Security tax collections far above benefit payments.

The supposed bad news is that government is not *saving* that surplus. Instead, it is using the excess receipts for spending on other programs, so when baby boomers retire in future years, they will find the Social Security cupboard bare. Workers of the next generation will have to pay much higher taxes in order that government can then provide benefits it had promised.

There are, indeed, myriad problems with Social Security. But what can it mean to speak of government "saving" in order to make future payments? "Saving" is generally defined as currently earned income which is not currently consumed. Government does not "earn" or produce income, so it cannot usefully be said to save. Social Security benefit payments are necessarily pay-as-we-go. But government *can* affect saving by the *rest* of the economy — and it can affect amounts and patterns of investment by the overall economy.

The problem is not that government spends today what it collects today through nominal taxing and borrowing. It cannot be otherwise! The *real taxation* by government is the *real spending* by government: government taxes by sequestering wealth of the rest of the community, regardless of the financial mechanisms through which it gets the dollars to buy the stuff. Since government absorption through spending on social output *is* taxation of society, the real government budget is always balanced.

What the community has available today for consumption, investment, and support of government is basically today's production. Only to a limited extent for a temporary time can we currently draw on previously accumulated wealth. Basically, we *use* today what we *produce* today.

Still, there *is* a time element. For what we produce, and thus have available, tomorrow will depend in part on what we do with today's resources. To produce a bigger pie tomorrow, some of our current output must be channeled into appropriate investment. And in directing today's production and allocating today's output, government policies can be critical. If government taxes and borrows heavily and clumsily, national *saving* will be curtailed; and if government spends heavily and unproductively on various forms of consumption, national *investment* will be curtailed and misdirected.

The economic fate of retired people — like that of us all — will be determined fundamentally by the productivity of the economy. Government inevitably plays a role. What is most critical here is not so-called government saving or dissaving, or so-called budget surpluses of deficits, but *how much* of the community output is sequestered by government and what government *does* with that output.

Tomorrow's productivity — and thus tomorrow's Social Security — will be weakened by excessive and poorly directed government spending.

Pension Funds: Financial Investing and Social Investing

ᴥᴥᴥᴥ

In a world of limited resources, in which it is not possible to satisfy all wants fully, we have decisions to make, selecting the seemingly best options available. But to choose, to trade-off some of this to get more of that, is, by definition, to bear cost. When faced with options, we weigh alternatives, comparing different costs with different returns, trying to attain what we deem to be the optimal balance. Rarely does one particular choice appear to be best by *all* pertinent criteria.

Difficulties and dilemmas of choosing are conspicuous in managing financial portfolios. There are many avenues of saving and outlets of investment. The traditional benchmarks include short-term price volatility, long-term risk, probable streams of income, and liquidity. Different people will attach different weights to the varied considerations, and a given person will attach different weights as circumstances change.

Increasingly, saving and investing is done for individuals through pension plans. By contributing to a pension fund, the saver can gain benefits of wide diversification and supposedly expert financial management. But then the criteria of the fund managers are substituted for those of the individual participants in the plan.

Conventionally, the controlling criterion is simply stated, if not easily satisfied: Invest the resources of the fund so as to generate appropriate returns with acceptable risks. But over the last decade, a number of funds have added the goal of "morality." Are "sound finance" and "social investing" mutually consistent?

It may be that we can do most good socially while doing as well financially. But, realistically, we can easily suppose that arbitrary social strategy and most fruitful investment strategy will *not* be compatible. There presumably will be *trade-offs*, giving up some monetary returns in order to invest in ways which, in the interests of making the world nicer, are often suspicious and sometimes certainly silly.

On the one hand, the obvious is sometimes admitted that *denying options* to the manager of the pension fund is a peculiar way to strengthen the economic quality of the portfolio. A high official of the

Labor Department warns of weakening funds by "using retirees' grocery money to achieve general non-pension goals."

On the other hand, the specific strategies adopted in seeking "non-pension goals" are not invariably attractive to all who provide the resources. A newspaper story sympathetic to "social investing" speaks of "putting your money where your morals are." But I can object to having *my* money put where *your* morals are. And when your morals lead you to support foolish international economic sanctions, to subvert nuclear power, and to weaken national defense, your morals are not mine.

Pension managers are to manage my money; I will manage my morals.

State and Local Financing

Rules of the Game or the Brooklyn Bridge

ℒℒℒℒ

A man who long was the supposedly impartial budget analyst for the State of California has provided a newspaper essay on managing government finances. The former official laments "a progressive loss of fiscal responsibility in state government," and he blames the loss largely on tax-and-spend restrictions adopted in response to great community pressure in the late 1970s.

But the citizens' revolt did not spring from a vacuum; it was not unaccountable aberrant behavior; it was a response — however clumsy — to a genuine and growing problem. In the twenty years, 1948-68, state and local budgets expanded proportionately much faster than the federal budget; in the next ten years, leading up to California's Proposition 13 and all that, the pace of expansion of state and local budgets rose still higher. Since 1978, the growth of taxing and spending by Little Brother has remained substantial but at a somewhat slower rate.

Voters have not been silly in complaining that there *is* a fiscal problem. And the first step to improvement is to acknowledge the enormous room for improvement. But to improve the situation, it is helpful to have some notion of why the problem developed. The source of the difficulty is *not* stupidity of government people. They are not dumber than most of us; indeed, they may be more clever than most in survival arts. Nor is it stupidity of the community, although people have been suckered and seduced into demanding much and ever more while complaining about the cost.

The problem is more the nature of the *game* than the nature of the *players*. At any rate, we are stuck with the players — in self-interest, they are willing to subsidize and to be subsidized at the expense of others and of future well-being of the group. At the same time, the rules of the game can be changed.

It is hardly surprising that the community would evince interest in reforms which promised to curtail the costly capers of government. But the government man complains that the constraints put on those capers are crude and unduly curtail. The reform formulas are tied to population and inflation, but he suggests that *all* expenses — education, health, welfare — should increase faster than people and prices.

So given the problem of growing government and given his discontent with the revolt, what does the budget analyst offer? Campaign reform! How clever!

All we need do is to lay down rules for genteel campaigns, in which the clear voice of an enlightened people will choose statesmen into whose hands we can appropriately and confidently place our fiscal fate with no strings attached! Yes, of course. No limiting rules, no imposed criteria, no minimization of activities are to guide or constrain government and its bureaucracy. No rules except election rules. Sure. And we all can get rich by buying the Brooklyn Bridge.

Government Grants and Government Waste

✍✍✍✍

Big Brother is not puny. But big and growing government is not confined to the feds. *Little* Brother — state and local government — also is big and growing. State and local government spending — close to 60 percent as large as federal — increased 40-times from the late 1940s to 1990, while federal outlays went up a mere 30-fold.

Why the astonishing expansion of state and local government, an expansion which doubled its share of GNP over four decades after World War II? At the level of the individual state, there is much of the "copycat," or "keeping up with the Joneses." A study by the National Bureau of Economic Research finds that one state will emulate spending of other states which are similar in some respects, especially in racial composition.

But, the National Bureau adds, "if no other factors change, then an additional dollar of *federal grant* money received will raise state and local spending by 66 cents." And there have been many additional dollars of federal grants-in-aid to lower-level governments, despite large federal budget deficits and large state-and-local surpluses.

Through the mid-1950s, receipts of federal funds amounted to some 10 percent of all state and local government spending. There was a swelling of federal grants from 1966 through 1978, when federal money covered more than one-quarter of state and local financing. With the widespread "tax revolt" beginning in 1978, federal grants expanded at a slower rate but still nearly doubled in the following dozen years.

It is apparent, says commentator Doug Bandow in a Cato Institute publication, why massive federal aid has bloated state and local spending. First, money is spent to establish a place at the federal trough by searching, applying, and lobbying for grants.

Second, a large proportion of federal gifts requires cost-sharing. State and local politicians who would not dare fund fully an overelaborate project of low priority will kick in a fraction of the cost when most of the dollars come from taxpayers in the rest of the country.

Third, so-called tax effort is a criterion in distributing federal largess. High taxes in a jurisdiction supposedly reflect great need for assistance, so tax a lot in order to attract a lot of federal money.

Fourth, the whole game of giving and getting, with some bureaucrats allocating other peoples' money to other bureaucrats who did not have to tax their own constituents to get the money, conduces "gold-plating" — overbuilt, oversophisticated, overpriced highway, urban development, mass transit, sewage, water, and airport projects.

Mr. Bandow speaks of bad projects badly done with slush funds in porkbarrel boondoggles. And so federal grants and state-and-local surplus continue, along with enormous governmental waste.

Budgetary Lessons To Learn

☙☙☙☙

Measured by budget, government in this Land of the Free is very big, and is not getting smaller. Over two decades, tax collections of federal, state, and local governments have averaged one-third of GNP. Expenditures — a more appropriate measure of the size of government

— have been even more awesome, as all of government has persistently had a budgetary deficit.

But the federal government and the state and local governments have had rather different histories. Stephen Moore, in a Heritage Foundation study, suggests that the relatively gratifying regional experience contains lessons which should be learned by the feds.

Interesting fiscal lessons found by Mr. Moore — with emphasis on experience of states — are of comparative nature within the group. Those states showing greatest budgetary prudence have fared best.

"Budgetary prudence" here is characterized by relatively *low rates* of taxation — especially low rates of personal and corporate *income* taxes; relatively level, *nonprogressive* income tax rates; and *reduction* of total tax obligations. Such states of smallest and falling tax burdens have had the fastest growth of income, jobs, and business investment.

The spending record of even state and local government is not a legitimate basis of great contentment, however. In the decade, 1978-88, the proportionate increase in federal spending *was* much larger than the state and local increase. But in the last three of those years, state and local expenditures rose faster than federal; indeed, state and local spending from 1985-88 rose at twice the rate of inflation.

A critical lesson — supported by both federal and state experience — is that an increase in government revenues does *not* reduce a budget deficit. Again and again over many decades, we find higher revenues triggering still greater increases in spending; the new spending becomes "a politically indispensable fixture," and, "as the budget balance deteriorates, pressures mount for [still] higher taxes."

Those pressures toward chronic deficits have been better resisted by Little Brother than by Big Brother. For more than 20 years, there has been an aggregate surplus in state and local budgets and a deficit in the federal accounts. Indeed, in the 1980s, the state and local surplus has averaged one-third as much as the federal deficit.

This budget-balancing success may be due largely — but certainly not entirely — to adopted rules of the fiscal game: 49 states have balanced-budget requirements, 43 give line-item veto power to the governor, 26 have tax and expenditure limitations.

Still, there are few limits in the ingenuity and inclination of politicians to evade statutory spending restraints, and many states — especially in the Northeast — persist in playing in fiscal quicksand. Evidently, not only does the federal government not learn from the experience of states, even state governments do not well grasp the lessons of their own experience!

Gambling on Education

ææææ

All across the country, lips are spelling out: "No new taxes." But state governments still gamble their way to higher revenues.

Nearly 30 states now have government lotteries. Many were sold to the public by promising much of the take for education. There is the Florida lottery introduced in January 1988. According to Susan A. MacManus, professor of public administration and political science at the University of South Florida, this lottery followed "a slick, high profile advertising campaign that sold Florida's voters on the notion that education was to be a big winner." Seven other states also obtained public support for lotteries by promising benefits to education. And in four states now considering spinning their way to bigger bucks, supporters stress alleged benefit for public schools.

But the expected bonanza may be little more than political hype. Says Professor MacManus: "Voters are frequently under the misimpression that lottery revenues increase funding levels above those of the pre-lottery days. However, what has actually occurred in many states is a fiscal-substitution shell game. Legislators simply substitute lottery revenues for those from sales and income taxes and use the tax revenues that previously funded education to support other functions."

So schools end up with no net fiscal gain. Indeed, in some states the proportion of the budget going to education actually declined after introduction of lotteries. Education's share of California's budget dropped 1.5 percent since introduction of the lottery in 1986 — even though the law earmarks 34 percent of all lottery funds for public schools.

Professor MacManus blames the decline on three factors. First, lotteries lose effectiveness in producing funds as their novelty wears off and as other states create competing casinos. Second, lottery revenues do not increase as quickly as sales and income taxes, which rise more directly with growing state economies. And third, if lottery revenues do rise, legislators usually cut other funds for education.

Compared with state and local income taxes, lottery revenues are puny. On average, the take represents only about 3 percent of state receipts. Moreover, much of the gross gambling revenue is eaten up by administrative costs and other expenses. Of 28 states with lotteries in 1988, says Professor MacManus, average disbursement of gross revenues was: 50 percent for prizes, 11 percent for administration, and 39 percent for various state uses, including education.

As a source of funding schools, state lotteries have been much oversold. And when citizens mistakenly believe that such financing is shoring up their schools, they are unlikely to support other measures of more appropriate financing.

Lotteries are supposed to be a sure bet for public schools. But they are really gambling with the education of our youth.

MONEY, INFLATION, AND MONETARY POLICY

The Federal Reserve: Techniques and Procedures

Monetary Analysis: Central Bankers, Senators, Seers, and Silliness

ᗰᗰᗰᗰ

There is much in economics — as in every other interesting area of research — which we do not know or understand only imperfectly. And it is tempting to bridge gaps in our comprehension with hope, camouflage, or extrapolation. In short, we fake it. But the stakes can be high in formulating policy. It is important that we do our honest, most clear-headed best. And so it behooves us to clutch to our bosom those elements of thought and implications of experience which do seem well-founded and persuasively tested.

Perhaps nothing of scholarship is so established as to be beyond challenge. If that is the case in physics and mathematics, it assuredly is true also in economics. But we have less uncertainty and confusion in some areas and on some propositions of economics than in others. A case in point is elemental monetary analysis and the guidance it can provide in determining and assessing monetary policy.

Over generations, even centuries, many ingenious thinkers have addressed questions of the linkage between the amount of money and more final variables, such as prices, employment, interest rates, and exchange rates. Directed commonly to policy issues in a changing institutional and psychological environment, the studies of money have not evolved a neat history of unbroken progress to Truth. There remains much work to be done.

Still, it is true also that we know much. For all the complexities of the world — including various and variable lags between cause and effect, lags both of political and administrative procedure and of market mechanism — it is well established that there is a connection between the amount of money and the level of money prices. We have learned that money can be created too fast and too slow — and that, as a matter of history, our money supply at any moment typically has been going up too fast or too slow. We know the linkage between money and prices well enough to do vastly better than we have done in trying to achieve a steady price level.

Despite the central and conspicuous role of money in determining the price level and other significant variables, many who should see with clarity feign blindness. I have heard one of the world's great central bankers speak for over half an hour on inflation without once mentioning money. I have heard one of the senior members of the United States Senate lecture for over half an hour on inflation without once mentioning money. I have read several hundred words on inflation in a report by a business forecaster without finding any reference to money. They allude to many things — inventories, management-labor relations, energy, productivity, foreign trade, budget deficits, regulation of business — but, with perverse genius, they manage to avoid reference to what matters most.

Why? Perhaps misguided by faulty toilet training, central bankers, senators, and seers have joined in a conspiracy of silliness.

Money and Open Market Operations

ℒℒℒℒ

Many have some notion that national money income is determined by the amount of money spending on output, that the amount of spending is determined largely by the amount of money, and even that the amount of money is subject to close control by the Federal Reserve.

But just *how* the Fed increases or decreases the amount of money is a widespread mystery. Journalists commonly wander astray, and occasionally they are joined in confusion by purported business economists. The Fed does not appear to try very hard to instruct the amateur economists in journalism and commerce.

Most money is created by bank lending — commercial banks create the deposits they lend. Banks are required to hold reserves equal to a minimum fraction of their deposit liabilities. They can hold *more* than the minimum, but banks earn income by making loans, so they do not sit long on "excess" reserves. If reserves increase, an increase in lending and money is not likely to be far behind. So the proportion of total reserves in the excess category has been perennially very small and very steady.

An increase in reserves *can* come from bank borrowing from the Fed. And there has been much amateurish attention paid to the interest rate charged by the Fed on its loans to banks. The impression has been created that changes in this so-called discount rate are the main means by which the Fed manages the money supply. That impression is incorrect.

Banks rarely borrow *much* of their reserves from the Fed regardless of the discount rate. And they rarely borrow much *more* when the Fed lowers the rate or much *less* when the Fed raises the rate. Since 1973, the discount rate has been jerked up and down again and again over an enormous range, but the ratio of borrowed reserves to total reserves — like the ratio of excess reserves to total reserves — has almost always been very small. Indeed, over the past three years, borrowed reserves have been virtually zero.

If banks have not *borrowed* much of their reserves, where did the reserves come from?

A number of things — including various actions by the public and by banks — can affect the amount of reserves in the banking system. But the dominating thing is "open market operations." The Fed often enters the government securities market. If the Fed buys securities from bond dealers, it thereby directly creates money dollar-for-dollar equal to the value of the purchase. More important, there will be additional reserves, on the basis of which banks can create a multiple of new checking deposits. There has long been an extremely large correlation between Fed purchases and sales of government securities, on the one hand, and the money supply, on the other.

If the real policy game is open market operations, why all the interest rate hocus pocus? It has been suggested that the interest rate diddling has been mainly a diversion, to distract Congress and the administration from silly, activist fiscal policy. But political tactics are in the realm of abnormal psychology, where civilized people dread to tread.

Alice in Deposit Insurance Wonderland

✍✍✍✍

With fractional-reserve banking, no bank is prepared to cover all its demand obligations. And the government deposit insurance fund is equal to only a fraction of its obligations. Viability of both — the individual bank and the insurance fund — rests on a small fraction of potential payments actually being required at any time.

The argument for the fund has been that its very existence will preclude massive claims. But the fund, as now established, can contribute to the likelihood of behavior which adds to risk and thereby to calls on the fund.

In relatively calm seas, the fund can have the desired effect of inspiring depositor confidence. But if institutions start to be seriously pinched, the fund can lead to dangerous tactics. If interest costs rise relative to interest income, with the capital ratio being diminished, institutions try to increase income; they do so by seeking higher returns; higher returns may be found with riskier investments — and if the risky investments do not work well, the fund will bail out the firm. For depositors, full guarantee eliminates concerns about the institution where they put their money. For institutions paying a flat, uniform fee, it is "heads-I-win, tails-I-don't-lose," as government bears the burden.

Reform proposals commonly call for higher capital requirements and/or larger deposit-insurance contributions. But increasing capital requires either increasing profitability (which makes greater risk taking attractive) or selling best assets (which increases the riskiness of the portfolio). And increasing premiums cuts profitability. So there can be contradiction in tactics — trying to increase profitability while reducing profitability; and the tactic — increasing capital while increasing premiums — induces firms to weaken themselves by taking on more risk.

As insolvency spreads, the government guarantee fund becomes a drag when premiums are raised. At the same time, it loses much of its protective and corrective significance as bailout requirements swamp the resources of the fund: The liabilities then fall vastly more on taxpayers than on the fund.

The situation would be basically different if so-called deposit insurance actually were insurance. With genuine insurance, premiums reflect the strength and the prudence of the insured firm. But the common fee now paid to the fund is not an insurance premium; it is simply a minor tax which gives failing firms access to unlimited taxpayer money.

What we call "insurance" is really not insurance, because it fails to link amount of risk with cost of protection from risk. We call "premiums" what actually are taxes, and we try to increase profits by taxing profits. And we try to curtail risks through devices and procedures which perversely encourage greater risk. Alice would recognize this as Wonderland.

Monetary Objectives and Policies

Money, Non-Money, and Reputation

❧❧❧❧

"Poor Professor Allen," murmured a commiserating Mouse Adam. "The dear man is disappointed, and irritated in his dismay."

"So what's new," cried Mouse Karl with cruel candor. "All economists are always unhappy."

"He has special reason to be annoyed," replied Adam. "On a trip some time ago, he leased a car from a leading rental firm. On returning the automobile the next day, the two clerks of the firm obviously were confused, and consulted with each other, but explained nothing to Professor Allen. He later discovered that they had charged his credit card an amount larger than the one initially quoted. A request was then made to correct the over-charge. Three months later, the firm acknowledged its error, apologized, and sent him a certificate of about the amount of the discrepancy which can be applied to a future rental."

"So, after a bit of a delay, the problem is perfectly resolved," trumpeted Karl. "Allen was initially charged too much, but now the money has been repaid."

"No," corrected Adam, "he was charged too much *money,* but he has *not* been reimbursed in *money.*"

"Don't be cute," criticized Karl. "I have heard you say that money is what money does, and that what money does is to pay for things. The certificate can pay for a car rental, so the certificate is money."

Adam tried to be patient. *"Anything* with market value," he said, "can be used in a swap for something else. But not everything is *money.* Money is so-called generalized purchasing power: it is a general claim which can be exercised by *any* holder to buy *any* good at *any* time from *any* seller. But the certificate is not transferable and can be used only by Professor Allen; it cannot be converted into cash and must be used only in renting a car from this company; and it must be used, if at all, within one year. The certificate is a claim, to be sure, but it is a very specific, not general, claim, and thus falls far short of being money. So the company still gains, and Professor Allen still loses, from the initial ineptitude of the company."

"I concede," conceded Karl, "that Allen has some reason for frustration. If money exists, it is because those things which make up money *are* different in some respects and in some degrees from non-money assets. The certificate is *not* money — and, for a given face value, obviously the certificate is not as valuable as the same amount of money."

"Money certainly facilitates trade," observed Adam. "By reducing the costs and inconveniences of transactions, it makes us more productive in our use of scarce resources. From the view of the community, it is thus a pity when a firm substitutes non-money for money in settling monetary obligations. The efficiency of the economy is thereby diluted — as is the reputation of the firm which tries too hard, but unwisely, for short-term gain and temporary advantage."

A Target of Permanent Zero Inflation

President George Bush does not favor a surge of inflation. But he does not seem to fear such a prospect as much as does Alan Greenspan, chairman of the Federal Reserve. Some go further than advocating simply maintenance of the present rate of inflation. The president of the Cleveland Federal Reserve Bank and several of his staff economists look with favor on gradual reduction in inflation from the current 5 percent to a level of zero.

Inflation is not required for prosperity; indeed, inflation can accompany slow growth of the economy. Over the past century, we have flourished most with either very moderate inflation or slight disinflation. This was the case from the 1890s to the first World War and in the 1920s, when the price level was approximately steady or even fell a bit; it was the case also from the late 1950s to the late '60s and during the mid- and late 1980s, when inflation was low. By contrast, from the early 1970s to the early '80s, inflation was large but the growth of output was small.

There could be some short-term costs for some in reducing the rate of inflation. Any change in major economic variables — such as inflation and interest rates — is likely to benefit some members of the community and make others worse off. Reducing the inflation rate would tend to favor creditors over debtors. Interest rates would tend to fall a bit as inflation anticipations are diminished, which would give current holders of securities a small, one-period gain. And there is the common concern — not entirely ridiculous even if often exaggerated — that even a short and gentle period of disinflation would generate a recession.

Such unevenly spread, but limited, transitional gains and costs would seem of small consequence compared to the major advantages of permanent establishment of virtually zero change in the price level. Keeping the inflation rate around zero would minimize various social and economic costs and increase productivity.

While some — through either deliberate shrewdness or unconscious good luck — can benefit economically and politically from inflation, the community generally can hardly gain. Rapidly and erratically rising prices do not increase the amount of our resources or improve the technology with which our resources are used. Rather, say the economists of the Cleveland Fed, the confusion and concern generated by inflation "... redistributes income arbitrarily, ... reduces national income by fostering inefficient decisions about production and consumption, ... induces people to use scarce resources both to forecast inflation and to protect themselves ..., and ... hampers growth of productive capacity by discouraging saving and investment...."

The Fed has just one fundamental policy purpose: stabilize the price level. It cannot much affect employment and output in the long-run, and it ought not to diddle and tinker with interest rates and exchange rates and short-term hyping and suppressing of economic activity. Well establishing an effective commitment to zero inflation would dilute the ability of the Fed to do things it should *not* do, while enhancing prospects of continuing success in doing what it *should* do.

Monetary Policy: Price Objective and Money Control

ꝏꝏꝏꝏ

Maintaining perennial — and thus easily predictable — stability of the price level would not, directly and by itself, solve our most basic economic problems. We could live poorly even with little price-level fluctuation. But while a flourishing economy requires much more than absence of inflation, we can do best in a hard world if not plagued by large and erratic swings in prices.

We have policy *tools,* and we can stipulate policy *goals.* Zero inflation is an attractive goal of monetary policy. But specifying a goal does *not* tell us how to use the tools, for there can be much slippage in the linkage between manipulation of the tools today and the uncertain repercussions a year or two down the road. We can state a long-term destination and still not know just what to do, step-by-step and day-to-day, in order to get there.

What we *can* do is use the tools and take the steps in ways consistent with analytic principle and coherent interpretation of history and of present circumstance. The very consistency of our tactics in trying to implement our strategy will help us along the path: Production and consumption decisionmakers would be comforted if persuaded that the goal of the Federal Reserve is zero inflation and that there will be ongoing policies of steady, non-erratic, empirically justified administration of those policy variables — mainly, the money supply — which are under our control.

Sensible, consistent, predictable monetary policy and its application will not generate unwavering zero inflation. There are too many variables, in addition to money, which affect inflation, and there are lags which are too long and too uncertain in the connections of cause-and-effect, to guarantee that steady money growth will mean a steady inflation rate. But those same complexities of the world — complexities of both social psychology and institutional mechanisms — make impossible the achieving of specified inflation by discretionary diddling with the policy tools.

Attaining with appreciable precision a stipulated inflation objective requires us to do things we cannot do well enough. Holding the rate of money growth *constant* (we can come close to doing that) will not yield a constant rate of inflation (zero or otherwise) in a changing world. But we do not know enough to *manage* the rate of money growth to offset those changes so as to generate a constant inflation rate.

Either we grandly decree the price level and then try somehow to *manipulate* money increase to meet and keep the price objective or we more modestly *stabilize* money growth and then let the price level settle down with minimal fluctuation. In trying for too much, we end with less than we could have had. It is shrewd to acknowledge our policymaking inadequacies and acquiesce in the feasible, to settle for the best we can do in a hard, imperfect, frustrating world.

Oil Shocks and a Long-Term Monetary Policy

✍✍✍✍

Much of the world has experienced a succession of "oil shocks" since the early 1970s. How shocking is an oil shock likely to be? What is the nature of the shock? And how are we best to respond?

The oil shock itself is a reduction in input supply. With curtailment of a key input, national *output* falls. With rising costs of production and transportation and resulting diminished output, *prices* tend to rise. *Interest rates*, too, can rise with anticipated inflation and with the public borrowing more to maintain its spending in the face of income loss.

This was the pattern in earlier oil crises — falling output, rising prices, some increase in interest rates. The current episode seems to fit into the same sort of picture. True, the American economy is much more energy efficient now than in 1973, as reflected in greater real output per unit of oil used, and this reduces the production and price impacts of sudden changes in the availability and cost of oil. Even so, the economy is hardly immune to shocks of oil supply and oil prices.

So economists of the Cleveland Federal Reserve Bank find that the Fed faces a policy dilemma. Should the Federal Reserve *increase* money growth to maintain *output* or *curtail* money growth to repress *inflation*?

A rise in oil prices by itself does not go far in generating inflation: with a constant money supply, increases in prices in some goods are likely to be accompanied by decreases in other prices. Still, even if the amount of money is maintained, there will be inflation if output falls. The decline in production increases the *ratio* of money to output, and the *relative* increase in money leads to higher prices.

Must output fall? No monetary policy can make more oil available. Reduced input means reduced output. And as output falls, there will be some rise in unemployment, for the economy's adjustment to the new circumstances of supply and prices will not be made instantaneously, without frictions and lags.

So what should monetary policy be? We cannot *both* expand and contract money growth at the same time. And in trying to fine-tune the economy, we are likely to hurt ourselves in the long-run while failing to help ourselves in the short-run.

An eminent group of non-government economists — the self-named Shadow Open Market Committee — urges a *steady long-term policy*. We cannot escape temporary wiggles in the price level and the rate of output. Indeed, in working on either of those problems, we probably will worsen the other — and even worsen *both* of them in the long pull. Don't try to fine-tune what is untunable.

But there is a third choice: Suffer with patience what is unavoidable in a period of transition, try not to make bad situations worse, and, instead, "maintain money growth at a rate consistent with *long-term* growth of output and declining inflation."

Determinants and Implications of Inflation

Inflation Control and Money Control

✍✍✍✍

Most people — including in that category politicians and editorial writers — advocate avoidance or elimination of inflation. We have had very modest inflation since 1981. Still, the inflation rate picked up a bit in 1988, and there is growing wonderment about the upward movement of the price level. But if we are to figure out how to stuff the bad genie of inflation back into the bottle and try to keep him there, it would help to understand how he so frequently has slipped out.

Lots of things are *not* directly and significantly responsible for the substantial and persistent increase of prices in general which can be called inflation. The noncauses of inflation include government budget imbalance, foreign trade imbalance, bad weather, international cartels, corporate pricing policies, labor union contracts, and consumer greed.

In terms of current production, the key relationship in determining the price level is between *total spending* on output and the *amount* of output. And, over time, if spending increases faster than output — if the ratio of spending to purchased goods and services increases — the price index necessarily rises.

The market value of the huge basket of output produced during a year is *price times quantity*: the weighted average price per unit of goods multiplied by the number of units. That market value of the basket — that price times quantity — is equal to, and determined by, spending on the basket. If spending increases at the same rate as the content of the basket increases, then the price per unit remains constant.

What, then, determines spending? Spending equals the number of dollars in the hands of the public times the average number of times during the year a dollar is spent on output. So spending is the *money stock* multiplied by the so-called *velocity* of monetary circulation.

During the fifteen-year inflationary period, 1966-81, money expanded at an annual rate of well over 6 percent, velocity rose at 3 percent, so expenditures went up at nearly 10 percent. It was not to be expected that output would rise that fast; Indeed, output expanded at less than 3 percent. With spending up at close to 10 percent and output up at less than 3 percent, prices inexorably soared at nearly 7 percent — a little faster than the expansion of money.

Since 1981, the spending rate has been dominated even more than before by money, for velocity has changed less than before, actually falling a bit. If the percentage change in velocity were *zero* — and it rarely deviates greatly from zero — then money and spending would move together proportionately. And if money (and spending) increased at just the same rate as output — typically about 3 percent — inflation would be zero.

If we are to control inflation, we must control spending; and if we are to control spending, we must control the amount of money. And we *can* adequately control the amount of money.

Inflation and Prosperity

◢◢◢◢

Is inflation a problem? Yes, of course. Inflation is *always* a proper concern. There have been extended periods when inflation was in remission, to be sure, but the disease can flare-up quickly when we get careless and cavalier.

After a flurry of rising prices right after World War II, the inflation rate was well contained for nearly twenty years — including the Korean War period — generally staying in the range of 1.5-3.5 percent. During the Vietnam mess — in the late 1960's and early '70s — inflation edged up to the 5-6 percent range. Then, in 1974 and '75, it exploded to 10-11 percent. And, after falling back a bit, it jumped again, this time to about 9-10 percent in 1979-81.

But ten years may be too long a time for some to remember lessons — if, indeed, they ever learn lessons in the first place. The editor of a newsmagazine finds it "silly to think that control of inflation is a higher priority than economic growth when many [producer] prices are falling." And a business economist tells us that "the biggest problem with inflation now is that we seem unable to shake our fears of it."

The economist alludes to nightmares of "the successive waves of inflation that characterized economic expansions before 1980." He should stop eating peanut butter and pickles before bedtime, for the nightmares are bad fiction: over the past century, our most conspicuous periods of prosperity have had either very little inflation or actually falling price levels. This was the case for a quarter of a century prior to World War I, in the Roaring 1920s, from the mid-1950s to the mid-60s, and during the mid- and late 1980s.

But if we need not bear the costs of high inflation in order to have high employment and output — if there need be no trade-off between low inflation and high production — then there is no issue of "priorities," no occasion to decide whether "control of inflation" is more or less important than "economic growth."

Not only does prosperity *not* require inflation, but our periods of greatest inflation have *not* been periods of high prosperity. The era of most massive inflation since World war II were the eight years from 1973 through 1981, when the average annual inflation rate was ridiculously well over 8 percent.

Economic prosperity and progress require more than a stable price level, of course. After all, we had essentially no inflation during the devastating depression of the 1930s. To live well, we must produce much. And to produce much, we must fully and effectively employ a productive labor force. But we have found that avoiding the inefficiencies and inequities of inflation can contribute greatly to high performance of our economy.

History: Inflation, Unemployment, and Output

✍✍✍✍

How much inflation is too much? A few want a target of zero inflation. Others — including the chairman of the Federal Reserve board — want zero inflation but would settle for a rate of 1 or 2 percent. With inflation of 2 percent, it would take some 36 years for the price level to double.

Still others agree that virtually zero inflation would be nice, but the price to obtain it is much too high. They say that the price of eliminating the increase in prices surely would be a recession. One economist presents a rule of thumb: a reduction of the inflation rate by one percentage point requires an increase in the unemployment rate by one percentage point for two years. So bringing the current inflation of close to 5 percent down to 2 percent would mean an additional 3 million people out of work for a couple of years.

A *Wall Street Journal* writer is impressed by the warning that substantial reduction of inflation must mean substantial increase in unemployment. "Unfortunately," he says, "those who see a painless cure for inflation haven't much history" on their side.

Well, let's look at our history since World War II.

Prior to the 1980s in that period, there were four instances in which inflation fell at least two percentage points in one year. But in three of the four cases, the unemployment rate *fell* over the next two years. The exception was the reduction of inflation by more than 9 points from 1948-49, and unemployment rose — but it rose less than 2 points, not 9 points. Further, in all four cases of appreciable fall in inflation, national real output *increased* some 8-10 percent during the next two years.

The early 1980s present a modified picture. Inflation reached record levels, and then for three consecutive years, the inflation rate was sharply reduced. The first two of those years, unemployment rose, and output went first down and then up by small amounts. But the third year of inflation curtailment saw the old pattern of falling unemployment and rising output.

Try an alternative historical view. Instead of looking at *changes* in inflation, unemployment, and production over *short* periods, look at *average* rates over *prolonged* periods.

Over the nineteen years, 1949-68, inflation was almost always below 4 percent, averaging under 2 percent. And the low inflation was accompanied by unemployment well below 5 percent and annual growth of real output of more than 4 percent. In the next nineteen years, 1969-88, inflation averaged close to 6.5 percent, more than three times greater than in the previous period; and this high inflation walked with high unemployment — more than 6.5 percent — and low production — 2.8 percent.

Low inflation and even falling inflation are typically associated with much employment and much output. That is what history really shows.

Work, Productivity, and Inflation

ØØØØ

How well we live depends on how much we produce. How much we produce depends on how *hard* we work and how *well* we work, on how *much* and how *efficiently* we combine our powers of muscle and mind with materials and machines. If we work a lot and work very productively, we will have much output.

Output is not everything, of course, and work is not the only proper activity. Civilized people work to live more than they live to work. If we obtain more goods simply by working more, we have less remaining time to enjoy what we produce. The more we produce per worker per hour, the more leisure we will have while producing a given stream of output. So no matter how much we work, it behooves us always to work productively.

Economist Michael F. Bryan, of the Cleveland Federal Reserve Bank, has reviewed the issue of "working more versus working better."

Many things of different natures help to determine our productivity. Those determinants range from the psychological to the physical — the mores and aspirations of the people, the institutional arrangements and property rights of the community, the education and the tools of the workers.

Mr. Bryan directs particular attention to *inflation*. Is a considerable and persistent rise in the price level conducive to greater productivity?

Many suppose so. They associate inflation with prosperity, even if they are vague on whether the inflation actually contributes to the prosperity or simply accompanies prosperity. In actuality, inflation and rising output have *not* been highly and positively correlated, and inflation can be expected to be a *hindrance* to robust economic growth.

In open economies of private property, saving and investment, production and consumption are guided by decisions of a great many people. People make those decisions in light of existing and anticipated prices of different goods. But during inflation, it becomes difficult to distinguish changes in the *general* level of prices from changes in *relative* prices of different items. The market price signals are camouflaged and garbled, leading to poorer market decisions and thus reduced rates of return. And more resources are devoted to trying to interpret the confusing signals and to seeking protection from capricious changes in the market setting.

All this means that inflation hurts productivity: Inflation leads us to use our resources less well. And that, in fact, has been the record since World War II: *Greater inflation* has been associated with *smaller* growth of *productivity*.

We have compensated by having more people work and by working more hours per week. But it is sobering that there is occasion for such compensation, for having to offset declining productivity growth with increasing work. It is a sad situation when we have to work harder just to maintain a rate of output expansion. And one way to offset declining growth of productivity is to keep inflation tightly under control.

Mouse Wisdom: Money, Production, and Control of Inflation

ØØØØ

"I know about all there is worth knowing about *inflation*," confidently confided Mouse Karl. "I know what inflation *is*, what *causes* it, and how to *cure* it."

"Do tell me," murmured Mouse Adam.

"Inflation," proclaimed Karl, "is a substantial, prolonged rise in the price level. It results from too many dollars chasing too few goods. And it is corrected by increasing the amount of goods being chased."

"Your three statements," replied Adam, "range from quite reasonable to pretty ridiculous. Most would agree that 'inflation' has to do with a persistent tendency for the price level to rise appreciably. It is a bit unpolished to say it stems from 'too many dollars chasing too few goods.' It is better to say that total expenditure on the nation's output rises faster than production of output — and add that changes in expenditure are generally dominated by changes in the amount of money."

"I accept your prissy precision," pouted Karl. "So the price level rises when spending outruns output. And we should control inflation by boosting the rate of output to match the rate of spending increase. If we produce enough, prices will not rise."

Adam rolled his eyes upward in appeal for patience. "Yes," he said, "*if* production were to expand fast enough, the price level would remain steady. But you forget that it is a world of scarcity and of producing by sweat of the brow. It is hard to increase output. Output rarely rises as much as 5 percent in one year, and, over substantial periods, it usually has grown at an annual rate of around 2.5-3.5 percent. In contrast, we easily and cheaply create money out of thin air, and almost always money is expanding faster than output."

"Hard to believe," sniffed Karl. "Our monetary authorities — who surely do not like inflation — would never allow money to grow much more than output."

"Look at the record," snapped Adam a bit impatiently. "In the nine years, 1972-81, the price level more than doubled, going up at an appalling annual average of over 8 percent. Why? The amount of money increased at 6.5 percent a year, and velocity — the rate at which money is spent — rose at more than 4 percent, so expenditure on output ballooned at close to 11 percent. But production could not grow at anything near 11 percent per year for nearly a decade. In fact, output went up at a modest rate of only 2.4 percent a year. With spending galloping ahead at nearly 11 percent and the output on which the spending was done chugging along at a little over 2 percent, we inevitably had inflation of more than 8 percent."

Karl was chastened. "We do live better as we produce much," he wisely said, "so production is very important. But we cannot expect to match irresponsible bloating of the money supply with massive increases in output. To avoid inflation, we must confine spending growth to output growth — and spending control requires money control."

Mouse Wisdom: Money and Mouse Work

ℒℒℒℒ

"The makers of monetary policy are dumb for keeping such a tight lid on the money supply," complained Mouse Karl.

"It's true," acknowledged Adam, "the money supply is smaller now than it was at the end of last year. The Federal Reserve has long alternated between too little and too much money growth. We all would benefit from a policy of *stable* growth of money at a prudent rate."

"Not now!" exclaimed Karl. "The Fed ought to pour money into the economy. With a greater supply of money and credit, interest will fall. Lower interest rates will then encourage businesses to invest more in new tools and technology. And with more and better equipment, the productivity of mouse work will rise."

"I agree," agreed Adam, "that more investment can increase mouse productivity. But I disagree that greater money growth will produce the increased investment."

"Nonsense!" snapped Karl. "If you were a good economist, you would know that more money always lowers interest rates, and lower interest rates always raise investment."

"Good economists," gently suggested Adam, "do not just wiggle their whiskers and ignore critical evidence. And evidence does reveal that greatly increased money growth causes *higher* (not lower) interest rates and *less* (not more) investment."

"I don't believe it," said Karl disbelievingly.

"Don't forget the relationship between money and inflation," cautioned Adam. "*Past* money growth — say, from two years ago — combines with *today's* real output growth to determine the rate of inflation. So when earlier money growth exceeds current output growth by a wider margin, monetary policy is more inflationary."

"And with more inflation," continued Adam, "interest rates rise as lenders add inflationary premiums to compensate for the cheaper dollars repaid to them in the future. More important, the uncertainties and distortions of greater inflation undermine incentives to make new investments in the first place. Overexuberent money growth generates inflation, and inflation is the enemy of investment.

"Consider the period since 1970. During these years, the growth of real net fixed investment generally moved opposite to the direction of monetary policy. When earlier money growth exceeded current output growth by a wider margin, investment grew more slowly."

"Or declined more rapidly?" asked Karl.

"Yes," answered Adam. "So if the Fed poured lots of new money into the economy now, the likely outcome would be more future inflation. And more inflation would mean *less* real investment."

"I suppose," supposed Karl, "that in the long pull we could have more investment if monetary policy did not lurch from one side to the other."

"Right," added Adam. "The Fed would encourage investment if it *consistently* aimed at producing a stable price level. And more investment would increase the productivity of mouse work...."

"And since earnings depend on the productivity of our work," concluded Karl confidently, "our standard of living would rise."

Money, Inflation, and Interest Rates

ΩΩΩΩ

Word is that the President and his Budget Director have been a mite miffed with the Federal Reserve. The Administration would like interest rates lower to inspire more investment in machinery and factories and induce more spending on cars and houses. But the Fed fears inflation and is reluctant to try to push interest rates down.

Inflation stems from excessive *spending*. Spending could increase not only because of lower interest rates, but because of a greater rate of increase in the amount of *money*. And the money supply could increase because that is the way the Fed operates on interest rates: the Fed cannot decree market interest rates; it can only nudge rates by diddling with money growth.

This is not the whole of the story. If the Fed were successful in getting interest rates to fall, that would discourage Americans and foreigners looking for high rates of return from buying U.S. assets. Allegedly, we have become hooked on net capital inflow, so there would be an unhappy side effect in reducing interest rates. At the same time, a smaller capital inflow would be accompanied by a smaller import balance of goods, and, allegedly, that would be desirable. By criteria of international finance and trade, therefore, it is unclear whether we should strive for lower or higher interest rates.

Even that is not the end of the complex story. Suppose the Fed decides to try to lower interest rates. So it directly and indirectly guns the money supply. The immediate, or impact, effect of that expansion of money and bank reserves and of bidding up of financial asset prices will tend to reduce rates. But if money increases fast enough long enough, prices in general will rise.

As the price level moves up, the community will expect still more upward movement. But the prospect of continuing inflation will lead lenders to add an "inflation premium" to the interest rates they charge. The premium is to compensate the lender for the lower-valued money with which borrowers later repay, after inflation has diluted the purchasing power of the dollar. So the attempt to reduce interest rates by greatly expanding the amount of money results in still higher rates.

Government types seem commonly to have trouble comprehending this sort of thing. Roughly a decade ago, interest rates reached uncivilized levels. Interest rates were bloated because *inflation* had reached uncivilized levels. Inflation was staggering because *aggregate spending* had reached uncivilized levels, and excessive spending resulted primarily from over exuberant creation of *money*. A large block of senators issued a proclamation demanding that the Fed lower interest rates by increasing the money stock — although rates were at horrendously high levels because money had already been increased too much!

This historical record is consistent with the logic. Since the early 1950s — at least to the early 1980s — the obvious trends of money growth, inflation, and interest rates have all been upward at closely comparable rates. Remember that when politicians call for the Fed to lower interest rates.

Inflation, Monetary Strategy, and Fed Tactics

Inflation and the History of the Fed

ᗝᗝᗝᗝ

The Federal Reserve has substantial control of the amount of money, and changes in money have repercussions on the price level, interest rates, output, employment, and exchange rates.

It is widely agreed that the immediate target of Fed policy should be prices. And it is widely agreed that the Fed can achieve rough stability of the price level. But the Fed has aimed at many targets at different times, and has slighted the primary goal of price stability. Ironically, success in maintaining price stability would have contributed more to such goals as low interest rates and robust production than have efforts to achieve such results directly.

The Fed has been with us for nearly eighty years. Its history overall is not a source of great contentment and confidence for those who take money and the price level seriously.

Milton Friedman points out that the price level is now some thirteen times its level in 1914 — an annual increase of 3.5 percent. An inflation rate of 3.5 percent strikes many as readily acceptable. At that rate, it would take about twenty years for prices to double, which looks good to a generation which saw inflation of some 14 percent just over a dozen years ago.

But that observation opens the way for the cat to escape the bag: the inflation record has been extremely erratic, with a strong tendency to worsen in the later part of the Fed's history.

From the beginning of the Fed through 1940 — over a quarter of a century — the average annual increase in prices was only about 1 percent. For the next quarter of a century or so — from 1940 through 1967 — the inflation rate rose considerably to 3.3 percent. And for the next twenty-five years, it ballooned to 5.9 percent.

But as Dr. Friedman emphasizes, these averages over quarter-century periods "conceal wide gyrations." Prices doubled in the World

War I period, fell sharply in the early 1920s, held steady in the roaring years of the '20s, collapsed in the early '30s, rose little in the rest of the '30s, took off during the World War II era, increased only moderately from the late 1940s to the late '60s, exploded from the late 1960s to the early '80s, and went up at 3.8 percent annually over the last ten years.

And contrary to what many suppose, high inflation and prosperity have not gone hand-in-hand, nor have low inflation and stagnation. Since World War II, as in most earlier periods, we have had by far our most robust productive activity when inflation was lowest. Inflation is the enemy of, not a price which must be paid for, a thriving economy.

"... the Fed's rhetoric is always anti-inflationary," notes Dr. Friedman, "but any relation in the past between its rhetoric and its performance has been purely coincidental." Some high officials of today's Fed have been speaking in terms of establishing *zero* inflation. We should hope that they are now serious and will be successful.

Banks, Money, and Policy

ᡒᡒᡒᡒ

In recent months, many financial writers and officials have spoken with seeming earnestness about a horrendous "credit crunch." Since the reference pertains to borrowing from banks, the so-called credit crunch is a "*money* crunch," for banks create money when they make loans. And, supposedly, there is a crunch because banks have quite abruptly — and mysteriously — begun to lend much less than they could lend. And this has caused a recession. Is all this consistent with analytic fundamentals?

Except in the most bizarre of circumstances, banks love to lend. The interest they get on loans they make is a major portion of their income. Banks are curtailed in the amount of lending they can do by reserve requirements. While banks must hold *minimum* reserves, they can hold *more* reserves than the minimum.

During the Great Depression of the 1930s, banks did hold vastly more reserves than were required: They found it more prudent to sit on "excess" reserves than to make loans which likely would not be repaid. But the depression was bizarre in the extreme, and for half a century, excess reserves have been kept very small.

We are, indeed, in a period of reduced rate of economic activity. But the slowdown is not recent and sudden. Both employment and national production rose rapidly during 1983 and early '84; they rose moderately form mid-1984 through '88; and they have risen very slowly since 1988.

It is not coincidence that growth of the money stock has followed a similar pattern. But the slow growth of money since mid-1988 has not stemmed from some perversity of the banks, which would be reflected in ballooning excess reserves. Virtually through 1990, there was *no* change in the long-established pattern of very small — indeed, minimal — excess reserves. Even with very recent modest increases in excess reserves, banks have continued to be essentially fully loaned up.

Banks cannot lend on the basis of excess reserves they do not have. Nor have they kept excess reserves low by greatly increasing conservative purchases of government and other securities rather than by riskier lending. In fact, the ratio of loans made to securities bought has barely fluctuated over these past three years. In short, when additional reserves have been made available, banks have correspondingly loaned.

But if banks are to have more reserves, the Fed will have to take the initiative to make them directly available, for the banks will not borrow reserves. For two generations, banks have borrowed hardly at all from the Fed, and that pattern, too, has continued. So lowering the rediscount rate — the interest rate charged by the Fed on loans to banks — cannot be expected to increase appreciably bank borrowing of reserves and subsequent lending.

Why, then, the great enthusiasm over recent cuts in the rediscount rate? Is it possible that — perhaps for sensible reasons — the Fed wishes to be *perceived* as following an expansionary policy while *actually* remaining neutral?

Inflation and the Tug of Money

✍✍✍✍

Through dense fog a tugboat pushes a line of barges along a winding channel. If the tug is to steer the barges around each curve, it must begin turning long before the channel bends. Yet the mist hides the twisting route. And tricky currents unpredictably magnify or minify the vessels' every turn. Even with valiant effort — and much good luck — the barges will probably be beached.

The tug's task is like that of the Federal Reserve: the Fed's current monetary steering does not turn the economy until some uncertain time in the unforeseeable future. And tricky economic currents unpredictably magnify or minify its efforts. So future turns in the economy cannot be accurately anticipated when the Fed's policy is decided. Even with dedication and good fortune, the monetary pilots at the Fed are apt to beach the economy.

Inflation is one way of running aground. True, higher oil prices, poor harvests, and other nonmonetary shocks can produce blips in the price level. But a persistent, substantial change in the rate of inflation is wholly unlikely unless the Fed raises or lowers the rate of money growth.

Still, a change in monetary policy will not alter the rate of inflation immediately or after a uniform lag. Indeed, today's inflation can be the result of monetary steering two years ago! So *past* money growth combines with *today's* economic current to determine the rate of inflation.

Consider the period, 1962-1988. For each of these years, subtract annual growth of real output from money supply growth of two years earlier. The difference between current growth of output and previous growth of money suggests the degree to which monetary policy has been turning the economy toward or away from inflation.

In 1980, for example, prior money growth exceeded present growth of real output by more than 8 percent. In contrast, the excess of money growth was less than 2 percent in 1984. Consequently, the economy was more likely to run aground on inflation in 1980 than in 1984. Indeed, consumer prices did increase in excess of 13 percent in 1980, while in 1984 they rose little more than 4 percent.

During the period since 1961, inflation generally has risen or fallen along with the Fed's monetary steering of two years earlier. When prior money growth exceeded current output growth by a wider margin, inflation generally increased. And when that margin fell, so also did the rate of inflation.

The relationship is not precise and invariant. Instead, changes in money growth affect inflation with unpredictable lags and intensity. So the piloting of those at the Federal Reserve can be perilous, indeed. By spinning the wheel first one way and then the other, they are more likely to wreck the economy on inflation than to save it.

The Well-Fed Stock Market

ØØØØ

Will Rogers knew how to make money in the stock market. Find a few good stocks, he advised, buy them when their prices are low, and sell them when their prices are high. And if their prices don't rise, don't buy them, of course.

Ol' Will was poking fun at our inability to foretell the future. While we try mightily today to pick only winners, tomorrow we still find lower prices for some of our stocks.

But we can reduce risk by diversifying. People buy shares in mutual funds, for example, because the funds pool investors' money to buy an assortment of stocks. The diversified investment allows gains of some stocks to cancel losses of others. With investment eggs spread among many baskets, investors sleep a little easier.

But not very easily, for the stock market overall can fall and unexpectedly break eggs in almost all baskets. In contrast, a rising market can lift most stocks.

Some say the best way to make the general market rise is for the Federal Reserve to gun the money supply. Hardly a day goes by when stock prices don't increase or decrease because investors are trying to guess the Fed's next monetary move.

But the daily guessing is shortsighted. True, the Federal Reserve can at times push stock prices up by increasing money growth — or pull them down by decreasing its growth. So when the Fed changes the money supply this way and that, it helps make stock prices jumpy. But the effect of money supply changes on the stock market is quite unpredictable and temporary. Indeed, greater growth of the money supply over a period of years is more likely to produce lower, not higher, stock prices.

The reason is that, over the years, substantially higher money growth tends strongly to increase the rate of inflation. And the higher rate of inflation directly and indirectly undermines national production and business earnings, which are the long-term supporters of stock prices.

Take the last 35 years, beginning in 1956 and ending in 1990. Compare the averages for rates of inflation, growth of the money supply, and changes in the real (inflation-corrected) Dow Jones Industrial Average.

The long-term comparison shows that inflation usually followed money growth up and down. It shows also that real stock prices declined when inflation was relatively high between 1965 and 1980. And at earlier and later times, real stock prices increased when inflation was relatively low or declining.

So a farsighted view of money and stock prices does not call for the Federal Reserve actively turning monetary policy this way and that. Rather, it has the Fed consistently and prudently trying to keep inflation at bay by containing and stabilizing money growth. Such a persistent and predictable monetary policy would strengthen the stock market because it would make the economy stronger.

Savings-and-Loans

Savings and Groans

ダダダダ

What caused the savings-and-loan fiasco? The popular answer is greed and deregulation. Freed from tight government regulation in the 1980s, managers looted their institutions and stuck taxpayers with the cleanup bill.

But the real cause of the savings-and-loan debacle is government itself. During the Great Depression of the 1930s, government began insuring deposits at commercial banks and savings-and-loan institutions. Government also directed thrift institutions to invest mostly in home mortgages with fixed rates of interest. Most of the funds for these investments came from deposits, which savers could withdraw at will. So savings-and-loans used *short-term deposits* to make *long-term mortgage loans.*

As long as interest rates were relatively stable, thrift institutions did well. But when rising inflation began to push up interest rates in the 1960s, thrifts had to pay higher short-term rates to depositors while earning lower fixed rates on existing long-term mortgages. To keep thrifts afloat, Congress in 1966 tried to contain rising interest costs by capping the rates they could pay to depositors.

But the financial band-aid could not stanch the hemorrhaging of savings-and-loans in the late 1970s and early '80s. When double-digit inflation pushed interest rates sky high, savers quickly put their money elsewhere to earn higher interest. Congress then had to junk its interest rate controls to allow thrifts to pay competitive rates to depositors. But thrift institutions still earned their money from past mortgages — made at much lower, fixed rates — so their incomes remained flat as interest costs soared.

As earnings sank, in 1982, Congress allowed savings-and-loans to invest in higher-yielding (and riskier) alternatives to mortgages. This act followed a reckless increase in deposit insurance in 1980, when Congress pushed coverage from $40,000 to $100,000 per account. No wonder large deposits began flowing into savings-and-loans. And no wonder depositors had little incentive to monitor how the thrifts were using their money. Best to put one's government-protected money into those thrifts paying highest rates — which usually were those taking biggest risks.

Many of the risks went sour, heaping even more losses on those suffered earlier, when inflation had pushed interest costs far above earnings on fixed-rate mortgages. But instead of assuring rapid closure or buyout of failed thrifts, some members of Congress, with an eye on their constituencies of thrifts and builders, delayed action and thereby made the cleanup cost mount.

So the savings-and-loan mess is a sad story about government — of paternalistic regulation, of ruinous inflation produced by government policy, of foolish risks by both depositors and thrifts encouraged by government guarantees, and of costly delays as government prevented the marketplace from closing failed thrifts or merging them with healthier ones.

S & Ls: Where Have All the Dollars Gone?

✍✍✍✍

Savings-and-loan institutions have lost about $200 billion since the mid-1970s. Where have all the dollars gone?

Tracking the money is tricky. But the *Wall Street Journal*, based on estimates of thrift authority Bert Ely, has made a stab.

The *Journal* discovered that homeowners were a major beneficiary. When interest rates soared because of higher inflation in the 1970s, savings-and-loans — or S&Ls — had to pay depositors higher rates. But earnings of S&Ls depended largely on fixed-rate mortgage loans made when inflation and interest rates were much lower. With earnings flat and interest costs soaring, thrift institutions began losing a bundle — in effect, transferring money to homeowners with low fixed-rate mortgages. These losses account for some 15 percent of the $200 billion. By the early 1980s, nearly 9 out of 10 thrifts were losing money, and the thrift industry as a whole had negative net worth.

Another 20 percent of the loss consists of bad real estate loans made in the 1980s after Congress allowed thrifts to seek higher returns to offset losses to homeowners. These dollars went to land sellers and to brokers, lawyers, and others who helped negotiate deals that turned sour.

How much went to crooked managers who defrauded depositors? Much less than most believe. The *Journal* estimates that fraud accounts for at most 10 percent of the total loss. And losses to issuers of junk bonds represent only about 2 percent.

To this point, these factors account for slightly less than half of the $200 billion. Another big chunk was caused directly by government's extravagant deposit insurance, which Congress increased 2.5 times in 1980 to $100,000. Knowing that government assured the safety of their money, big depositors shopped for S&Ls paying higher rates and ignored the condition and tactics of these institutions. But the highest-paying thrifts were usually the sickest, which should have been promptly closed. Instead, their losses mounted as many depositors — and the brokers who often pooled their money — raked in dollars from premium rates paid by insolvent S&Ls. Losses from paying bloated rates account for about 10 percent of the total.

And deposit insurance and government-induced delays in closing down insolvent thrifts continued to pump money into dead institutions. So the thrift industry lost even more, representing another 22 percent of the $200 billion debacle.

The remaining 20 percent or so of the total loss went to excess thrift expenses, government administration of the bailout, and liquidation losses.

In total, the $200 billion tab is "one of the biggest transfers of wealth in U.S. history," says the *Journal*. And its cause lies largely with government policies — policies that spawned inflation, offered lavish insurance to deposits, and delayed closure or merger of failed savings-and-loans.

GLOBAL THINKING: TRADE, FINANCE, DEVELOPMENT

Trade: Purposes, Experiences, and Policies

Truth and Free Trade

✍✍✍✍

"You may think me a bit slow," said Mouse Karl slowly, "but when I do see the truth, I firmly clutch it to my bosom."

Talk of bosom-clutching tends to make Mouse Adam a bit nervous. "So long as you adhere only to genuine truth," he said, "I applaud."

"You should agree this time that it is truth," Karl said reassuringly, "for you taught it to me. I refer to trade. Trade is a very good thing. It must be, for everyone does it. And no mouse would participate in exchange if he did not gain from it. No one will trade unless he himself puts a greater value on what he *receives* than on what he *gives up*. Since *each* participant in the swap deems himself to be better off, then it is unambiguous that trade is terrific. And an activity which benefits everyone involved ought not to be curtailed."

"We may reasonably say," Adam said cautiously, "that the burden of proof is on those who propose to prevent freely consenting mice from trading. But not everyone agrees that it is unequivocally desirable to permit the buying and selling of everything."

"Then they are demented mice," cried Karl caustically. "If some gain and none lose from an activity, it is crazy to forbid it."

"Still, the community *does* forbid or restrict selected trading," Adam pointed out. "It can be claimed that some traders do *not* well know their own preferences; and some supposedly know their preferences *now* but will be disappointed *later* by their actions today; and some do know what they want, but *should* not have those preferences; and some trades which are beneficial to the traders will have bad side effects on third parties. I doubt that anyone is a full-fledged free-trader, unwilling to accept *any* restrictions on *any* possible trade."

"All you are saying," said Karl, "is that the woods are full of blue-nose and dictatorial types who are eager to impose their arbitrary standards and preferences on the rest of us."

"One mouse's idealist is another's ideologue," observed Adam. "Is trade in naughty pictures and sinful activities and gambling unsponsored by government and mind-blowing drugs a good thing? Many quite rational and reasonable mice fear that such transactions harm not only the immediate traders but also others in the community. How about required licensing of professions? Probably most believe that untrained people, equipped with only an ice pick and a fingernail file, should not be permitted to do brain surgery — even if the patient is willing. College students — all of whom are ever so liberated — will riot over a university contract for research in national defense."

"Sigh," sighed Karl. "I do understand the *explanation* of trading activity. But to *account* for trade is not in itself to *condone* trade. The theory of trade tells us much about *why* and *how* trade takes place; it does not pass final *judgment* on the ultimate *desirability* of trade. And it is well to understand what theory explains — and what it does not explain."

The Trade Deficit and Cheap Foreign Labor

ᵍᵍᵍᵍ

Cheap foreign labor is responsible for our enormous trade deficit. That is what many Americans believe. This myth persists with the tenacity of a hungry dog gripping a bone. It would help to bury it — the myth, not the bone.

First, the simple contention ignores differences in labor productivity. If, on average, foreign workers produced half as much per hour as do Americans, then foreigners could earn a wage no more than half as much if their unit costs are not to be higher. If you are paid $10 for making 10 pins in an hour, then each pin has a labor cost of $1. The unit labor cost is the same if I receive just $5 for making only 5 pins per hour. Foreign hourly *wage* rates below ours do not mean that foreign production *costs* and *prices* also will be lower.

Second, foreign workers are paid in their own currencies, not dollars. If a South Korean worker receives 2,000 won per hour, is that wage more or less than the $10 earned by an American? It depends on the rate of exchange between the won and the dollar. If the dollar could buy 2,000 won, then the Korean wage would be equal to $1. In that case, the Korean worker would earn less than the American. But if the dollar buys only 100 won, then the hourly wage of 2,000 won would equal $20, greater than the American wage. Whether the Korean earns more or less than the American thus depends on the rate at which dollars and won can be traded.

What do exchange rate gymnastics have to do with the argument about cheap labor and our trade deficit? If the gap between foreign and American *wage rates* rises above the gap between *worker productivities* — if the American money wage more than offsets the American edge in physical productivity — then foreign labor would be relatively cheap. With American wages high relative to Korean, our imports would rise, our exports would fall, and the trade deficit would grow.

But here is a further point often ignored. As foreigners buy fewer American goods, they demand fewer dollars. And as we import more, we supply more dollars. The result is a surplus of dollars in international markets. This dollar surplus would cause the prices of the dollar to fall in terms of foreign money. And if it takes more dollars to equal a given foreign wage, then the dollar measure of that wage will rise. Foreign wages — measured in dollars — would rise until they reflected the difference between foreign and American productivities.

Given international productivity differences and the money payments to workers here and abroad, freely adjusting exchange rates will keep the general level of American wages competitive with foreign wages, even though foreign incomes generally are smaller in purchasing power.

Our trade deficit has ballooned in recent years, and some worry about that. But cheap labor abroad — reflecting lower productivity abroad — is not the cause of the deficit.

Foreign Lessons

♨♨♨♨

Foreign trade is not a simple subject. So it's not surprising that many find it ... well, foreign. And they are inclined to agree with proposals that superficially seem sensible yet actually produce misery.

Take the popular belief about imports and jobs. Layoffs in the auto industry and elsewhere seem to confirm that imports are destroying jobs of our workers. So why not put Americans first and protect their employment by restricting imports?

One problem is, such a policy is more likely to hurt than help American workers. No wonder a group of over 1,000 economists petitioned President Hoover in 1930 to veto the Smoot-Hawley bill, which proposed huge hikes in tariffs. At the time, its cosponsor, Rep. Hawley, argued that, "The Tariff...is for the purpose of maintaining our industries, protecting our labor, sustaining our agriculture and promoting the general prosperity of this country."

Economists knew that Hawley's argument was wrong. But the bill sailed through Congress, and President Hoover, with an eye on the upcoming election, signed it. The massive tariffs then helped to constrict world trade, reduce production and employment, and promote the horror of the Great Depression, with the related fallout of World War II.

This was not the outcome intended. But Americans, and others, poorly understood (and politicians never admitted) that greater foreign trade usually means more, not less, production and employment in our country.

Recent experience confirms such a relationship between imports and employment. To measure employment, consider the number of employees in manufacturing, construction, and mining, the so-called goods-producing industries. And to measure imports, take the value of imported merchandise as a percentage of national output.

Over the past decade and a half and longer, these two measures closely moved together. When imports increased as a fraction of national output, employment in American industries producing goods went up, not down.

Put simply, trade helps make the economic pie bigger. When we buy imports, we pay dollars to foreigners. Some of those dollars come back to us when foreigners use them to buy U.S. stocks, bonds, and other assets. More funds then become available for our businesses to invest in new tools and technology, and the greater investment boosts production and employment here.

Most of the dollars spent abroad return when foreigners spend them on our output. True, our imports can cause production and employment to shrink in some areas. But foreigners' purchases from us expand production and employment in others. American workers then move to more efficient industries and businesses, where they are more productive and can earn higher wages.

Foreign trade promotes our nation's wealth. That was an important lesson that President Hoover and Congress found so alien in 1930. But is the lesson any less foreign today?

The Trade Balance and the Economy

ØØØØ

For most of the past century, we were comforted by our net exports of goods and services. But now we are in our eighth straight year of deficit. In response, some are having a cow.

Are net imports a bad thing? What causes them? And if the import balance is to be eliminated, what other adjustments in the economy may be required?

Imports can't be all bad. We have imports because domestic residents want to obtain foreign goods, and wanting stuff — for consumption or production — is not crazy. Further, if we buy more from foreigners than they buy from us, then their output contributes more to our living than our production contributes to theirs. Whether a country is prospering or stagnant or recovering from catastrophe of war, there is much to be said for having the rest of the world, on balance, working for it.

Of course, a net inflow of foreign goods is accompanied by a net inflow of foreign capital. A country, like an individual, which spends more than current income must borrow or sell assets to cover the difference.

Now, how is the flow of investment into or out of a country related to the domestic economy?

Broadly, net foreign investment equals the balance of domestic saving and investment. But saving includes the government budget imbalance. If the budget is in *surplus*, with receipts greater than spending, the government is said to be saving, and the surplus is added to private saving to get total saving. But with a *deficit*, government is a dissaver, and the deficit is deemed on offset to private saving.

During most of the period since World War II, the investment/saving differences and the spending/revenue differences were small and largely offsetting, so the net foreign capital flow did not amount to much. But beginning in 1983, the excess of saving over investment (averaging about $15 billion per year) has been swamped by an average government deficit of $117 billion, so there has been annual net foreign investment in the U.S. of over $100 billion.

Despite the fact that the gains from trade stem from imports and that exports are a cost to the economy, suppose you instinctively abhor a negative trade imbalance. But how to reduce the net inflow of foreign investment? Do you increase exports or reduce imports? And do you increase saving or reduce investment, and do you increase taxes or reduce government spending?

Trade restrictions and promotions can affect the *pattern* of trade, the *composition* of trade, and the aggregate *volume* of trade. But tariffs, quotas, and subsidizations can have no effect on the *balance* of trade unless they somehow modify saving, investment, taxes, and government spending.

Poor Senator Snort, who takes it on faith that eliminating an import balance is desirable and that it is readily accomplished by trade controls imposed directly and in isolation from the rest of the economy. His objective is misconceived, and his tactics are misdirected.

Foreign Trade and Terrifying Bargains

ﾉﾉﾉﾉ

Most of us enjoy a spot of competition on the playing field. When it comes to our employment and income, however, we are not playing, and it would be nice to be a monopolist. But not many attain and retain monopoly status, especially in international trade.

So how to cope with foreign competitors? *Outcompeting* competitors — producing products which are relatively attractive to consumers — is hard work. And we might fail. It is more convenient and certain to get government to *curtail* competition. We can't lose a game which is not played because the other team is kept off the field! But when the game is competitive economic activity, not playing means we do lose production efficiency and consumption options, which means we live less well.

Oh, Daddy Warbucks and Senator Snort assure us that they really are gung ho competitors. All they ask for is "fair" trade. And trade which is "fair" is not necessarily "free." Among their dastardly tricks, foreigners are all the time "dumping." For two generations, the United States has pretended to protect its economy with anti-dumping laws.

"Dumping" certainly does not sound nice. But not everyone agrees on just what it is, and few have any coherent notion of why it occurs or what its consequences are or how public policy should cope with it.

Dumping by foreigners has to do with charging us a price for the good in question which is in some sense *low*. The price may be lower than foreign production *costs* or lower than the *price* charged in the foreign country or lower than foreign *market value*.

All those benchmarks are dubious and difficult. How do we get detailed data on foreign costs? And we seek what costs of what producers under what circumstances for what rate of output? Even price presents problems: the pertinent price includes what charges, taxes, commissions, and discounts? And foreign market value — if not the same as price — is an ethereal notion fit only for philosophers.

Whatever the particular criterion of the lowness of price, isn't a low price attractive to buyers? As economists Leland Yeager and David Tuerck have emphasized, the *existence* of a low price is more fascinating than the *cause* of the lowness. Foreign sellers may discriminate in our favor with relatively low prices as a strategy which is entirely reasonable in light of different market demands and costs here and abroad. And those different costs can reflect different natural endowments, different social experience and personal attributes, and different public policies and private strategies. Whatever the cause of the low price we are charged, a bargain is a bargain.

This is hardly the whole story. A current low price of foreign-made widgets will not be applauded by our own producers of widgets. But price is of some interest to consumers — and each of us is a consumer. We are not obliged to be terrified by bargains.

Farm Aid and Foreign Blockade

ΌΌΌΌ

Federal farm subsidies distort and suppress markets: They yield chronic surpluses that bloat government granaries; they sow largess mainly among wealthy farmers; and they shrink total national production through inefficient use of resources. Further, federal farm subsidies batter markets abroad: Bad domestic policy becomes also bad foreign policy.

Leading the assault on foreign markets are so-called marketing loans. Actually, these euphemistically labeled "loans" are grants which do not require repayment. Consider cotton or rice. American farmers sell each product at its world market price. The federal government then grants farmers the difference between the market price and a higher government-stipulated amount known as the target price.

Suppose the target price for cotton is 80 cents per pound, and world market price is 30 cents. Cotton farmers can sell all they want at the market price of 30 cents, but the government guarantees them the target price of 80 cents by paying the 50-cent difference.

That difference is financed by the American taxpayers. For both cotton and rice, the subsidies encourage farmers to produce more for the world market. And as world supplies of the goods rise, their market prices plunge.

Lower prices are of no concern to American cotton and rice farmers, of course, for government subsidies continually assure the higher target prices. But foreign farmers are harmed because they receive lower prices for their cotton or rice. "For example," states the 1987 *Economic Report of the President*, "high target prices for U.S. rice coupled with marketing loans have resulted in large U.S. exports imposing significant costs on Thailand, a major rice exporter. The same basic policies for cotton have generated similar ... effects for Egypt, Bangladesh, Mexico, Guatemala, Paraguay, and other cotton-exporting countries." James Bovard, of the Cato Institute, cites similar punishment of poor foreign cotton growers in Malawi, Cameroon, and Sudan.

But the global harm inflicted by farm subsidies is not limited to marketing loans for cotton and rice. Strict import quotas for sugar inflict considerable injury, not only on American consumers, but among friendly nations by limiting their sugar sales in the U.S. The quotas reduce incomes in the Philippines, Brazil, and Caribbean and Central American nations.

The result is an embarrassing conflict between America's farm policy and foreign policy. As the editors of *The New Republic* magazine state: "What is the point of trying to help incipient capitalism with one hand if, with the other, we're hurting it?... If we would get out of the way, and let developing nations freely take the first step toward capitalism, maybe we wouldn't have to subsidize the trip so heavily."

The government ought to get out of the way by ending farm aid that blocks the development of foreign economies while weakening our own economy.

Sanctions, Sense, and Sticks

ⱰⱰⱰⱰ

The world is quite a naughty place. Much of the naughtiness is committed through and in the name of national governments. Governments prepare for aggressive war and invade neighbors, they shamelessly exploit citizens, they brutally suppress domestic dissent and foment revolution abroad, they wish us ill and aid our enemies, they monopolistically charge too much for their exports and buy too little of our goods.

How are we to impress proper behavior upon such abhorrent and recalcitrant characters? How can we persuade or pressure them into moral rectitude, political gentility, military quiescence, and economic cooperation? A common response has been: *economic sanctions*. We will squeeze the villains with curtailment of foreign trade and investment. Economic pressure supposedly is quickly effective, can be directed precisely, and is not expensive to apply.

The United States has a busy record over many decades of trying to use sanctions as a foreign policy lever. The record is not one of total failure — not quite. But successes have been few and generally very limited, while failures have been much more common, sometimes being humiliating and resulting in net loss. Sanctions have been imposed in situations where they have been readily circumvented or diluted to triviality. They have then been a mode of petty political posturing more than a procedure of applying power.

John Train, an analyst of foreign and military affairs for *The Wall Street Journal*, is the latest to review the conditions to be satisfied if sanctions are likely to succeed.

First, the imposer of the sanctions had better be vastly more *powerful* than the target country, and systematically *vigorous* in implementation of the sanction. Even being economically much larger is not enough in the absence of effective (although often reluctant) international cooperation with potential *alternative suppliers* of the embargoed goods.

Second, not only may the target country draw on alternative suppliers of a good, it may turn to *substitute goods*, some produced domestically. So embargoed goods had better be of strategic significance.

Still, the *goals* of the sanction policy are best kept modest. The more ambitious the objectives, the more conspicuous and serious are likely to be the repercussions of the embargo — including unintended repercussions on third countries. And history shouts that a community under significant siege tends to coalesce and adapt in support of the governmental regime we set out to weaken. At the same time, major sanctions are likely to be economically and politically divisive at home.

All this suggests why we have succeeded in so little and failed in so much as we try to swagger with sanctions while avoiding a fight. "Sanctions may go wrong," Mr. Train tells us, "because they are ill-considered expressions of political outrage rather than the result of careful calculation. But ... great-power statecraft is too grave a matter, and the ultimate sanction, war, always too close, to permit silliness. The U.S. looks weak when it inverts Teddy Roosevelt's admonition to walk softly and carry a big stick."

International Finance and Capital Movements

Mouse Wisdom: Foreign Trade and Investment

ŚŚŚŚ

"I'm worried," worried Mouse Karl.

"What is it this time?" asked Mouse Adam patiently.

"I worry about the huge deficit in foreign trade," replied Karl, "and I worry about foreigners no longer investing in our country."

"Your worrying worries me," answered Adam. "Why don't you go to the cheese festival and have some fun?"

"Their displays are full of imported cheese," fretted Karl, "and the festival is housed in a building owned by a foreign investor. Even there, I can't escape trade deficits and foreign investments. I will rest only when the trade deficit comes down and when foreigners assure us that they will not suddenly pull the plug on all their investments here."

"The trade deficit is not great cause for alarm," Adam said assuringly, "but I do know how to reduce the import balance and even convert it into an export balance."

"How?" shrieked Karl.

"By reducing or even reversing foreign investment in our country," answered Adam.

"But that is one of my worries!" cried Karl.

"I know," said Adam. "But you *can't* reduce the trade deficit unless foreigners stop investing so much here."

"Economic mumbo-jumbo," snapped Karl.

"It is an accounting fact," insisted Adam, "that our import trade balance is the mirror image of net foreign investment here. If the import balance of trade gets bigger, so does the inflow of capital from abroad. If foreigners invest less here, we reduce our net imports of goods. And if, on balance, capital moved out of our country, it would be accompanied by net *exports* of goods."

"You are making my head hurt," complained Karl.

Adam was sympathetic. "I am saying simply," he said, "that things are paid for with things in two-way exchange. When we get things, we give up things. We pay for imports of things with exports of things."

"Obviously," agreed Karl.

"Now," Adam continued, "if the things bought and the things sold internationally are both merchandise — if we simply swap exported goods for imported goods — then trade is balanced and neither country is borrowing from or investing in the other. But suppose we finance the purchase of foreign goods only partly by export of our goods, making up the difference by export of bank accounts and ownership titles of office buildings. It is still the case that we are exporting things to pay for imports of things, but what we export can include claims on and ownership of assets in this country. And that export of claims and ownership to foreigners *is* foreign investment here."

"I am convinced," conceded Karl. "If we import more goods than we export, then foreigners *will* gain investments here. And if foreigners were to reduce their investments here, we *will* have an export balance of goods. The balance of payments does balance. The only question is *how* it balances: do we have *import* balances of goods and capital or *export* balances of goods and capital? And the present pattern of getting, on balance, both foreign goods and foreign capital has its attractiveness."

Adjustment Mechanisms: Letting Variables Vary

♱♱♱♱

It is not to be anticipated that the money value of a country's exports of goods and services over a year will exactly equal the value of its imports. But a trade imbalance will be financed somehow.

An import balance can be paid for by income earned on investments abroad or drawing down accumulated claims on foreigners or foreigners increasing their claims on us or sending gold to foreigners or receiving gifts from foreigners. In one way or another, the total of transactions with the rest of the world — the balance of international payments — will balance.

Still, some ways of financing cannot go on forever. A country has only a finite accumulation of investments abroad and of gold to draw on, and foreigners may not be willing to continue indefinitely to lend or to make gifts on a large scale.

These financing constraints give rise to market corrections. The trade imbalance itself triggers changes in market variables which will either eliminate the trade imbalance or confine the imbalance to a dimension which will be sustained by profitable actions of international investors. That is, the market embodies an "adjustment mechanism" — *if* market variables are permitted to vary.

But the spontaneous equilibrating orchestration of market variables can be thrown into disharmony by government suppression or manipulation of the variations of those variables. The broad variables involved in international markets include both national incomes and prices, with prices including wage rates, interest rates, and exchange rates along with prices of goods. And government loves to tinker with all of them.

Increasingly since the outbreak of World War I in 1914, governments have tried to keep national income high and rising, they have diddled with individual prices and tried to suppress inflation with direct controls, and they have tried to put floors on wages, ceilings on interest rates, and straight-jackets on exchange rates.

We can have a market-induced, self-correcting international mechanism when *some* variables are pegged or manipulated, but *no* machinery can operate if no variables can vary.

But for a quarter of a century after World War II, with the International Monetary Fund, we were cursed with both pegged exchange rates and governmental management of incomes and prices. Leaving *no* market variables free to vary is a *decreed arrangement*, not an *equilibrating mechanism*. And — with the shortages and surpluses, uncertainties and divisiveness which always result from controls — it makes us poorer than we need be.

Price Control in the Foreign Exchange Market

ℬℬℬℬ

A market is a procedure through which something is bought and sold at a price.

A market is a very useful institution: it brings demanders and suppliers together for exchanges which benefit both parties of the trade. And, if people in the market are free to bid and offer as they please, the exchanges are not only mutually beneficial, but also equilibrating: prices are agreed to at which buyers can buy and sellers can sell all they want at those prices — the market is cleared.

The foreign exchange market really *is* a market. The commodities traded are currencies of the world; and the prices are exchange rates — the dollar price of the yen, the peso price of the mark.

The foreign exchange market is a smooth-operating mechanism, for the commodities are standardized (a dollar is a dollar, but wheat comes in different grades), and communication is virtually instantaneous. So if the foreign exchange market is not hamstrung by government, it is readily cleared, and market participants are not frustrated by shortages and surpluses.

Although equilibrium prices are generated by the intermingled activities of the people in the market, no person — private trader or government manipulator — can know at the beginning of the day what those equilibrium prices will turn out to be. So only by accident could a price-pegging operation establish a market-clearing price. There is no formula or procedure — not even a wetted finger in the breeze or meditation over frogs' entrails — which will reveal before the fact what exchange rates an unencumbered market would provide today, tomorrow, and all the following tomorrows.

And since an open market will efficiently equilibrate, with changing prices quickly reflecting changing supplies and demands, why are there always interventionists eager to decree prices? There is no reason to suppose that monetary authorities can do the market's job better than can the market.

We do not require discretionary intervention by bureaucrats to clear the market; indeed, such intervention precludes equilibrium for long, if it permits equilibrium at all. Even if the interventionists happened to specify an equilibrium price — which the market would have yielded, anyway — that price will not remain the equilibrium price. As incomes and preferences and prices and interest rates and technologies and input supplies and business practices and government policies change, the equilibrium exchange rate value will change; and if we are stuck with the old pegged price, then the foreign exchange market will no longer be cleared.

If the busybodies eventually wish to pull the peg and impose a different price — for it is costly to buck the market, defending and living with artificial prices — then they are back in the fog of uncertainty about where to replace the peg. And they do not know how long to wait before changing the peg, whether the change in the price should be done gradually or precipitously, or how best to make do in the intervening imbalance.

Price-control of currencies — like price-control of wheat and apartments — does not give us equilibrium prices, and it does not help to correct disequilibrium prices. Markets are made less useful by the tinkerings of price controllers.

False Fears About Foreign Investment

✍✍✍✍

Foreigners have been buying buildings, stocks, and other American assets. Many believe such foreign investment is dangerous. In a 1988 poll, more than four-fifths of respondents opposed foreign purchases of domestic businesses and real estate. In another survey, more than half thought greater foreign investment in the United States threatens American economic independence.

Americans had long invested more abroad than foreigners had invested here: America was a *net* owner of foreign assets. But the roles began to reverse after 1981. Foreign investment here soon pushed ahead of U.S. investment abroad. By 1985, official data show foreigners owning more assets here than we owned abroad. The figures greatly exaggerate the change, for they understate the relative value of foreign assets owned by U.S. citizens. Still, the Department of

Commerce *officially* reports that in 1988 foreigners were *net* owners of $532 billion of U.S. assets.

What are the dangers that net foreign investment is thought to present? One is that foreigners will control us politically. Yet, eminent economist Milton Friedman suggests that foreign investors are actually putting themselves at the mercy of our government: "They are gambling," he says, "that the U.S. will not expropriate their assets, or prevent them from benefiting from their dollar earnings." The U.S. did expropriate German assets during World War II.

Still, couldn't foreigners dominate us by threatening sudden withdrawal of their investments? If foreigners wanted to take out their investments, they would first have to sell them. The rapid sale of stocks, real estate, and other holdings would reduce their prices, so foreigners would lose wealth when selling them.

Moreover, upon selling their assets, foreigners would obtain dollars, which they would then have to exchange for other currencies. But as they demanded more yen, marks, and such, foreigners would bid up the dollar prices of those currencies. The dollar would then buy fewer amounts of other moneys, so foreigners would again lose considerable wealth when selling.

Foreign investors are not likely to inflict these financial wounds on themselves. And they are not likely to act simultaneously with such single-minded purpose. They are many independent individuals scattered about the globe whose only common characteristic is to seek the best returns for their investments.

Those returns have been offered by American assets in recent years. Foreigners have benefited from investing in these attractive assets, but so have Americans.

With today's highly integrated world financial market, it is not surprising that U.S. annual private domestic investment and net foreign investment in the U.S. have been strongly correlated. Nor is it surprising that since the early 1980s, world investors — both American and foreign — have found the U.S. economy to be a choice place for investment. And that investment has made the American economy still more attractive.

Patriotism and Capital Imports

✍✍✍✍

Love of homeland is not ridiculous. But perhaps feeling for national family has led some to fear investment here by foreigners, and naive fear can convert patriotism into chauvinism. Some sensible perspective on inflow of foreign capital is in order.

First, what *magnitudes* are involved? Capital movements into and out of the U.S. are not puny, but they hardly dominate our enormous economy. Over the past decade, the average annual net inflow of capital from abroad has been just over 2 percent of the GNP, and that ratio has been falling since 1987. And the proportion of federal debt held by foreigners remained within a range of about 13-15 percent all through the 1980s.

Second, what has *caused* the considerable capital inflow of these past eight years? The mechanisms of the market and the logic of accounting make capital inflow inevitable when there is an import balance of goods, services, and investment income. An American import of a widget is financed by the U.S. importer drawing down a previously accumulated demand deposit in a foreign bank or by the foreign exporter building up a deposit in a bank here. And either a reduction in U.S. claims on the rest of the world or an increase in foreign claims on us is a capital flow into the U.S.

The most glamorous form of international investment is so-called *direct* investment — the acquisition of foreign buildings and land rather than demand deposits and bonds. The net flow of direct investment was into, rather than out of, the U.S. during the 1980s. Indeed, in the early '80s, the U.S. actually reduced its direct investment abroad, for the American economy has been one of the world's most attractive places for American as well as foreign investors.

But even if the U.S. has looked good to global investors, we have a final question: Does foreign direct investment help or hurt the American economy?

Economists Cecil E. Bohanon and T. Norman van Cott, of Ball State University, consider who gains and who loses when Mr. Brown, the owner of XYZ Corporation, sells his firm to the highest bidder, a Japanese company. The investor considered the deal advantageous, for otherwise he would not have made the offer. Future profits of XYZ will go to the Japanese instead of to Mr. Brown, but the rest of us are not claimants to those profits in any case. And taxes will continue to be paid by the new owner, so government is not affected. Mr. Brown gains, for otherwise he would not have sold his property.

The Japanese were prepared to make the highest offer because they believe they can make the largest profits. They expect to do so either by providing more or better services or by reducing costs. With a more attractive product, XYZ customers benefit; with lower costs, XYZ absorbs fewer resources, so the American economy gains.

In sum, with unrestricted investment, many have gained, and no one has lost. Even a patriot can smile.

International Debt: Rescues and Reforms

ØØØØ

The international debt crisis of Mexico, Brazil, Argentina, and many lesser economies became abruptly apparent in mid-1982. Their massive foreign debts did not materialize overnight, of course, but few were prepared for announcement that such potentially wealthy countries could not continue interest payments.

It was widely supposed in creditor countries that this was only a transitory difficulty. After all, world oil prices had softened after 1979, and interest rates had risen along with inflation. So the preferred prescription for the debt problem was somehow to reduce interest rates, to increase demand for exports of debtor countries by world economic recovery, and meanwhile to continue lending to the debtors by banks and international agencies.

But Anna J. Schwartz, distinguished financial analyst, finds that the debt problem was not temporary concern stemming from simply a recession in industrialized economies and a rise in short-term interest rates. It was a genuine crisis of *solvency*, not a passing tightening of *liquidity*. The cause of the crisis was not so much breakdown in the world economy as miserable management of the debtors' economies, abetted by peculiar policies of the world's lenders.

Borrowing can be sensible. But this requires sensible use of the borrowed funds. The resources acquired through borrowing must be productively employed, creating income out of which the debt can be serviced and ultimately repaid. In the current, ongoing episode, a huge proportion of the borrowed funds was not used well: much went into consumption rather than investment, much was sunk into unprofitable state enterprises, and much left the borrowing countries in "capital flight." Foolishness, inefficiency, and corruption wasted a great deal of what was borrowed as the debts continued to grow.

An internally collapsing situation can be sustained only by external propping. Unwise borrowing has been feasible through imprudent, if not utterly unconscious, lending, largely by private banks. And after 1982, creditors found themselves holding a tiger by the tail, hardly daring to let go. So new money has been loaned in order to enable debtors to pay interest on old money, hoping — typically in vain — to buy time in which half-finished investment projects might be completed.

Bankers belatedly began to realize that nonperforming loans are made by poorly performing lenders. But they were cajoled and coerced by their governments and international agencies to paper over the genuine problems of the debtor economies and to support "the facade that the foreign borrowers were faced only with a liquidity problem."

The prescription of the early 1980s has not been adequate: interest rates *have* fallen, the world economy *has* generally flourished, and lending to debtors *has* continued — but so has the problem. Reforms have not been made, and stop-gap rescues cannot work.

Economic Growth

The Goal of Growth

ꬽꬽꬽꬽ

We are not likely to go far in attaining a goal when we are not sure what the goal is and what may be entailed in attaining it.

Is "economic growth" good? Other things given, having more goods is better than having less. But there can be nebulousness in the concept, the objective, and the required strategy of growth. We can agree that Utopia is fine — provided that each of us is free to make his own specifications of Utopia and how best to get there.

The meaning of growth is commonly couched in terms of a persistent, substantial rise in output — *per capita*. Perhaps we should add reference to *distribution* of the social output. If, in a community of 1 million, the incomes of 999,999 people remain constant while that of one person increases, national income rises. Indeed, national income could rise while each of the incomes of the 999,999 falls. Is this to be deemed a "growing" economy? If not, then how many of the million must have how big an increase in income for the economy to qualify as a "grower"?

At any rate, we want lots of output. What is here required is, in broad outline, quite apparent.

First, *use all resources as much as possible*. With respect to the human factor, perhaps an 18-hour workday, at least six days a week and 51 weeks per year, beginning at age five and continuing to the grave, seems about right.

Second, *use all resources as effectively as possible*, largely by providing powerful incentives for producers — even if this requires highly uneven incomes and selective use of the thumb screw.

Finally, *consume currently as little as possible*, in order to devote maximum resources to capital formation, thereby making output tomorrow greater than that of today.

Further, the three ingredients may not be wholly compatible. The prospect of working less hard in the future is a present incentive, but the incentive may lose force if the prospect is never realized. Again, drastic and indefinitely prolonged curtailment of consumption seems hardly the way to induce greatest effort. One may even wonder about an unending passion for capital accumulation: if we save today, it is in order to consume more tomorrow — but does tomorrow ever come?

The real issue seems to be whether the economy is producing the biggest possible bundle of goods of the *sort it desires* with the resources it has available and *chooses to employ*. But this — maximizing desired output with selected resources — is the notion of *efficiency*. Much confusion and arguing at cross purposes would be abated if the discussion were in terms of (properly defined) efficiency instead of (ill-, or un-, defined) growth.

Determinants of Economic Growth

✑✑✑✑

Some peculiar types find economic growth dangerously simple and seductively easy, for, to them, growth is not desirable, with greater wealth enhancing our ability to do stupid and naughty things. A larger number find growth attractive and also simple and easy enough as long as Big Brother decrees and directs the activity. Most agree that producing more of what we want most is a good thing; but they can see that growth is complex in prerequisite and process and hard to sustain in a stingy world.

What *are* the immediate determinants of economic growth? Many things. Some analysts — including economist Arnold Harberger in a publication of the Institute for Contemporary Studies — have tried to classify them.

Economic growth entails production, and production entails combining productive inputs into commodity outputs. Given climate and endowments of nature, aggregate output depends on the *quantity*, the *quality*, and the *efficiency of use* of scarce labor and capital. What, in turn, determines the quantity, quality, and efficiency of labor and capital?

The quantity of labor is a function not only of the size of population but also of the proportion of the population in the labor force and of the proportion of the labor force which is employed. The amount of capital stems from net rates of saving and investing, not only domestically but also by world financial partners.

Questions of quality are more subtle. The quality of labor services is affected by health and age composition and occupational distribution, by education and technological knowledge and general cultural attributes, by on-the-job training and work experience and managerial direction. The quality of capital is intertwined with the quality of some kinds of labor. It reflects at any given time the state of the industrial arts — the level of production knowledge applied from the accumulation of knowledge available. And over time, in global competition, just to stay in the same place, a community must run fast through improvement in designs and technical innovation.

For growth, resources of substantial amount and of high quality still must be used efficiently. Somehow — through processes of acquiring information and of applying optimal decision rules — we are to shift workers and capital from lower-productivity to higher-productivity activities, developing appropriate specialization and division of labor, exploiting economies of scale, and innovating new products.

More than two centuries ago, Adam Smith concluded that the *quality* of resources and the *efficiency* of their use are more important than their *quantity*. The poorest nations, he noted, have the largest working proportions of population. What primarily determines how well we live is, as Smith put it, "the skill, dexterity and judgment with which [our] labor is generally applied." That is still true.

Markets, Investment, and Growth

ᔑᔑᔑᔑ

Good teaching of economics is hard. Good testing of competence in economic analysis may be harder.

An economics multiple-choice exam for high school students around the country has been heavily criticized. Not all the criticism has been crazy. One of the questions pertains to promotion of "economic growth" by "a developing country." Officially, the correct answer is: "increase investment"; but *The Wall Street Journal* prefers another of the choices: "use the market system."

Investment — along with the saving which provides investable resources — is, indeed, part of the development process. We can produce more — and thereby save, as well as consume, more — with greater income. So greater income makes feasible still greater income.

But *greater* income need not mean *great* income. Very poor communities can save and invest and thus initiate or continue development. We know that, for it has happened. Indeed, to reach current levels of wealth, it *had* to happen, for initially no community was wealthy. Some communities *have* become relatively wealthy, partly through saving and investment, but Adam and Eve were destitute when ejected from the Garden.

We did not start with capital. It has been laboriously accumulated. *Why* would poor people forego consuming some of their little current income in order to direct resources into production of capital? Critical here is the *quality* of people — their attitudes and aptitudes, their sense and sophistication, their boldness and initiative. This is not a matter wholly of genes and hormones. It reflects also their past experience and current prospects, and the prospects and options of strategy and activity are shaped by institutions and ground rules.

It is provincial and mechanistic to speak simply of investment being the basis of growth. Given appropriate ambitions and inducements, determined mainly by the nature and assurance of property rights, investment will come. There are many connected links in the chain of growth causation, but "investment" is not the first link.

Not only the *amount* of investment is ultimately strategic, but also the *kind* of investment and for *whom*. Presidential palaces, steel mills, and a national airline are forms of investment — but they do little to promote growth of a poor country. And from *where* do the investment resources come? *How* are they sequestered and directed? Foreign aid, heavy taxation, expropriation, inflation are ways of channeling resources into some kinds of investment. All such ways have big problems of both efficiency and equity, and they cannot be expected to be the basis of prolonged, substantial growth.

First come the human and institutional prerequisites of growth ambitions and strategies; then come investment and other growth activity in the market; finally, there comes growth. The market system inspires hope of personal betterment and makes growth plans feasible. From markets comes investment; and from market-generated and market-directed investment comes growth.

On Closing of Income Gaps

⊗⊗⊗⊗

Three authors have investigated growth records of nearly 100 nations. They dubiously conclude that per capita income growth is determined basically by just three factors: income growth is reduced by large population increase but raised by greater saving and more education. And they indicate that world living standards will converge — the poor will begin to catch the wealthy — if the rates of population growth, saving, and education investment become similar everywhere.

But if countries come to have similar rates of economic growth because they evolve similar profiles of population, saving, and education, then the international income gaps can not be eliminated. If the United States and country Alpha both grow at the same *rate*, then the initial money income gap will get ever *larger*.

There is a further problem. If per capita income grows at *any* faster rate in Alpha than in the U.S., then *eventually* Alphian income will match U.S. income and finally grow larger. But is it realistic to believe — as do these writers — that *half* of the gap will be eliminated in only *35* years?

The larger is Alpha's output relative to U.S. output initially, the smaller need be her rate of growth to reduce the gap by half in that period.

Suppose that U.S. output per person is valued at $20,000 in 1990, while Alpha is a basket case with per capita output of only $2,000 — a difference of $18,000. And suppose that over the coming 35 years, the U.S. grows at a mediocre rate of 2 percent annually. U.S. output will thus double to $40,000 in year 2025. If the gap is to be cut to $9,000 — half the initial difference — then Alpha would have to grow over this considerable period at a highly implausible rate of more than 8 percent.

If Alpha were to grow at a more realistic but still impressive rate of 4 percent, it would require well over a century to cut the income gap in half.

Or let Alpha's income start at $10,000, half the U.S. figure. Even then, reducing the income difference by half within 35 years would require an Alphian growth rate of close to 4 percent.

Granted, if the gap actually is halved in only 35 years, it would then take only another five to ten years to close the difference completely.

But, as the U.S. and Alpha start the income race, the original gap would *not* begin to fall *immediately*. Even with the U.S. growing at only 2 percent from an income of $20,000 and Alpha growing remarkably at over 8 percent from a level of $2,000, the gap would *increase* for the first sixteen years.

It should be appreciated that economic growth is difficult, involving much work, sacrifice, and luck. And the closing — or even the reducing — of large international income gaps will take, at best, many years.

Fantasy Axioms of Foreign Aid Policies

ØØØØ

How to account for great international disparities in income and the stubborn persistence of poverty over much of the world?

Whatever the diagnosis, many — in both the wealthier and the poorer nations — have a ready prescription: foreign aid. The record of aid effectiveness is discouraging, so increase the amount of aid and hope it is better used. And if aid still fails to induce much *economic development*, it is to be provided as a procedure of international *income redistribution*.

The stakes in the development issue are high, and the amount of resources already expended in aid is not trivial. It is in order to reexamine widely parroted axioms in support of governmental foreign aid. We can be instructed by Peter Bauer and Basil Yamey, of the London School of Economics.

Professors Bauer and Yamey see the maximum possible benefits of aid received to be very modest and the likely waste and actual harm of aid to be impressive. They find that, actually but not surprisingly, foreign aid has imposed costs, political as well as economic, on the givers of aid while failing to conduce, and often even constraining, development by the recipients of aid.

Expanding efficient economic activity requires resources, to be sure. But the resources required are not limited to immediate inputs of production: more basically, "economic achievement has depended, as it still does, on people's own faculties, motivations, and mores, on their institutions, and on the policies of their rulers" — "in short, ... on the conduct of people...."

Further, the necessity of resources does not imply the necessity of receiving aid. No history of national economic development can be written in terms of external donations. When foreign resources can be used productively, they will be available from self-interested lenders. Lenders will not irrationally provide resources which would be wasted; if foreign governments *give* resources which investors would not *lend*, the transfer is not converted from irrationality to rationality, and the waste is not transformed into efficiency.

The contribution of aid, then, can be no greater than relieving the recipient of repayment, with interest, of productive loans. At best, this is a marginal contribution in the context of total gross national product. But even modest aid can bulk large in the resources of the *government* of the receiving nation.

Public foreign aid does go to the governments, not directly to the people. Typically, those governments are not efficient organizations for the promotion of economic development. Indeed, there is little reason to suppose that broadly shared economic gain is a major objective of the self-serving government officials of these heavily hierarchical, politicized societies.

The sober and sobering conclusion of Professors Bauer and Yamey is that the "... contribution [of official Western aid] to Third World development cannot be significant, and is much more likely to be negative. ... And it will not help the West."

Index